**The Tyndal**

PROFESSOR D. J. WI

222.32 07 C912 1968
Cundall, Arthur Ernest
Judges & Ruth

D0372204

# JUDGES & RUTH

# JUDGES
*AN INTRODUCTION AND COMMENTARY*
by
**ARTHUR E. CUNDALL**, B.A., B.D.
*Lecturer in Old Testament,*
*The London Bible College*


# RUTH
*AN INTRODUCTION AND COMMENTARY*
by
**LEON MORRIS**, M.SC., M.TH., PH.D.
*Principal, Ridley College, Melbourne*

INTER-VARSITY PRESS
Downers Grove, Illinois 60515

© 1968 by The Tyndale Press, London, England. Published in America by
InterVarsity Press, Downers Grove, Illinois, with permission from Universities and
Colleges Christian Fellowship, Leicester, England.

All rights reserved. No part of this book may be reproduced in any
form without written permission from InterVarsity Press,
Downers Grove, Illinois.

InterVarsity Press is the book-publishing division of Inter-Varsity Christian Fellowship,
a student movement active on campus at hundreds of universities, colleges
and schools of nursing. For information about local and regional activities, write
IVCF, 233 Langdon St., Madison, WI 53703.

Distributed in Canada through InterVarsity Press, 1875 Leslie St., Unit 10,
Don Mills, Ontario M3B 2M5, Canada.

ISBN paper 0-87784-257-4
ISBN cloth 0-87784-896-3
Library of Congress Catalog Card Number: 68-31426

Printed in the United States of America

| 19 | 18 | 17 | 16 | 15 | 14 | 13 | 12 | 11 | 10 | 9 | 8 | 7 | 6 | 5 |
|----|----|----|----|----|----|----|----|----|----|----|----|----|----|----|
| 93 | 92 | 91 | 90 | 89 | 88 | 87 | 86 | 85 | 84 | 83 | 82 | 81 | | |

# GENERAL PREFACE

THE aim of this series of *Tyndale Old Testament Commentaries*, as it was in the companion volumes on the New Testament, is to provide the student of the Bible with a handy, up-to-date commentary on each book, with the primary emphasis on exegesis. Major critical questions are discussed in the introductions and additional notes, while undue technicalities have been avoided.

While all are united in their belief in the divine inspiration, essential trustworthiness and practical relevance of the sacred writings, individual authors have freely made their own contributions within the limits of the space available. These restrictions on length – essential if the books are to be produced at reasonable prices – bear more hardly on authors handling larger books. This is one reason why commentaries in the series will differ from each other in treatment, a fact exemplified by the two contributions brought together in this volume. Another is the impossibility, and indeed undesirability, of imposing detailed uniformity of method in the handling of such varied subject-matter, form and style as the books of the Old Testament.

In the Old Testament in particular no single English translation is adequate to reflect the original text. The authors of these commentaries freely quote various versions, therefore, or give their own translation, in the endeavour to make the more difficult passages or words meaningful today. Where necessary, words from the Hebrew (and Aramaic) Text underlying their studies are transliterated. This will help the reader who may be unfamiliar with the Semitic languages to identify the word under discussion and thus to follow the argument. It is assumed throughout that the reader will have ready access to one, or more, reliable rendering of the Bible in English.

There are signs of a renewed interest in the meaning and message of the Old Testament and it is hoped that this series will thus further the systematic study of the revelation of God and His will and ways as seen in these records. It is the prayer of the editor and publisher, as of the authors, that these books will help many to understand, and to respond to, the Word of God today.

D. J. Wiseman

# JUDGES

*AN INTRODUCTION AND COMMENTARY*

by

ARTHUR E. CUNDALL, B.A., B.D.

*Lecturer in Old Testament,*
*The London Bible College*

# CONTENTS

## AUTHOR'S PREFACE

FEW periods in Israel's eventful history are as important as the period of the judges. During these centuries the nation took the wrong turning that led to her downfall and near-destruction. The apostasy of the later generations has its origin in the early years of the settlement, and there is a clear line between the time when the nation first went after Baal and the dark age when the Jerusalem Temple itself was defiled with all the trappings of the Baal worship, not excluding cultic prostitutes (2 Ki. 23:4–7). There is much in Judges to sadden the heart of the reader; perhaps no book in the Bible witnesses so clearly to our human frailty. But there are also unmistakable signs of the divine compassion and long-suffering. It may be that the modern reader of Judges will hear the warning voice of the Spirit, 'This is *not* the way, walk ye *not* in it.' Or, as the lives of these lesser-saviours are considered, there may be a realization of the need in modern times of a greater Saviour, of unblemished life, who is able to effect a perfect deliverance, not only in time but for eternity.

I am conscious of the limitations of this commentary, especially when the need for brevity has led to an over-simplification of some of the problems, but I trust that the advanced student will not be misled, even if discussion of some technical points has had to be curtailed. An endeavour has been made to set the history and religion of the period in the wider sweep of the biblical revelation. Many students shrink from the very immensity of the Old Testament, including as it does 39 books, covering over 1500 years and involving so many other nations besides Israel. But there are rich rewards waiting those who make the effort to grasp the detail of the historical revelation. Books that were treasured before will shine with a new lustre and the Bible itself will come alive in a new way. Incidentally, Judges is one of the books where the use of a good Bible atlas is essential.

I am deeply grateful to Professor D. J. Wiseman for a

number of helpful suggestions which I have incorporated into the text, and to the publishers for their encouragement and assistance throughout. Finally, I would like to acknowledge the continued encouragement and help of my wife, not least in the typing of the manuscript.

ARTHUR E. CUNDALL

## CHIEF ABBREVIATIONS

Albright      *Archaeology of Palestine* by W. F. Albright (Pelican, 1960).
AV            English Authorized Version (King James).
Bruce         See *NBC*, below.
Burney        *The Book of Judges*² by C. F. Burney (Rivingtons, 1920).
*DOTT*        *Documents from Old Testament Times* edited by D. W. Thomas (Nelson, 1958).
Driver        'Problems in Judges Newly Discussed' by G. R. Driver, in *The Annual of Leeds University Oriental Society*, IV, 1962–3.
Heb.          Hebrew.
*IB*          *Interpreter's Bible*, Vol. 2 (Leviticus–Samuel) (Nelson, 1953). Exegesis on *Judges* by Jacob M. Myers.
*JBL*         *Journal of Biblical Literature.*
*JSS*         *Journal of Semitic Studies.*
LXX           The Septuagint (pre-Christian Greek version of the Old Testament).
mg.           margin.
Myers         See *IB*, above.
*NBC*         *The New Bible Commentary*² edited by F. Davidson, A. M. Stibbs and E. F. Kevan (I.V.F., 1954). Commentary on *Judges* by F. F. Bruce.
*NBD*         *The New Bible Dictionary* edited by J. D. Douglas, F. F. Bruce, J. I. Packer, R. V. G. Tasker, D. J. Wiseman (I.V.F., 1962).
Noth          *The History of Israel*² by M. Noth (A. & C. Black, 1960).
RSV           American Revised Standard Version, 1952.
RV            English Revised Version, 1881.
*VT*          *Vetus Testamentum.*

# INTRODUCTION

## I. TITLE AND PLACE IN THE CANON

THE book of Judges derives its English title from the Latin *Liber Judicum* which itself rests upon the LXX *Kritai* ('judges'). The Hebrew title is *šōp̄eṭîm*. The English title is apt to be misleading, since it conveys the idea of a group of men whose principal task was in the legal sphere, arbitrating in disputes between men. A cursory reading of Judges will show that this was, in fact, a subsidiary function of its leading characters. The clue to the connotation of the Hebrew may be found in 2:16, 'And the Lord raised up judges, which saved them out of the hand of those that spoiled them' (RV). The judges were primarily the 'saviours' or 'deliverers' of their people from their enemies. Nowhere in the book is the noun *šōp̄eṭ* used directly of an individual, but the associated verbal form is found in connection with Othniel (3:10), Deborah (4:4), Tola (10:2), Jair (10:3), Jephthah (12:7), Ibzan (12:8,9), Elon (12:11), Abdon (12:13,14) and Samson (15:20; 16:31). In 11:27, in the context of the Ammonite oppression, the Lord is described as a *šōp̄eṭ*. This conception may be said to form the background of the book: the Lord is the *real* Judge of His people; it is He who gives them into the hands of their oppressors; it is He who raises up deliverers for them; it is His Spirit, coming upon men, which equips them for their tasks (3:10; 6:34; 11:29; 14:6,19; 15:14).

This raises a point of considerable importance. These men who were raised up to be the saviours of their people were characterized by peculiar qualities which were believed to be the manifestation of a unique endowment from the Lord. The people could recognize this quality as it was revealed in life and action, its most spectacular manifestation being in delivering Israel from foreign domination. This attitude was not confined to the period of the judges. Saul was marked out by this charismatic[1] quality (1 Sa. 11:6) which was displayed openly when he delivered the citizens of Jabesh-gilead from the Ammonites. David received such an anointing (1 Sa. 16:13) which accounted, in measure, for his mighty exploits and his success in battle, a fact not overlooked by the northern tribes when they invited him to be their king (2 Sa. 5:2). It was not until the establishment of the dynastic principle in Judah that the evidence of charismatic qualities in its leaders became less significant; in Israel, with its many successful rebellions against the reigning king, the exercise of these unusual qualities probably continued to be a factor in the acceptance or rejection of a contender for the throne.

Military prowess was, however, not the only way in which this divine endowment could be revealed, for wisdom and discernment were equally the gifts of God. No warlike deeds are recorded of any of the minor judges (apart from Shamgar, 3:31). In all probability they were distinguished from their fellows by mental and moral qualities. It is possible that they became the guardians and interpreters of that portion of the Mosaic tradition concerned with the casuistic laws, applying them to local disputes. But it would be unwise to attempt to make too precise a distinction between the military and the pacific judges. Deborah was already established as an arbiter in the everyday affairs of her countrymen when she was called to take the lead in delivering her people from the Canaanite oppression (4:4,5). Similarly Samuel, whose position as a judge as well as a prophet reminds us that the period of the judges is not coterminous with the book of Judges, both delivered the nation from the Philistines and acted as a magistrate (1 Sa. 7:3–14; *cf.* 7:15–17). Conversely it should be observed that we have insufficient information about the minor judges to be able to state dogmatically that they were totally devoid of the military qualities of the better-known judges. Indeed, it is recorded of one of them, Tola the son of Puah, that he 'arose to

---

[1] This word conveniently describes this unique quality of the judges. It derives from the Greek noun *charisma*, meaning a 'free favour', 'gift' or 'endowment', and was first used in this connection by the prominent German sociologist, Max Weber.

save Israel' (10:1, RV). One further factor to be noted is that the high priest, by virtue of his position at the central shrine, may be regarded as a judge, since the sanctuary was the traditional place for the settlement of disputes as well as the place where the blessing of God was sought before a military campaign.

Thus the book of Judges derives its name from the term used to describe the activities of its leading characters. These men (and, of course, Deborah) possessed outstanding qualities of leadership which were conceived to be the result of God's Spirit coming upon them. The more spectacular evidence of this possession, and therefore the most likely to be remembered by posterity, was the shattering of the yoke of an oppressor. Other qualities assumed prominence when the national emergencies receded, and those who manifested these gifts were respected and sought out by those in need of advice or arbitration. While there are parallels to the functions of the judges in the *suffetes* of Phoenicia and Carthaginia and, to a lesser extent, in the consuls of Rome, the concept of the direct action of God's Spirit upon men made this group unique in ancient history.

In the English Bible the book of Judges would be classified amongst the historical books, but in the Hebrew Bible it is placed in the second of the three sections, the Law, the Prophets and the Writings. This section is itself divided into two, the Former Prophets and the Latter Prophets, each containing four books. Judges is the second book in the Former Prophets, following immediately after Joshua. The implication of the inclusion of dominantly historical books amongst the Prophets should be carefully noted, for it reveals a fundamental attitude of the Israelite historians. They were not concerned merely to compile an authoritative record of their nation's history; their motive was to draw out the religious truths which were implicit in that history. This in turn witnesses to their developed sense of the sovereignty of God, whose mind and will were discernible through historical events as well as through the words of His servants the prophets.

A view which is widely held today is that Judges is part of the 'Deuteronomic History' which includes the books of Deuteronomy, Joshua, Judges, Samuel and Kings.[1] It must be objected that the reasons for removing Deuteronomy from its traditional place in the Pentateuch are slight, yet there is some justification for this view. Deuteronomy looks forward as well as backwards and so leads on naturally to the period of settlement in the Promised Land. Moreover, the attitude of the editors responsible for the collecting and shaping of Israel's history reflects clearly the spiritual principles set out in Deuteronomy. These will be dealt with in the relevant sections of the text. At the moment it may simply be noted that Judges forms part of the *official* historical record of Israel.

## II. COMPOSITION, STRUCTURE AND DATE

A cursory reading of Judges reveals that it is, in the main, a compilation of independent stories, most of which centre on an individual. This applies particularly in the central and major portion of the book, namely 2:6–16:31, where it is apparent that these stories have been carefully integrated into a framework of editorial introduction and comment. The opening and closing sections of the book, 1:1–2:5 and 17:1–21:25, do not fit into this pattern and must be considered separately, thus making three main divisions. Before attention is given to each of these individually, two points may be observed. First, that even in the second and major section of the book events have been selected. Whether the editor had access to a larger corpus of historical information is a matter of conjecture. What has been preserved provides an insight into conditions at different times and in different parts of the country, as will become clear when the chronology of the period is considered. Secondly, the period of the judges did not terminate until Saul's accession to the throne. 1 Samuel 12, which reiterates the principles of God's dealings with Israel in the pre-monarchic period and applies them to the changed situation, may be regarded as marking the end of an era. A complete discussion of the period of the judges must take 1 Samuel 1–12 into account and also the book of Ruth.

[1] *Cf.* Noth, p. 42.

*a. The settlement in Canaan* (1:1–2:5)

In this section we have a number of incidents connected with the Conquest of the land, the focus being upon the individual tribes. The part played by the tribes of Judah, Simeon and their associates in the conquest of the south receives attention in 1:1–20 and the capture of Bethel by the Joseph tribes is dealt with in 1:22–26. The greater part of the remainder of the first chapter is concerned with the incomplete nature of the Conquest, and a catalogue is made of the unconquered territory in each of the tribal portions. The fragmentary nature of the record makes it virtually certain that we have here selections from a settlement narrative which is independent of the account in the book of Joshua and therefore of great value.

There are close parallels between the two accounts, *e.g.* Judges 1:10–15,20 (*cf.* Jos. 15:13–19); Judges 1:21 (*cf.* Jos. 15:63); Judges 1:27,28 (*cf.* Jos. 17:11–13); Judges 1:29 (*cf.* Jos. 16:10). The minor points of difference will be dealt with in the commentary on the text. But what appears to be a major difference is that in Judges attention is given to the individual participating tribes, particularly Judah, whereas in Joshua the Conquest is viewed as the work of the united tribes under one leader. The difficulty cannot be sidestepped by the supposition that Judges 1 is a history of the *later* stages of the Conquest after the death of Joshua, as would appear from 1:1a. Such a view would increase rather than reduce the problem, since the parallels with events in Joshua are too close.

It is possible, however, to magnify the differences and regard the record in Judges as a contradictory account of the Conquest as some scholars maintain. This view is occasionally linked with the theory of a composite invasion of the land, the main thrust coming from the 'Rachel' tribes but with two other movements coming respectively from the north (the 'hand-maiden tribes') and the south (the 'Leah' tribes). Scholars who support this concept of a three-pronged invasion suggest that in Judges 1 there is the record of Judah's infiltration and invasion from the south. But this overlooks the fact that, while in this whole section (1:1–36) the movement is from south to north – dealing successively with Judah and Simeon, the house of Joseph and, finally, the northern tribes – in the section which recounts the exploits of Judah and Simeon the movement generally is from north to south, beginning at Jerusalem. This would be inexplicable if Judah and Simeon had not entered the land with the remainder of the tribes and *then* moved southwards to possess their inheritance. When certain other considerations are borne in mind the differences between the accounts of Joshua and Judges become less significant and they are seen as complementary rather than as contradictory. They are:

1. The attention given to the southern tribes, particularly Judah, in Judges 1:1–36, probably indicates that this is an extract from a *southern* version of the Conquest, placing particular stress upon the part played by its own members.

2. This section is, in itself, generally acknowledged to be incomplete. The reason for its inclusion lay in the fact that its delineation of unoccupied territory serves as the background to the events which followed when Israel, lacking cohesion between its constituent tribes, was itself the object of attack by some of the nations it failed to subjugate. Too much weight must not be placed upon the *selection* of events introduced here.

3. It is inaccurate to suppose that the book of Joshua depicts a *complete* conquest and occupation of the whole land in a relatively short space of time. In the speeches of Joshua reference is made frequently to the incompleteness of the occupation (*e.g.* Jos. 13:1–13; *cf.* 16:10; 17:12, 13, 16–18; 18:2–4) and earlier on in the narrative there are hints that the campaign was a protracted one (*e.g.* Jos. 11:18). Victories are indeed claimed over the armies of many of the cities listed in Judges, but the defeat of an army and the death of its king, even the destruction of a city, does not involve the *occupation* of the city. There may well be a certain idealization in the record (*e.g.* Jos. 11:23; 21:43–45; 23:1) and reference to these passages alone could be used to support the view of a complete conquest and occupation. But certain sections do not support this view and the tension of evidence suggests a great victory but an incomplete one.

4. It must be borne in mind that the account in Joshua does

not come from a writer whose sole concern was the accurate setting out of the facts of history. This does not mean that it is unhistorical, but it does mean that caution must be used in applying the methods of twentieth-century historians. Hebrew history is theocratic history; its emphasis is religious rather than military and political, but it does not differentiate between political, religious and social elements. Stress is placed upon the Lord as the One who had given them the land and upon Joshua His chief representative. The book of Joshua, when taken as a whole, does not give a misleading picture; the fact is openly noted that 'there remains yet very much land to be possessed' (Jos. 13:1).

5. Joshua, as the commander-in-chief of the Israelite forces, may occasionally be given the credit for action carried out by the individual tribes. Thus the operation of the tribe of Judah noted in Judges 1:1ff. may well have followed soon after Joshua's campaign against the southern confederacy of Jerusalem, Hebron, Jarmuth, Lachish and Eglon (Jos. 10), forming part of the over-all strategy.

Before passing on to the next section some explanation must be given concerning the opening words of the book, 'And it came to pass after the death of Joshua' (RV). The opinion has already been expressed that the events of 1:1–2:5 are to be connected with the invasion under Joshua's command and are therefore before, not subsequent to, his death. A comparison of Joshua 24:28–31 with Judges 2:6–9 suggests strongly that the first section of the present book of Judges, although contemporary with the events narrated, was included at a later date and so interrupts the continuity of Joshua and Judges 2:6ff. The death of Joshua is noted in Joshua 24:29 and Judges 2:8. It is likely that, when the book of Judges assumed its present form, the opening words were added not with reference to the section which followed immediately afterwards (*i.e.* 1:1b–2:5) but with a more general application to the whole book as dealing with the situation in the post-Joshua age. Indeed, the suggestion that the opening words were the original title of the book is most plausible and entirely in accordance with Israelite usage.

## b. Israel's judges (2:6–16:31)

In this central section we are introduced to the twelve main
characters from whom the book derives its name: Othniel
(3:7–11), Ehud (3:12–30), Deborah, with Barak in support
(4,5), Gideon (6–8), Jephthah (10:6–12:7) and Samson
(13–16). These are usually regarded as the major judges
while the minor judges, considered in far less detail, are
Shamgar (3:31), Tola and Jair (10:1–5) and Ibzan, Elon and
Abdon (12:8–15). The stories of the major judges are recounted with great animation and vividness, which has made
them popular with teachers and preachers down the ages.
Who has not wondered at the craftiness of Ehud, at the
transformation from timidity to highest courage in Gideon,
or at the potentiality and degeneration of Samson?

It is apparent that the stories themselves are older than the
framework in which they are set. They may be regarded as
contemporaneous with the events described and it is likely
that they were handed down in oral form for some time
before they were committed to writing. It is probable that
this period was brief, since modern archaeological research
suggests that oral and written sources were contemporary in
the tradition of the Ancient Near East. Our increasing knowledge of the accuracy with which traditions of ancient peoples,
such as the Israelites, have been handed down through the
ages guards against the assumption of major deviations
occurring in the narratives themselves during this period.
In the case of oral tradition there would always be the check
of a large number of others who would know these stories off
by heart. Thus there was probably a considerable period during
which the stories were transmitted in both written and oral
forms before they were gathered together into the present
selection. Possibly there were other, earlier collections.
'The Book of the Wars of the Lord' (Nu. 21:14) or 'the
Book of Jashar' (Jos. 10:13; 2 Sa. 1:18) may have been among
the sources used, but there can be no certainty of this.

A further suggestion is that some of the narratives preserved
in Judges are compounded of two or even three variant versions: the stories of Gideon and Jephthah, in particular, have

frequently been examined in an attempt to discover the underlying strands. Persistent endeavours have been made by other scholars to show that in Judges there is a continuation of the two main strata which are still widely held to underlie the Pentateuch – the Yahweh source, emanating from the south, and the Elohist source, coming from the north at a later date and lacking some of the vigour of the earlier version. But the whole documentary theory of the origin of the Pentateuch is being seriously challenged at the moment. While it still commands substantial support, it has been subjected to considerable modification and is now no longer regarded as 'cut and dried', as it was by an earlier generation. The conservative view that the Pentateuch is substantially the work of Moses commands greater respect today than it has for some generations. Of particular interest is the fact that the attempt to analyse the books of Joshua and Judges into clearly distinguishable strata has now been generally abandoned.[1]

We must admit that we do not know whether or not our editor had access to one or more documents or traditions, nor need it concern us. As we shall see, the final selection was made by an editor or editors who were concerned to impress moral and spiritual truths which they conceived to be fundamental to God's dealings with His chosen people. Subsequent generations have seen here and in other parts of the Bible a divine oversight of selection and presentation which makes it in a real sense the Word of God.

It should be observed that we must not lightly import our western methods of investigation and analysis into our study of Ancient Near-Eastern documents. For example, no fewer than five reasons are advanced in the book of Judges for the failure of the Israelites to occupy the land of Canaan. It was because of the superior arms and fortifications of the Canaanites (1:19); because of Israel's disposition to make alliances with the inhabitants of the land (2:1–5); because Israel had

[1] C. A. Simpson, *The Composition of the Book of Judges* (Blackwell, 1957), is one of the exceptions to this statement. The author claims to detect three main sources (J1, J2, and E), with a further subsidiary source (chapters 19–21) which he calls C. Few contemporary scholars would be so confident of tracing the underlying sources with such precision.

sinned and must be punished (2:20,21); because God was proving Israel's faithfulness (2:22,23; 3:4); and finally, it was so that Israel might be instructed in the arts of war (3:1–3). To suggest that there is inconsistency here would do despite to the basic Hebrew approach to life, with its highly developed conception of the sovereignty of God. Israel had failed to occupy the land for very good reasons and so the former inhabitants remained in the land, but God overruled even this for His people's good. There is no need to allege two or more traditions; all five reasons could have suggested themselves to the same Hebrew mind at various times and in differing contexts. Or again, we could cavil at the way in which Israel is said to have been given into the hand of a certain oppressor and subsequently delivered and governed by a particular judge, whilst the context makes it clear that only a minority of the tribes and a relatively small area of the land were affected. An explanation of this may lie in the Hebrew conception of racial solidarity.

Attention has already been drawn to the carefully ordered framework into which the narratives are placed. A similarity of pattern is exhibited in two ways:

1. In the introductions to the stories of Othniel (3:7ff.), Ehud (3:12ff.), Deborah (4:1ff.), Gideon (6:1ff.), Jephthah (10:6ff.) and Samson (13:1).

2. In the conclusions to these narratives, where the overthrow of the oppressing nation is noted together with the period during which the land had rest (*e.g.* 3:11,30; 4:23; 5:31; 8:28). A variation is sometimes introduced, in which the period of office of a particular judge is noted (*e.g.* 10:2,3; 12:7,9,11,14; 15:20; 16:31).

Chapter 2:6–3:6 may be regarded as an introduction to the stories of the judges, setting out the general principles operative throughout the period. The historian sees a pattern of events which forms a recurring cycle containing four elements: the children of Israel do that which is evil in the sight of the Lord; the Lord delivers them into the hand of an oppressor; in their distress they cry to the Lord; the Lord raises them up a deliverer. Thus there is a cycle of apostasy, servitude, supplication and salvation. It is this process which is followed closely in the succeeding chapters.

This section of the book of Judges can be said to be interpretative history and we are indebted to the historian for elucidating the spiritual principles inherent in his nation's traditions. The editorial comments, as would be expected, highlight these principles more clearly than the narratives themselves. Indeed, there are occasions where the leading characters were less than praiseworthy. Gideon, in the course of delivering the nation, took the opportunity to settle a blood-feud (8:18–21); Jephthah appears as an opportunist with but a scanty knowledge of the Lord's requirements; whilst some of the exploits of Samson have often been likened to practical jokes. These facts themselves are important as witnesses to the decadence of the age. But there are evidences that the principles delineated by the historian are not alien importations into these ancient traditions but rather a fundamental element in the relationship between God and Israel. For instance, in the Song of Deborah the impoverishment and disorder of the nation is attributed to its apostasy (5:6–8).

*c. Appendices* (17:1–21:25)

In the final section of the book there are two unconnected incidents: Micah and the Danite migration (17,18) and the incident of the Levite's outraged concubine and its sequel (19–21). There is much here of an unsavoury nature, yet the documentation of the debased religious and moral standards of the age is of first-rate importance, as are also the allusions to the prevailing social and political conditions. The standpoint of the writer is clear; the oft-repeated observation 'there was no king in Israel' (17:6; 18:1; 19:1; 21:25) shows that he looked back from the time of the monarchy and accounted for the disorder of the earlier period by the absence of the firm rule of a king. These editorial comments are not of the same kind as those in the second section of the book and this has led many to suggest a different editor. But it may be that the vastly different subject-matter is sufficient to account for the absence of comment of a more specifically religious nature – the stories speak for themselves. It is possible that they were handed down in Danite and Benjamite circles respectively before being incorporated into the larger collection of Israelite traditions. Not all scholars would give assent to this, however, since the stories do not reveal the tribes of Dan and Benjamin in a particularly complimentary light.

We are now in a position to attempt a reconstruction of the way in which the book of Judges assumed its present form. The successive stages may be noted:

1. An oral stage, closely following the events themselves, the traditions being transmitted amongst those tribes affected by the events described.

2. The reducing of these traditions to writing. The most likely time for this is a matter of dispute, but the earlier period of the monarchy has the strongest and most consistent claim. Obviously the combining of these traditions could come about only when there was the consciousness of a national unity and this would be a feature of that period. Moreover, the time of David and Solomon was the golden age of the nation in which it prospered to such an extent that the Israelite Empire was possibly the greatest power in the Fertile Crescent[1]. Such an age would be creative in the realm of the arts and there would also be a vital interest in the nation's traditions. Attention has already been drawn to the standpoint of the editor of Judges 17–21. Clearly he looked upon the monarchy as the solution to the ills of the former age. Such order and stability were more the features of the early monarchy than the later monarchy, and, if precision be not too presumptuous, of the earlier part of David's rule over the united kingdom. Tradition, recording the literary activities of Samuel, Nathan and Gad, lends some general support to this view (1 Ch. 29:29; 2 Ch. 9:29). Indeed the Talmud preserves the tradition that Samuel *was* the author of Judges, which is unlikely since Samuel's attitude to the monarchy (*e.g.* 1 Sa. 8) is at variance with that of the editor of Judges 17–21, where the monarchy is viewed in a favourable

[1] The usual designation for the region extending from Egypt, through Palestine, Syria and Mesopotamia to the Persian Gulf.

light. A date for the book of Judges about 980 BC seems not unreasonable, although dogmatism is out of place.

3. It is likely that the first draft of Judges contained the majority of the present book, *i.e.* 2:6–21:25. As has been pointed out, chapters 17–21 have been regarded as a later addition and there are certain other sections in the book, notably the Abimelech episode (9) and the final chapter of the Samson stories (16) which, because of the absence of the usual editorial comment, are not held to be original in the view of a few scholars. As well as this view, *i.e.* that these sections are later interpolations, there is the view that there were two editings of the book, these sections being omitted from the first edition but re-incorporated in the second edition, thus escaping the editorial treatment that was characteristic of the earlier version. The conjectural nature of this hypothesis is apparent, and it is sufficient explanation to assume that these stories, because of their nature, did not lend themselves to the religious editorial comment that was employed elsewhere.

4. The final stage came with the addition of 1:1–2:5, which was, as has been noted, an extract from an ancient account of the Conquest and settlement. It is likely that this was added at a very early date, possibly by the original historian, and that this is the only extant trace of this independent account.

5. We cannot rule out the possibility of further editorial shaping, probably of a minor nature, when the book of Judges was incorporated into the complete official history of Israel from the settlement in Canaan to the destruction of Jerusalem in 587 BC, *i.e.* the books of Joshua, Judges, Samuel and Kings. It is likely that this history was completed in the earliest period of the Babylonian captivity by a Jew who had access to the secular and religious records of the nation and who saw clearly the principles involved in the Lord's rejection of Judah.[1]

6. While the foregoing sections provide a reasonable ex-

[1] It has been observed that the point of view of the whole narrative is often called 'deuteronomic' because its finest expression is found in Deuteronomy. Our use of the adjective, however, does not automatically indicate an acceptance of a late date for the promulgation of Deuteronomy. There has been increasing support in recent years for an early date for Deuteronomy.

planation of the composition of Judges, a case can be advanced for an even closer relationship of the constituent parts. We have referred to the *editor* of Judges, indicating that he made use of already existing material. The word *author*, however, could well be used, since the material is so carefully integrated into a purposeful whole. In the first section of the book (1:1–2:5) there is a selection of events indicating Israel's failure and culminating in the charge that the nation had broken the covenant with the Lord. In the second section (2:6–16:31) the writer shows that this act of apostasy was repeated in the following generations in the recurring cycle already observed. But it is not an entirely regular cycle, for as the period wears on there is a marked deterioration. 'From Abimelech's time on, the land does not recover its peace; deliverance is less complete; Jephthah fails where Gideon succeeded in avoiding civil war. If the Samson episode is regarded as part of the central theme – and this is implied by 10:7–9 – then at the very end there is lacking something which is normally regarded as basic to this theme; for Samson is a judge in Israel, but he does not effect any real liberation from the foreign enemy.'[1] The Abimelech episode, normally regarded as outside the general pattern of the main narrative, witnesses to conditions in the vicinity of Shechem, where the worship of Baal-berith was dominant (8:33; 9:4,27,46). In the final section (17:1–21:25) the two stories are sufficiently indicative of the moral and spiritual condition of the age to need no comment from the writer. Thus viewed, there is the skilful assembling of the various parts that make up our present book, with the creation of an atmosphere which anticipates the revival in Israel's religion which accompanied the institution of the monarchy, particularly in the time of David.

### III. THE HISTORICAL LIMITS AND CHRONOLOGY OF THE PERIOD

There is fairly general agreement today amongst scholars that the Conquest of Canaan took place in the latter part of the thirteenth century BC. This consensus of opinion comes after

[1] J. P. U. Lilley, 'A Literary Appreciation of the Book of Judges', in *Tyndale Bulletin*, 18, 1967, pp. 98f.

decades of controversy between the protagonists for a fifteenth-century BC date for the Exodus and Conquest and those who supported a thirteenth-century date. There is no place here for a full discussion, but amongst the evidence that has led to greater support for the later date we may note:

1. The Tell el-Amarna correspondence of the fourteenth century BC between Egypt and her vassal city-states in Canaan points to a period *before*, not after, the main Israelite invasion.

2. The events associated with the Israelite bondage in Egypt fit easily into the period of the XIXth Egyptian dynasty, *i.e.* from about 1310 BC.

3. The kingdoms of Edom, Moab and Ammon emerged during the early thirteenth century BC and the relationships noted between Israel and these would be impossible at an earlier date.

4. There is strong archaeological evidence for the destruction of a large number of Canaanite cities in the latter part of the thirteenth century BC. Amongst cities which have been sufficiently excavated to reveal a pattern of destruction, usually by fire, are Hazor, Eglon, Bethel, Lachish and Debir. It must not be assumed that every city was destroyed by the Israelites, but a general pattern of invasion and destruction is observable which links closely with the biblical record. Egyptian power was at a low ebb in this period, apart from one incursion into Canaan by Merenptah in *c.* 1220 BC, and this prevented aid coming to her vassal city-states and allowed Israel to become established in the land.

It is significant that in most recent accounts of Israel's history the late date for the Exodus and Conquest is assumed, no mention being made of a possible fifteenth-century alternative.[1] An approximate date for the Conquest may therefore be accepted as *c.* 1230 BC.

[1] As well as the books listed in the Selected Bibliography the following may be consulted concerning the dating of the Exodus and Conquest. Supporting the fifteenth-century date for the Exodus are J. W. Jack, *The Date of the Exodus*, 1925, and T. H. Robinson, *Expository Times*, XLVII, 1935–6, pp. 53–55. Supporting the thirteenth-century date are C. F. Burney, *Israel's Settlement in Canaan* (Schweich Lectures), 1917, and H. H. Rowley, *From Joseph to Joshua* (Schweich Lectures), 1948, pp. 11f. All three books listed in section III of the Selected Bibliography support the later date.

At the other end of the judges' period there is the reign of Saul. The length of this is a matter of considerable dispute but a date of *c.* 1020 BC for the coronation of Saul is perhaps best supported. Deducting thirty years for the latter years of Joshua and the elders who outlived him (Jos. 24:31), a not unreasonable estimate in view of the age at which Joshua died (Jos. 24:29; see note on Jdg. 2:6–10), approximately 180 years can be allowed for the judges' period, *i.e.* from *c.* 1200 to 1020 BC. We are immediately confronted with a problem of chronology when we consider the figures which are found in the book of Judges, as may be seen from the following table:

| | |
|---|---|
| The oppression of Cushan-rishathaim | 8 years |
| The period of rest following Othniel's deliverance | 40 |
| The Moabite oppression | 18 |
| The period of rest following Ehud's deliverance | 80 |
| The oppression of Jabin | 20 |
| The period of rest following Deborah's deliverance | 40 |
| The oppression of Midian | 7 |
| The period of rest following Gideon's deliverance | 40 |
| The reign of Abimelech | 3 |
| The judgeship of Tola | 23 |
| The judgeship of Jair | 22 |
| The oppression of Ammon | 18 |
| The judgeship of Jephthah | 6 |
| The judgeship of Ibzan | 7 |
| The judgeship of Elon | 10 |
| The judgeship of Abdon | 8 |
| The oppression of Philistia | 40 |
| | 390 years |

To this figure there must be added an estimated 20 years for Samuel's judgeship, giving a total of 410 years. Admittedly there are problems. The oppressions of Ammon and Philistia may have been contemporaneous (10:7,9; *cf.* 13:1) and it will be observed that we have included the 20 years of Samson's judgeship (16:31) *within* the period of the Philistine oppression, which we suggest was broken by Samuel at Ebenezer (1 Sa. 7:5–13). No allowance whatever has been made for Shamgar (3:31), and the 40 years of Eli's judgeship (1 Sa. 4:18) has also been excluded. But, in spite of these adjustments, the figure remains impossibly high. It is frequently observed by scholars that the editor is influenced in his chronology by the 480 years noted in 1 Kings 6:1. We do not accept this view, since to the figure of 410 years there must be added (to conform to the requirements of 1 Ki. 6:1) the 40 years of the wilderness period, approximately 20 years for Saul's reign (some scholars would put this as high as 40 years; *cf.* Acts 13:21), a further 40 years for the reign of David (2 Sa. 5:4) as well as the 4 years of Solomon's reign (1 Ki. 6:1), a total of 514 years. This, the lowest possible figure, can hardly be reconciled with 480 years.[1]

Various attempts have been made to reduce the over-all total, *e.g.* by including the years of foreign domination within the periods of the individual judges, or by omitting the years of the minor judges and the usurper Abimelech, but such solutions are highly conjectural. Nor need we resort to such speculation in an attempt to remove the difficulty, for a simpler solution is obvious: it is that in Judges there is a *relative* rather than an absolute chronology. Flinders Petrie is probably too precise in his view that there were three groups of judges in the north, east and west of the land respectively, with the chronologies relating to the relevant parts of the country.[2] We may simply note that the period of any two judges may have overlapped, a view supported by a consideration of the area of the country affected in each foreign oppression:

1. *Cushan-rishathaim.* No specific detail is given apart from the mention of Othniel, whose tribe was connected with Judah.

---

[1] The most reasonable explanation of the 480 years of 1 Ki. 6:1 is that it represents twelve generations, possibly the great national leaders Moses and Joshua, the six major judges, and Eli, Samuel, Saul and David. That this figure is approximately correct may be deduced from the priestly genealogies (1 Ch. 6) which note eleven or twelve generations.

[2] W. M. Flinders Petrie, *Egypt and Israel* (S.P.C.K., 1925), pp. 54ff.

2. *Eglon*. Limited encroachment from Moab which affected the territory of Benjamin and Ephraim.

3. *Jabin and Sisera*. A larger number of tribes than at any other time in the period co-operated under Deborah and Barak. Ephraim, Machir, Issachar, Naphtali, Benjamin and Zebulun shared in the deliverance, Reuben, Gilead, Dan and Asher were censured for their non-participation, only Judah and Simeon are not mentioned.

4. *Midian*. Manasseh, the tribe of Gideon, was the tribe chiefly involved, with Asher, Zebulun, Naphtali and, at a later stage of the operation, Ephraim.

5. *Ammon*. The oppression was limited to Gilead, east of Jordan, although Judah, Benjamin and Ephraim were affected in earlier raids (10:9).

6. *Philistia*. Samson's activity was a one-man operation against the Philistine infiltration. No tribes are noted as co-operating with him, nor is he ever represented as the leader of an army. The tribes principally affected by the Philistine incursions were Dan, the tribe of Samson, which was forced to vacate its tribal portion and migrate northwards (18:1ff.), and Judah (15:9–11).

A careful examination of a map of Israel will show that, with the exception of the oppression of the Canaanites which was broken by Deborah and Barak, only a relatively minor portion of the country was affected during each emergency. The general accuracy of the figures in Judges may be accepted, therefore, but care must be taken in interpreting them. Possibly the frequency with which the figure 40 or its multiples occurs suggests that it is a round figure representing a generation. The following table gives an approximate chronology for the period of the judges:

| 1230 | The entry into Canaan |
| 1200 | Othniel |
| 1170 | Ehud |
| 1150 | Shamgar |
| 1125 | Deborah and Barak |
| 1100 | Gideon |

1080   Abimelech
1070   Jephthah
1070   Samson
1050   The battle of 1 Samuel 4
1020   The accession of Saul

One further difficulty must be mentioned, which illustrates the problem of ascertaining a precise chronology. Jephthah (11:26) refers to a period of 300 years between the Conquest and his own time. This appears to be related to the chronological data already given in the book of Judges up to this point. The total of the figures supplied is 319 years, and this may be reduced to 301 years if the 18 years of the Ammonite oppression be subtracted. Various attempts at a solution of this problem are given in the commentary on the text. This verse is important evidence for those who support a fifteenth-century date for the Conquest, but the balance of evidence remains in favour of a thirteenth-century date.

### IV. ARCHAEOLOGY AND THE PERIOD OF THE JUDGES

Archaeological research has underlined the disparity between the Canaanite culture and the Israelite occupation which succeeded it. 'The contrast between the well-constructed Canaanite foundations and drainage systems of the thirteenth century and the crude piles of stones, without benefit of drainage, which replace them in the twelfth century, especially at Bethel, can scarcely be exaggerated.'[1] But whilst this fact is admitted, another fact of greater importance must also be noted: it is that the Israelites *settled down immediately* in the territory which they occupied without any transition period, which suggests strongly that they were not typical nomads. It is clear that the Israelites could not break the power of the Canaanite city-states in the valleys and coastal plains, as noted in the biblical records. However, the development of a water-proof lime-plaster made possible an efficient water storage in large underground cisterns and this in turn facilitated the opening up of the hitherto sparsely-populated, central hill-

[1] Albright, p. 119.

country. Thus archaeological evidence tends to confirm the Israelite dominance of the mountainous region, with a continuation of the Canaanite occupation of the low-lying areas, where chariots could be effectively employed.

No Israelite sanctuary of the period has yet been discovered. This may be due to the inferior constructional techniques of the Israelites, resulting in a lack of archaeological evidence. Or it could witness to the divine prohibition against the indiscriminate erection of sanctuaries (Ex. 20:24–26; Dt. 12:1–7). Similarly, Israel's religion was an imageless faith (Ex. 20:4–6) and it is a remarkable fact that no representation of a male deity dating from this period of Israelite occupation has been found, although many clay figurines, akin to the Canaanite goddess of fertility but without the insignia of a goddess, have been discovered, witnessing to the attraction which the Baal cult exercised in Israel.

Of major importance are the archaeological discoveries at Megiddo which make it possible to pin-point Deborah's crushing victory over the Canaanites 'at Taanach, by the waters of Megiddo' (5:19) about 1125 BC.[1] So also is the light thrown upon the Philistine culture and their influence upon their Israelite neighbours. Philistine pottery was so distinctive that the degree of its distribution in sites which have been excavated gives a reasonably clear picture of the extent of their influence, either by trade or through conquest. This is particularly marked in the Shephelah (a term used to designate the range of lower hills rising to the east of the coastal plain, including part of the territory of Dan, Simeon and Judah), which is precisely what we would expect from the traditions recorded in Judges. Finally, archaeology bears its mute but eloquent testimony to the destruction of Shiloh about 1050 BC. This fact is not noted in 1 Samuel but it is attested elsewhere in Scripture (Ps. 78:60; Je. 7:12; 26:6) and undoubtedly followed the double defeat inflicted on the Israelites at Aphek and the capture of the ark (1 Sa. 4). The destruction of other towns in Judah at the same time shows the extent of the Philistine domination over Israel towards the end of the period of the judges.

[1] Albright, pp. 117, 118.

### V. THE IMPORTANCE OF THE BOOK OF JUDGES

The period of the judges was of crucial importance in the history of Israel, for it was a period of transition. The nation which had been welded together from a rabble of slaves and other diverse groups had entered the Promised Land, with high ideals and austere moral standards, and is seen in Judges settling down in an environment dominated by Canaanite culture and religion. Moreover, there was pressure from the surrounding countries, of an occasional nature but sometimes strong. Israel was shaped by these factors and the future course of her history was, in measure, determined by the events of these two vital centuries. These trends are documented in Judges and they may be considered under various headings.

*a. Politics*

Israel's political structure when it entered Canaan can be described as an amphictyony, *i.e.* an assembly of tribes united together by a religious bond which found its focal point in a central sanctuary with its associated cultus. This structure may be observed elsewhere in the Mediterranean area, but an unusually strong centripetal bond amongst the tribes of Israel derived from the covenant event of Sinai, with its background of the miraculous deliverance from Egypt. Israel's traditions witness uniformly to this kind of political structure and there is incidental testimony as well. For example, during the wilderness period there was a prolonged sojourn in the vicinity of Kadesh-barnea, the name Kadesh (sanctuary), indicating that the focal point of their settlement was the sanctuary. During the first two centuries in the land the central sanctuary was located successively at Shechem, Shiloh (for a limited period), Bethel and, finally, again at Shiloh. In our commentary on the text it will be observed how this system operated. There were forces in the period of the judges, however, which tended to break down the strong political and religious bond which, ideally, ought to have characterized the amphictyonic league:

1. The incomplete nature of the Conquest made full co-operation between the tribes almost impossible. There was one group of unreduced Canaanite cities in the Esdraelon valley and a second in the Aijalon valley leading up to Jerusalem. The effect of these two wedges of Canaanite influence was to divide the tribes of Israel into three groups, northern, central and southern.

2. Geographical factors had a profound influence, since it was in the valleys and coastal plain that the main areas of Canaanite settlement were found. From west to east Palestine is divided into the coastal plain, the central mountain range, the Jordan valley and the Transjordan plateau. From north to south the three main divisions to the west of the Jordan are the region best known as Galilee, the central hill-country and the southern mountains which merge into the desert-wastes of the Negeb. As in ancient Greece these geographical factors made effective unity between inter-related groups extremely difficult.

3. These divisions made it difficult for the amphictyonic sanctuary to exert its cohesive force and some tribes must, for all practical purposes, have been dissociated from their fellows. Thus, in periods of foreign pressure, individual tribes or groups of tribes found themselves fighting for their lives with no help forthcoming from the amphictyony. We have already noted the limited areas affected by the various oppressing nations. Ideally all Israel ought to have come to the succour of the beleaguered tribes, but in practice intertribal co-operation was limited. Only in the crisis faced by Deborah and Barak do we find six of the tribes combining to face the menace; of the remainder, four put their own interests first, and two, Simeon and Judah, were so cut off from the stream of national life that they are not even mentioned.

4. It was this breakdown of the intertribal organization that led ultimately to the adoption of the monarchy, in conscious imitation of the surrounding nations. A king could summon the tribes to action and his personal leadership could weld the disparate elements together in an effective unity. The antecedent of this may be observed in the case of Gideon who,

following his victory over the Midianite menace, was offered the crown, a position he ostensibly declined.[1] The events which followed his death show the inclination towards the monarchy, at least in certain parts of the land. But the Midianite menace, acute as it was, was not sufficient to overcome the deep-seated aversion to the monarchy of the average Israelite, with his strong sense of independence. This was not to come until the Philistines threatened the very existence of Israel and then the nation, going against Samuel, the Lord's chief representative, clamoured for and secured the appointment of a king. Thus the book of Judges is a highly important witness to the breakdown of the traditional political structure and to the initial steps towards the adoption of the monarchy.

### b. *Religion*

When Israel entered into the land of Canaan its religion had already assumed its basic form and customs. It was a near-miracle that this religion survived the searching test of the crucial first centuries in Canaan. It would have been more than a miracle had such a religion developed *after* the settlement, with all the forces making for disintegration and deterioration pressing in upon it. In the formation of Israel's distinctive religion the part played by Moses cannot be overestimated. He, under God, was used to weld an undistinguished, dispirited multitude into an organized and carefully regulated unity. It has already been observed that this organization took the form of an amphictyony, a union of twelve tribes sharing a common faith and grouped around a common sanctuary. Their god was Yahweh, who had brought them out of slavery in Egypt by the manifestation of His power and had entered into a covenant with them at Sinai. Their part in the covenant-relationship was to be loyal to Him and to keep His commandments, which may be divided into two categories. There were the casuistic laws, which have many parallels in other law-codes of the second millennium BC, those of Israel being distinguished by a more humanitarian note and by an emphasis

---

[1] A full discussion of this point will be found in the commentary on 8:22,23 (see p. 120).

on persons rather than on property. The second group contains what are known as apodictic or apodeictic laws, the feature of these being their categoric character. They are introduced by 'Thou shalt...' or 'Thou shalt not...'. Israel was to obey these laws without question because Yahweh so willed. It is generally agreed that this class of law is distinctively, if not uniquely, Israelite. The cultus of the nation had a background of the harvest festivals which were commonly observed throughout the Fertile Crescent, but they received through Moses a complete reorientation and were made to celebrate the saving acts of God on behalf of the nation. It is of the highest importance to observe that the stress in the genuine Israelite religion was on a God in history, not simply, as in the cults of Canaan and elsewhere, on a god in nature. Similarly the sacrifices of Israel can be paralleled amongst her neighbours, as has been made abundantly clear through archaeological discoveries at Ras Shamra, the ancient Ugarit.[1] But again the genius of Israel's faith is apparent in the adaptation of these already existing forms.

It may be assumed, once the basic historicity of the events narrated in the book of Exodus is accepted, that Moses was conversant with the kind of religion that was practised in the land which he planned to occupy. This religion was, basically, a nature cult, designed to enlist the aid of the Baal pantheon and ensure the fertility of the land. This took the form of a mimetic ritual in which male and female cult-prostitutes featured, seeking to promote the action of the gods in the wider sphere of nature. In Canaan in particular, the religious life of the community had been debased to the lowest level. It is against this background that the command to exterminate the Canaanites must be seen. Israel, with its more austere morals and loftier faith, became the agent of divine judgment upon the Canaanites. Since God is both sovereign and righteous, and therefore active within history, this is only to be expected and it has been paralleled in the history of the nations many times subsequently. But the divine command

---

[1] D. J. Wiseman, 'Archaeology', in *NBD*, p. 70. The whole article is probably the best general introduction to the subject of biblical archaeology.

was also prophylactic. It was designed to safeguard the life of the nation from the corroding influences of Canaanite life. And since the purposes of God through Israel were redemptive, a redemption in which the whole world was ultimately to share, the importance of an Israel dedicated and uncontaminated is apparent.

This, then, in broad outline and with inevitable generalizations, was the situation which existed at the beginning of the period of the judges and we trace in the book of Judges the failure of Israel to remain loyal to her God.

1. It is clear that not all Israelites shared the lofty faith and high ideals of their leaders, Moses, Joshua and the elders. This is hardly surprising when the background of servitude in Egypt is considered, together with the presence of the mixed multitudes which attached themselves to Israel. The grumbling and the disobedience of the wilderness period were ominous portents of the future life in Canaan, whilst Joshua 24:15 shows that a living memory of past paganism lingered in the minds of many.

2. The incomplete conquest and the failure to exterminate the inhabitants of the land was Israel's undoing. Joshua, towards the end of his life, had exhorted his hearers that they 'come not among these nations, these that remain among you; neither make mention of the name of their gods, nor cause to swear by them, neither serve them, nor bow yourselves unto them' (Jos. 23:7), but the measure of their failure to comply with his commands was the measure of their failure to achieve all that God had promised them. They were content to settle down amongst the Canaanites and they lost the incentive to possess the whole land. Judges records both the fact and the effect of mixed marriages (3:5,6), in which the question of the relationship of Yahweh and the Baal gods would become an acute family problem. Whenever two groups of peoples come into contact there is an inevitable tendency to syncretism, the gods become identified, or, in the case of a conquered country, their gods find an inferior place in the pantheon of their conquerors. This process is not conscious or deliberate, but it is nevertheless real. In the case of Israel there would seem

39

to be a very specious reason why she should give attention to the gods of the land into which she entered. The God of Israel, Yahweh, was to the majority of the Israelites associated with the wilderness in which they had spent the earlier part of their lives. His superiority over the Baal gods had been demonstrated in the victories gained over the inhabitants of Canaan. But the gods of the land controlled the rain, springs and vegetation on which they would depend in their future settlement, at least, so the average Israelite, scarcely removed from polytheism, would argue. There was no conscious forsaking of Yahweh, but mixed marriages, the need to give deference to the forces controlling fertility, and the powerful appeal of Canaanite worship to the lower and more sensual nature, were all factors which led inevitably to an easy-going syncretism. Baal was identified with Yahweh, and Yahweh was worshipped, in degree, with the forms of Baal worship. This was, in fact, to be characteristic of the nation until after the destruction of Jerusalem in 587 BC. The prophets Hosea, Isaiah and Jeremiah in particular speak of their worship in terms of spiritual adultery, as 'going after Baal', a charge hotly repudiated by a people who were unconscious of the fact that they were not true Yahweh worshippers. In the course of the commentary we shall observe the course of this moral and spiritual declension. At the moment we are concerned to point out the fundamental nature of this apostasy. During the judges' period the nation, heedless of the clear warnings of its earlier leaders, took a wrong turning that was to have disastrous consequences.

3. Closely associated with the foregoing, there was a decline in the standard of leadership. The editor observes that 'the people served the Lord all the days of Joshua, and all the days of the elders that outlived Joshua, who had seen all the great work of the Lord . . .' (2:7). From that point on there was no-one remotely comparable with Moses, Joshua or Phinehas until the Lord raised up Samuel. Our appreciation of these stirring tales of the judges does not blind us to the blemishes in their characters, although the strength of their underlying faith in the Lord is unquestioned. Ehud was but a cowardly

assassin; Gideon led the people astray after his victory over the Midianites; Jephthah, with his unfortunate personal background, appears as an opportunist, in spite of his many admirable qualities; and the stories of Samson sadden rather than inspire and leave us wondering what he might have achieved, if he, like Caleb, had 'wholly followed the Lord'. We observe here the basic honesty of the narratives of the Bible. There is no attempt to whitewash the principal characters; their faults are clearly depicted and the focus throughout is on the infallible God, not fallible man.[1]

4. A point noted already must be briefly repeated here. The forces which made for disunity and division had a corresponding effect in reducing the effectiveness of the central sanctuary. Where there is a strong, central authority controlling the political, social and religious life of the community, there is little possibility of deviation. This did not obtain during the major part of the period of the judges and there was little to check the drift away from the standards set in the law of Moses.

5. It is possible, of course, to overdraw the picture and, as a corrective, we must observe that the tribal structure itself remained intact. Chapters 20 and 21 show the amphictyony in action against the offending tribe of Benjamin, and, just beyond the period of our text, we observe that external pressure from the Philistines, together with the leadership of a true man of God, Samuel, were to bring in a new unity which had been largely absent in the preceding century and a half. Even this unity had its limitations, for there was an irreparable gulf between north and south that stemmed from the period of the judges; it manifested itself frequently during the reigns of David and Solomon and was ultimately to issue in the formation of the rival kingdoms of Judah and Israel.

*c. Moral problems raised by the book of Judges*

Frequent references to the moral and religious shortcomings of the judges will be found in this commentary. These are dealt with in their context, but a more general discussion of the

---

[1] See also section *c.*, below.

issues involved is necessary. Unquestionably the problem becomes acutest in connection with Samson, a charismatic individual, yet one who appears sensual and completely irresponsible. He seems to have little, if any, religious fervour and his Nazirite vow, irregular and limited as it was, did not separate him from evil. Even his patriotism is suspect, for his actions seem to have been actuated by purely selfish motives. It is not surprising, therefore, that some Christians have found the stories a real embarrassment. The difficulty is increased still further by the fact that Samson is included in the list of the heroes of faith in the New Testament (Heb. 11:32).

There is also a particular problem within the general problem. It was when the Spirit of the Lord came upon Samson that some of his questionable feats of strength were performed (*e.g.* 14:19). We are accustomed to think in terms of New Testament doctrine which associates the possession of the Spirit of God with uprightness of character (*e.g.* 1 Cor. 3:16,17; 6:18–20). What was the association of Samson's anointing with morality of life? Was he responsible for his actions when possessed by the Spirit of God? What is the relationship between these narratives and the teaching of the New Testament? These are some of the questions which suggest themselves to the reader. It may be that no answer can be given which will fully satisfy every enquirer, especially within the limitations of this discussion. But the following suggestions and observations are advanced:

1. Samson was a man of his age, and that age was one of declension and apostasy. In these narratives we have a mirror of the prevailing conditions which is of inestimable value, albeit negatively. Not only was this a period when New Testament standards were still far distant, but even the standards of the Mosaic covenant were lightly regarded. The book of Judges is a faithful witness to this sombre but significant fact.

2. The purpose of the editor must be taken into account at this point. We have observed in our consideration of the structure of the book of Judges that there is a framework of editorial comment of a religious nature. This is less evident in

the Samson narratives. It has been suggested that 'they became so firmly fixed in tradition that even the editor of our book could do little to adapt them to the needs of the age in which he lived'.[1] Might it not be that he did not wish to adapt them in this way? If his concern was to trace the moral, political and religious decline of the period, these stories give eloquent support to his thesis without adaptation.

3. It was widely believed throughout this period that unusual power of any kind was a unique endowment from the Lord and an evidence of the working of His Spirit. Conversely, any abnormality was attributed to the possession of, or by, an evil spirit from the Lord, as in the case of Saul (1 Sa. 16:14ff.). Samson was a man of supernatural strength; therefore he was a man supernaturally endowed by the Spirit of the Lord. But it is too facile an explanation to leave this point simply as the popular (and possibly erroneous) reason advanced for Samson's great strength. We must ask whether this is a valid conception. Or is its validity limited to the unenlightened views of this period?

Throughout the Old Testament we find that events are related directly to God Himself. Thus the Lord is said to harden Pharaoh's heart (Ex. 4:21; 7:3,13, *etc.*); it is, as we have already mentioned, an evil spirit from the Lord that troubles Saul (1 Sa. 16:14); the Lord puts a lying spirit in the mouths of the false prophets (1 Ki. 22:23). This has created problems for the Christian. Some would explain these phenomena by reference to secondary causes, or by the laws of psychology, or to God's permissive will. Yet the witness of the Old Testament is accurate. For if God is sovereign, then that sovereignty must be taken seriously and all events and facts must be considered in relationship to it. Similarly, any reference to the laws of psychology is valid; but it must be realized that all law which is true must be an expression of God's sovereign manifestation within the universe. It is in this realm of ideas that the difficult expression of 14:4, 'he was seeking an occasion against the Philistines', finds its explanation. This incident, wherein Samson sought a wife from among the Philistines,

[1] Myers, p. 776.

was part of God's overruling of history. We have discussed elsewhere[1] the part played by Samson's lone exploits against the Philistines. He himself was not actuated by worthy motives, but without his exploits Israel could easily have succumbed to Philistine influence.

4. It is apparent that God may make a man a vehicle of His revelation, or a channel of power, quite apart from the quality of life of the individual concerned. In the Old Testament we find Him employing the most unlikely agents. He used Balaam, a time-serving, non-Israelite prophet (Nu. 22–24); there is the possibility that Shamgar was a non-Israelite (Jdg. 3:31); the heathen monarch Nebuchadnezzar is described as His servant (Je. 25:9; 27:6; 43:10); Cyrus, the Persian king, is styled 'my shepherd' and 'his anointed' (Is. 44:28; 45:1), although it is specifically pointed out that 'you do not know me' (Is. 45:4). There is an inscrutable element in this fact of God's choice which is not completely open to man's understanding. From the human standpoint we may question how God could equip and employ a man like Samson. But the fact is that He did, and while the details of Samson's life may cause embarrassment to the modern reader, the value of the part which he played in the history of Israel is evident.

It is equally clear that, in this period, the coming of God's Spirit upon a man is not to be equated with the fuller teaching and revelation of the Holy Spirit in the New Testament period. A charismatic anointing did not necessarily produce holiness of life. A certain limited range of activity was employed for the out-working of the divine will. The man so endowed was still accountable to God and his life ought to have been lived in conformity with the revelation and instruction already given. Samson failed abjectly at this point.

5. Finally, the book of Judges must be seen in the total context of the revelation of God in and through the Scriptures. This revelation is redemptive in its nature and purpose. It covers the unfolding of God's character and it culminates in the New Testament. In the Old Testament period God was dealing with material which was often intractable and un-

[1] See p. 154.

responsive. Whilst there were periods of great spiritual advance, such as the Mosaic period, or the time of the great eighth-century prophets, there were also times of regression. The Old Testament period is not a plane. It is a pathway, often tortuous, sometimes descending rather than ascending. But it is not aimless, and with the New Testament it forms one great and complex movement. The ages of spiritual and moral degeneracy are delineated accurately. The period of the judges was one of the 'dark ages' of Israel's history and the irregularities and problems contained therein must be set against this general background. In its own way it is a faithful witness to the fact of man's frailty and to his need not of a merely temporal deliverer, but of an eternal Saviour who can effect a perfect redemption.

### d. *The permanent religious value of Judges*

1. *God is righteous.* Attention has already been drawn to the sombre nature of the narrative which we are studying, and an attempt has been made to account for the moral and spiritual decline traced by the historian.[1] Some parts of the Old Testament make a positive appeal to us, exhorting us to the life of uprightness and integrity by direct command and instruction, or by illustration and inspiration in the life of a godly man. But in Judges the appeal is negative. As the reader observes the results of a nation's apostasy he is warned rather than edified. This is not formulated in abstract principles but in living examples, particularly in the last five chapters. One can almost hear the warning voice of the Holy Spirit, 'Beware lest you also fall into temptation and a similar fate befall you.' But behind this record of a nation which had lost its first love, vision and purity there is the unmistakable picture of a righteous God. It is true that the low standard is accounted for in part by the absence of authoritative human leadership, with every man doing 'that which was right in his own eyes'. But the editor underlines the fact that the misery which overtook the people was due to their forsaking of a holy God. Their sin was not an insignificant thing, to be passed over lightly; it

[1] See pp. 39ff.

was an affront to God's righteous being and as such was visited by stern and painful judgment. A nation that forsakes the Lord, or lowers and compromises His standards, cannot hope to prosper in any ultimate sense.

2. *God is sovereign.* This facet of the eternal character of God is, of course, implied in the preceding paragraph. He orders all the forces of nature and history in accordance with His own righteous will, thus working out His judgment upon the nation. This sovereign power, however, is also revealed in His saving activity through the various judges who are men upon whom His Spirit has come. This supernatural endowment means that deliverance is gained from nations numerically stronger than Israel itself. The account of the reduction of Gideon's army from an original 32,000 to an insignificant 300 and the consequent crushing of the host of the Midianites is a telling illustration of the view that the victory was the Lord's who fought for them (*cf.* Ps. 20:7; 118:6,7). The same truth is illustrated vividly in the Song of Deborah, where the forces of nature are depicted as participating in Israel's sweeping victory over Sisera. The book of Judges recounts the exploits of the judges, but the focus of attention is not on the individual but on the ever-present and all-powerful God. Gideon, the greatest of the judges, was conscious of little but his own inability and lack of qualifications (6:11–15), but the key to the situation was the divine promise, 'But I will be with you, and you shall smite the Midianites as one man' (6:16). Throughout Israel's long and chequered history the Hebrew historians, prophets and poets retained a profound consciousness of the Lord's sovereignty. It may well be necessary to remind the people of God in our own troubled generation that this sovereignty remains unimpaired. He is still on the throne.

3. *God is gracious and longsuffering.* The cycle of sin, servitude, supplication and salvation is repeated so frequently in Judges that it almost becomes monotonous. We must be on our guard against such an attitude, for it could so easily blind us to fundamental truths. The first is the downward bias of the human heart, mind and will and man's incurable reluctance to profit by experience, either his own or that of a previous

generation. One wonders how Israel *could* be so blind to the evident lessons of its history until one looks at one's own heart and experience. But there is a reverse side to this coin. In contrast to man's multiplied misdemeanours there is the constancy of a God who is always ready to hearken to the cries of His wayward people and to intervene on their behalf. He does not act precipitately to blot out the very name of a nation that had treated Him so shabbily. His arms are stretched out still to welcome the penitent supplicant. The forbearance of God and the wonderful possibility of a new beginning through His grace strikes a glad note in this book which cannot be silenced by the discordant sounds which appear to predominate.

4. *The importance of faith.* As we consider the characters of the individual judges we shall not discover much of moral grandeur to inspire us, but we shall often observe that quality of faith which co-operates with the Lord and enables Him to reveal His might. It is this aspect which the writer of the Epistle to the Hebrews takes up when he includes so many of the judges in his catalogue of the heroes of the faith. 'And what shall I more say? for the time will fail me if I tell of Gideon, Barak, Samson, Jephthah . . . who through faith subdued kingdoms . . .' (Heb. 11 : 32, 33, RV). Thus these men who achieved so much as God worked through them witness to our own generation, reminding us that the people that know their God (and how immeasurably greater is the revelation of God granted to us!) and have faith in Him can do mighty things (*cf.* Dn. 11:32).

## VI. THE HEBREW TEXT AND THE SEPTUAGINT

### a. *The Hebrew Text*
The small number of footnotes in the Revised Version of Judges indicates its excellent state of preservation. In a commentary of this kind it is impossible to enter into minute detail concerning the minor errors that may be detected, but it may be noted generally that almost all of these may be attributed to scribal errors in the transmission of the text. The exception to this is

the Song of Deborah, a very ancient poem which poses many problems to the modern scholar.

### *b. The Septuagint*

The book of Judges is of peculiar interest in connection with the Septuagint and it has frequently been maintained that there were two Greek versions of this book, represented principally in Codex Alexandrinus (fifth century) and Codex Vaticanus (fourth century), resting upon distinct Hebrew originals. Scholars are at variance as to which version is to be preferred and this has led, on occasion, to the unusual recourse of printing both versions side by side.[1] The recent discovery of the Dead Sea Scrolls confirms that there were considerable variations amongst the Greek texts of Judges.

[1] A full discussion of these problems may be found in Burney, pp. cxxii ff.

# SELECTED BIBLIOGRAPHY

## I. COMMENTARIES

F. F. Bruce, 'Judges' (*NBC*²) (I.V.F., 1954).

C. F. Burney, *The Book of Judges*² (Rivingtons, 1920).

G. A. Cooke, *The Book of Judges (The Cambridge Bible)* (Cambridge University Press, 1913).

J. Garstang, *The Foundations of Bible History: Joshua, Judges* (Constable, 1931).

C. F. Keil and F. Delitzsch, *Joshua, Judges and Ruth (Biblical Commentary on the Old Testament*, Vol. IV) (T. & T. Clark, 1887).

G. F. Moore, *A Critical and Exegetical Commentary on Judges*² (*International Critical Commentary*) (T. & T. Clark, 1903).

J. M. Myers, *The Book of Judges (IB*, Vol. 2) (Nelson, 1953).

G. W. Thatcher, *Judges and Ruth (The Century Bible)* (Caxton Publishing Company, 1904).

## II. INTRODUCTIONS

A. Weiser, *Introduction to the Old Testament* (Darton, Longman & Todd, 1961).

E. J. Young, *An Introduction to the Old Testament* (Tyndale Press, 1960).

## III. HISTORICAL BACKGROUND

J. Bright, *A History of Israel* (S.C.M. Press, 1960).

R. K. Harrison, *A History of Old Testament Times* (Marshall, Morgan and Scott, 1957).

M. Noth, *The History of Israel*² (A. & C. Black, 1960).

## IV. GENERAL

W. F. Albright, *Archaeology of Palestine* (Pelican, 1960).
*The New Bible Dictionary* (I.V.F., 1962).

R. de Vaux, *Ancient Israel* (Darton, Longman & Todd, 1962).

# ANALYSIS

# COMMENTARY

## I. THE INCOMPLETE CONQUEST OF CANAAN
### (1:1 – 2:5)

### a. The conquest of southern Canaan (1:1-21)

These verses supplement the account of the Conquest preserved in the book of Joshua and as such are of great value. Some of the difficulties concerning the inter-relationship of the accounts have already been dealt with in the Introduction.[1]

**1:1a. Introduction.** As the death of Joshua is dealt with in greater detail in 2:6–9, the most likely explanation of the first section of this verse is that it is the title and general introduction to the whole book; *i.e.*, it is concerned with the history of the post-Joshua age. 1:1b–2:5 actually deal with events during the lifetime of Joshua but are presented in such a way as to provide the background for the main part of the book of Judges.

**1:1b-7. Initial success.** The tribes of Judah and Simeon were blood-brothers (Gn. 29:33–35) and are uniformly depicted as acting in the closest relationship. The inheritance of Simeon was within the borders of Judah (Jos. 19:1) and it appears certain that Simeon soon lost its tribal identity, being absorbed in the more powerful tribe. After the consolidation of a secure base in the central highlands it is likely that the individual tribes were allowed a certain freedom of action in conquering and occupying their own allotted territory, although it may be surmised that Joshua kept these individual thrusts as integral parts of the over-all strategy. No certain location can be given to the scene of the first success of Judah and Simeon, although Bezek has been tentatively identified with the modern Khirbet Bezqa in the vicinity of Gezer, west-north-west of Jerusalem. Adoni-bezek (the name means 'lord

[1] See p. 19.

of Bezek') has been confused with Adoni-zedek of Joshua
10:1, a confusion increased by the LXX which has Adoni-bezek
in both verses. But in Joshua, Adoni-zedek is said to be the
king of Jerusalem and the leader of the southern confederation
of Canaanite cities against the Gibeonites, who had entered
into an alliance with the Israelites. In Judges Adoni-bezek was
defeated at Bezek and was brought to Jerusalem after being
mutilated.

**1b.** Enquiry is made of the Lord as to which tribe or tribes
should lead against the Canaanites. This enquiry doubtless
involved the manipulation of the oracle, the exact form of which
is uncertain but which probably consisted of small, flat,
inscribed stones which were used rather akin to the dice in
modern games, the various combinations allowing for alternative answers. This method appears unsatisfactory to the
Christian who has the Holy Spirit to guide and direct him,
but it was widely used throughout the Ancient Near East
and is found in New Testament times before the descent of the
Spirit of God at Pentecost (Acts 1:24–26). It was firmly
believed that the Lord controlled this device and made
known His will thereby. *Cf.* Proverbs 16:33, 'The lot is cast
into the lap, but the decision is wholly from the Lord.'

**2.** The Lord's answer indicated His sovereignty. There was
much hard fighting ahead, but the final outcome of the
conflict was not in doubt.

**4.** The term *Canaanites* usually designates all the inhabitants
of the land at the time of the Israelite invasion. Occasionally
a distinction is made between the Canaanites and the Amorites,
the former being noted as occupying the valleys and coastal
plain and the latter as dwelling in the mountains (*e.g.* Nu.
13:29). The *Perizzites* are unknown, but as they are mentioned
in conjunction with the Canaanites it is likely that they were
an aboriginal group rather than merely the local name of the
Canaanite population.

**6, 7.** The mutilation of *Adoni-bezek* not only humiliated
him, but rendered him an impotent cripple who could not
wield any weapon effectively. Such treatment, which to the
modern reader seems so harsh, and was only infrequently

employed by Israel, was accepted almost philosophically by
the king, such was the strength of the *lex talionis*. The law of
'an eye for an eye and a tooth for a tooth' was set aside by
Christ (Mt. 5:38,39). The reference to *seventy kings* (RSV) is
doubtless hyperbolic, indicating a great, rather than a precise,
number. The incapacitated ruler of Bezek was no longer a
danger to the Israelites and was brought to Jerusalem by his
own followers, where he died. But the security of the city where
he found refuge was soon to be shattered by the same army
that had defeated him so decisively.

**1:8. Jerusalem.** The city of Jerusalem is one of the oldest
cities in the world, having been occupied almost continually
for a period of 5,000 years. Archaeological investigation of its
lower levels has been hampered because of this continuous
occupation, but it is certain that it existed *c*. 3000 BC, when it
was little more than a mountain fortress on the hill Ophel,
south of the present Temple area. It is mentioned in Egyptian
execration texts of the nineteenth century BC and in the Tell
el-Amarna correspondence of the fourteenth century BC,
when it was an important city-state. There is no reason to
doubt that the Salem over which Melchizedek ruled as priest-
king is to be identified with Jerusalem (Gn. 14:18). Its capture
and destruction recorded here is complicated by the reference
in verse 21 that Benjamites did not drive out the Jebusites from
Jerusalem, and by Joshua 15:63 which notes that Judah did
not expel the Jebusites from Jerusalem. Probably the city,
after its destruction, was not occupied by the Israelites and
was subsequently reoccupied by the Jebusites. Or, less likely,
it may have been recaptured by the Canaanites because of its
important position on a main line of communication (see the
note on verse 35). The centre of the tribe of Judah was
located much further south in Hebron. The apparent confusion between Judah and Benjamin can be readily explained
on this hypothesis, for as the city of Jerusalem lay close to the
dividing-line between the two tribes, when it was reoccupied
by the Jebusites it formed an enclave, a 'no man's land'
between the two that either might legitimately acquire, al-

though, strictly speaking, it was part of the possession of Benjamin (Jos. 18:16). It was not conquered again until the time of David (2 Sa. 5:6ff.), when it became the politically-acceptable capital of both the northern and southern sections of his kingdom largely because it was on 'neutral' territory. It must be remembered that the Israelites were not sufficiently strong numerically to occupy all the territory and cities they conquered (Ex. 23:29, 30; Dt. 7:22–24).

**1:9–20. To the south and west of Jerusalem.** The AV of verse 9, *in the mountain, and in the south, and in the valley*, does not make sufficiently clear that these refer to the three major divisions of the southern part of the land. The first is *the hill country* (RV, RSV) which describes the mountainous region between Jerusalem and Hebron; the second, *the South* (RV) or *Negeb* (RSV), is the semi-arid area between Hebron and Kadesh-barnea; the third, *the lowland* (RV, RSV), often called the Shephelah from the Hebrew word used here, is the region of foot-hills running north and south between the coastal plain and the central mountain range. There is here a summary (amplified in the following verses) of the movements of Judah and her allies.

**10.** *Kiriath-arba* means 'city of four', pointing to its probable origin in a federation of four cities, a view strengthened by the fact that *Hebron* itself means 'confederacy' or 'association'. It can readily be appreciated that such unions were made because of the mutual strength they afforded in time of need (*cf.* Jos. 9:17; 10:3). *Hebron*, 19 miles south-south-west of Jerusalem, had associations with Abraham (Gn. 13:18, *etc.*). Later on it was to be the capital of Judah during the first seven years of David's reign (2 Sa. 5:5). *Sheshai, Ahiman* and *Talmai* are described in verse 20 as 'the three sons of Anak'. The Anakim, being proverbial for their great stature, were feared by the Israelites (*cf.* Dt. 9:2)[1]. Tradition uniformly associates Caleb with Hebron (Jos. 14:6ff.; Jdg. 1:20). Possibly

[1] E. C. B. MacLaurin, in *VT*, XV. 4, 1965, pp. 468–474, produces strong reasons for assuming a connection between the sons of Anak and the Philistines.

it was that portion of the land which was his particular responsibility to reconnoitre when the spies went on their mission (the detail of Nu. 13:22 indicates a source in either Caleb or Joshua himself).

**11.** *Debir*, 11 miles south-west of Hebron and strategically situated between the Negeb and the Shephelah, was the next principal target. The earlier name *Kiriath-sepher*, meaning 'the city of books' or 'city of records', has found no convincing explanation although it may suggest that it was the repository of a library like those of the great Mesopotamian cities. Debir, the modern Tell Beit Mirsim, is one of the more important centres of archaeological interest. It was a strongly defended city, approximately 7½ acres in extent, which was destroyed by fire *c.* 1220 BC. No break in occupation followed, but the architecture and culture in the succeeding decades was of a greatly inferior standard.

**12-15.** (*Cf.* Jos. 15:15-19.) It is not clear in this section whether *Othniel* was the nephew or the younger brother of *Caleb*: the grammatical connection permits either alternative. Caleb is called 'the son of Jephunneh the Kenizzite' (Nu. 32:12). The Kenizzites were an Edomite clan (Gn. 36:11) associated with the tribe of Judah. It is of considerable interest and significance to observe that both Caleb and Othniel were able to rise to positions of prominence in this truly classless society. Caleb, whose pedigree went back to Edom rather than to Israel, was a prince in Judah and was actually chosen as its representative in the reconnaissance of Canaan (Nu. 13:2,3,6). Caleb, although an old man, had shown conspicuous bravery in the capture of Hebron; now, at Debir, it was Othniel's turn and his success was rewarded by his marriage to Achsah. The city appears to have been given to Othniel and his bride as an inheritance, but Achsah asked of her father a dowry, a field with *springs of water*, so essential in such a semi-arid area.

**16.** The adjectival *Kenite* cannot refer to an individual without the article, which suggests that a name has dropped out, probably either Jethro (as in Codex Vaticanus) or Hobab (as in Codex Alexandrinus). The Kenites were a nomadic group closely connected with the Amalekites (*cf.* 1 Sa. 15:6);

but whereas the latter had shown themselves the implacable foes of the Israelites (Ex. 17:8–16), the former had lived harmoniously with them. A further difficulty arises because, while Hobab is connected with the Kenites (Jdg. 4:11), Jethro is elsewhere associated with the Midianites (Ex. 18:1). An explanation may be found in the nomadic character of the Kenites whose wanderings could associate them with both the Amalekites and the Midianites. Another well-known difficulty is the relationship between Reuel, Jethro and Hobab (*cf.* Ex. 2:18; 3:1; Nu. 10:29; Jdg. 4:11). The Hebrew words for 'father-in-law' and 'brother-in-law' have exactly the same consonants, and as the system indicating the vowel sounds was not completed until the sixth to the ninth centuries AD, some confusion does exist. The most plausible explanation is that Hobab is synonymous with Jethro as Moses' father-in-law and that Reuel was a remote ancestor.

*The city of palm trees* elsewhere indicates Jericho (3:13), but that identification is ruled out here by the context. Possibly it was located at the southern end of the Dead Sea. *Arad* was approximately 16 miles due south of Hebron, in a very desolate region. An earlier Canaanite king of Arad had enjoyed limited but short-lived success against the Israelites when they first approached the Promised Land, before their lack of faith led them to fall back into the wilderness (Nu. 21:1–3). The Amalekites were to be found in this area and many scholars emend *the people* to read 'the Amalekites' (the Hebrew word 'people' is formed with the first two consonants of the word 'Amalek'), suggesting that the Kenites settled in the vicinity of the Amalekites, with whom, as has been noted, they were closely connected.

**17.** The verse recalls the earlier incident (alluded to in the note on the preceding verse) recorded in Numbers 21:1–3, which some scholars feel should precede the mission of the spies (Nu. 13,14), since in Numbers 14:45 the defeated Israelites fall back upon Hormah, suggesting its capture at an earlier date. In any case there is no need to suggest confusion between the two accounts, nor to maintain that they prove a separate invasion, from the south, by Judah and her associates.

Archaeology shows that some towns (*e.g.* Debir) were destroyed more than once and the forty years between these events would have given Hormah a chance to re-establish itself. The continuity of occupation at a particular site is influenced strongly by such factors as availability of building materials, ease of defence and an adequate water-supply. *Hormah,* located about 20 miles south-west of Hebron, has a name derived from a verb meaning 'to devote to destruction', *i.e.* to destroy everything, animate and inanimate, as an offering to the gods (the custom was widely observed by nations other than Israel). The background of this custom is the religious one of covenantal obligation or promise to the deity. Its apparent brutality is mitigated by the fact that it did eliminate many of the evils associated with war, *e.g.* pillaging, raping, *etc.*

**18, 19.** The two verses, taken together, appear contradictory, since Gaza, Ashkelon and Ekron were on the low-lying coastal plain indicated in verse 19. Probably the Israelites, having taken these towns and their suburbs (AV *coast* refers to 'suburbs' or *territory*, RSV), were forced back into the hill-country where the Canaanites could not employ their chariots effectively. The Israelites feared the chariot as a weapon of war and rarely matched the Canaanites in combat waged on level ground, unless, as in the battle noted in Judges 4, 5, the chariots were immobilized as a result of torrential rain (5:4,5). Thus Judah *took possession of the hill country, but he could not drive out the inhabitants of the plain* (RSV). The Canaanites, and later on the Philistines, were able to work in *iron*, whereas Israel did not emerge from the Late Bronze Age until the time of David. It is likely that verse 19 is a general reference including both Canaanites and Philistines. Later on the Israelites viewed the use of chariots with reserve, as indicating dependence upon human power rather than the divine might (*e.g.* Ps. 20:7). David was quite unable to utilize the chariots captured from Hadadezer (2 Sa. 8:4) and not until Solomon's reign was effective use made of this weapon (1 Ki. 9:19; 10:26). We should all be better off today if we bore in mind that, in an age when the chariot has long since been superseded as a weapon of warfare, a faithful (and righteous) reliance upon the Lord is the stoutest weapon in the armoury of a nation or an individual.

The reference to *Gaza*, *Ashkelon* and *Ekron* relates to a period before the main Philistine settlement in the coastal plain. The Philistines were part of a complex migratory movement from the Aegean area a generation or so after Israel's entry into the land (*i.e.*, *c*. 1200 BC). These 'people of the sea' settled in large numbers in the coastal plain. Egypt, keeping them at bay with difficulty, allowed them to settle and form their pentapolis (Ekron, Ashdod, Ashkelon, Gaza and Gath). This does not preclude the probability of earlier, but smaller, settlements of Philistines noted in Genesis 21:32; 26:1.

**1:21. The Benjamites and Jerusalem.** (See note on verse 8.) The *Jebusites* were the Canaanite inhabitants of Jerusalem and its immediate environs, Jebus being an alternative name of the city (19:10,11). The reference *to this day* does not necessarily involve a date before David's capture of Jerusalem (2 Sa. 5) about 993 BC, since the Jebusite population was allowed to continue in the city after its capture (*cf.* 2 Sa. 24:16).

**b. The capture of Bethel (1:22-26)**
This ancient account of the capture of Bethel raises the question of its connection with the narrative of the Conquest in Joshua, which nowhere tells of the capture of Bethel but which includes the men of Bethel as allies of the men of Ai (Jos. 8:17). The two cities were very close together (Jos. 8:9,12), but archaeology shows clearly that the site of Ai was unoccupied from *c*. 2200 BC. It is unlikely that a mistake has been made in the identification of the site or that a Middle or Late Bronze Age town has been completely eroded. This problem has led many to conjecture that the names Ai and Bethel were used to refer to the same place, or, less likely, that the men of Bethel used the ruins of Ai (the name itself means 'a ruin') as an armed outpost against the advancing Israelites. The involvement of all the men of both cities (Jos. 8:17) demands some correlation of the two accounts. The sending up

of spies is a point that both have in common (1:23–25; Jos. 7:2,3), but this was a stratagem frequently employed by the Israelites, as in the case of Jericho (Jos. 2:1ff.). There is a broad parallel with the campaign against Jericho in that the informer and his family escaped the destruction which overtook the town. Notice, as in the case of Judah (1:2–4), that the presence of the Lord (22) was the guarantee of victory. *Bethel*, associated with the patriarch Jacob (Gn. 28:19), was to become one of the principal sanctuaries of the period of the judges. Afterwards, following the death of Solomon and the Disruption, it became the national shrine of the northern kingdom. Its name means 'house of God', using not Israel's distinctive name for its deity (Yahweh) but a designation common amongst Israel's neighbours; El was the nominal head of the Canaanite pantheon.

The *Hittites* (26) were a people of Indo-European descent who established a great Empire in Asia Minor and Syria during the period 1800–1200 BC. Archaeologists have discovered many connections between incidents in the patriarchal and Mosaic periods and Hittite laws and observances, notably in the Hittite suzerainty treaties which have thrown light on the earlier period of Israel's history. The area of Syria was known as 'the land of the Hittites' at the time of the Conquest (Jos. 1:4), while later Assyrian and Babylonian records refer to Syria and Palestine as the 'Hatti-land'. The man who betrayed Bethel may have been a Hittite, left behind at the decline of the Empire, who returned to his own race after this incident. The location of *Luz* is completely unknown.

## c. A catalogue of unoccupied territory (1:27–36)

**27, 28.** The cities mentioned in verse 27 controlled one of the most important trade-routes of Canaan, which passed through the valleys of Jezreel and Esdraelon and formed a wedge between the Israelites occupying the hill-country to the north and south. Whilst victories were recorded (Jos. 12:21,23) against the kings of some of these cities it is clear that the Canaanites were able to dominate the low-lying areas, where they were able to deploy their chariots effectively (*cf.* Jos.

17:11–13). A glance at the map, however, will show that these cities were widely separated, so that, while the Canaanites were able to maintain control of the valley itself, there would still be a considerable freedom of movement between the Israelites in the adjacent highlands. *Beth-shean* was an important fortress commanding the junction between the Jordan valley and the valley of Jezreel. It is known that an Egyptian garrison was maintained here until the time of Rameses III (1175–1144 BC), whilst at a later date there are indications of a Philistine occupation (*cf.* 1 Sa. 31 : 10). The phrase *and her towns* (AV, RV; lit. 'daughters', RV mg.) refers to the surrounding suburbs or *villages* (RSV) which would associate themselves with the mother-city for reasons of trade and security.

*Ibleam* controlled the southern exit of the Esdraelon valley to Shechem and Bethel. *Taanach* was 5 miles south-east of *Megiddo*, with which it was often associated (Jos. 12:21; 17:11; Jdg. 5:19; 1 Ki. 4:12), and these two cities dominated the south-western pass from the Esdraelon valley to the Plain of Sharon and beyond. Megiddo was under Egyptian control until the middle of the twelfth century BC when it was suddenly destroyed, remaining unoccupied for a considerable period; hence the oblique reference in 5:19. *Dor* was situated on the Mediterranean coast just south of the Carmel promontory. Its position in the text interrupts the general westward movement of the description; possibly it came last originally, as in 1 Chronicles 7:29. The final reduction of these Canaanite enclaves was not achieved until the time of David, who used their non-Israelite population as a source of cheap labour, as did Solomon after him. The ultimate effect of this was that a considerable Canaanite element was eventually assimilated into the northern section of Israel, which must have accelerated the Canaanization of its worship.

**29.** *Gezer* was strategically situated on a low spur of the Shephelah, some 18 miles west of Jerusalem, in the extreme south-west of the tribal portion of Ephraim. It is mentioned several times in Egyptian inscriptions, including the recording of its capture by Merenptah on his 'Israel' stele, *c.* 1220 BC. Obviously a town of some consequence, it was not held by

Israel until the time of Solomon, when Pharaoh captured it and annihilated its inhabitants and then presented it to his son-in-law as a wedding present (1 Ki. 9:15-17).[1]

**30.** Neither *Kitron* nor *Nahalol* has been positively identified. The territory of *Zebulun* is noted in Joshua 19:10-16.

**31, 32.** Whilst most of the tribes were able to occupy at least some part of their allotted territory, the tribe of Asher seems to have failed completely to dislodge the Canaanites, hence the significant change *the Asherites dwelt among the Canaanites* (*cf.* verses 27, 29, 30). The same situation applied in measure in the tribal portions of Naphtali and Dan (verses 33-35). It should be realized that this makes for a certain idealization in the lists in Joshua which delineate the tribal boundaries. What was intended was never achieved and the consequent disorganization affected the tribal boundaries in areas which *were* completely occupied, as tribes which could not occupy their designated territory encroached on that of their neighbours. This means that there are sometimes difficulties in ascertaining the original boundaries as noted in Joshua, which is hardly surprising in the circumstances.

The first four cities listed in verse 31 were all situated on the coast north of Mount Carmel. In this area the Canaanite inhabitants of the land retained the virility which was lost elsewhere, and this region developed into the important maritime kingdom of Phoenicia, with which David and Solomon entered into alliance (2 Sa. 5:11; 1 Ki. 5:1-12). It was a Phoenician princess, Jezebel, who introduced the worship of Baal-melqart into Israel following her marriage to Ahab (1 Ki. 16:31), with disastrous results.

**33.** The sites of the two cities are unidentified, but the names are suggestive. *Beth-shemesh* ('house of the sun') was probably a sanctuary dedicated to the worship of the sun-god; *Beth-anath* ('house of Anath') was dedicated to Anath, the Canaanite goddess of fertility and the consort of Baal. Variants

---

[1] An obvious problem is how a Canaanite city so close to David's capital could remain uncaptured during his long and successful reign. It has been plausibly conjectured that the reference to Gezer should read Gerar, a town probably situated 11 miles south-east from Gaza and noted in Genesis 26:1, 8 (*cf.* Gn. 21:32, 34) as being in the 'land of the Philistines'.

of these names are not uncommon in the land settled by the Israelites.

**34, 35.** The Danites, like the Asherites, failed to occupy their territory. Their position was precarious in the extreme, however, for, unlike the Asherites, they were not permitted to settle in the midst of the inhabitants of the land. Instead, they were under continual pressure and were forced up into the territory properly belonging to Judah. So acute was their predicament that a considerable number of them eventually migrated to the extreme north of the land (18:1ff.).

An evidence of design on the part of the writer may be observed at this stage. He notes the increasing deterioration of the situation; in verses 27–30 the Canaanites dwell amongst the Israelites and are eventually reduced to the status of slave-labourers; in the case of Asher and Naphtali (31–33) the Canaanites dominate but the Israelites remain; but in verse 34 the Danites are completely dispossessed. It is likely that the *Amorites* were themselves under pressure from the Philistines who, settling in the coastal strip in large numbers *c.* 1200 BC, drove its surviving inhabitants into the foot-hills, so that the Danites, denied a place in the lowlands, were eventually ousted from the hill-country. The Samson narratives show the effect of direct Philistine pressure in this movement. *Aijalon,* 11 miles north-west of Jerusalem, is the only city positively identified, although *mount Heres* (AV, RV; *Har-heres,* RSV, 'hill of the sun') has been suggested as equivalent to Beth-shemesh ('house of the sun', not to be confused with the city of the same name in verse 33) some 15 miles west of Jerusalem. The three cities probably dominated the main route from Jerusalem and the central highlands to the coastal plain, thus driving another lesser wedge into Israelite territory and increasing the isolation of Judah in the south.

**36.** The *going up to* (or *ascent of*) *Akrabbim* is the pass to Akrabbim (lit. 'scorpions') which is usually identified with the main pass to Beersheba from the region just south of the Dead Sea. The mention of the border of the *Amorites* in this area is perplexing and its connection with the preceding verses is obscure. The difficulty is probably caused by the fact that these verses are a selection from a fuller account, detailing the frontiers of the tribes, which may have ended with this verse. Some scholars favour the reading of several manuscripts of the LXX which read 'Edomites' for 'Amorites' (the change in Hebrew is very slight), in which case the reference would be to the border between Judah and Edom.

### d. The effect of the broken covenant (2:1-5)
In this section the Lord faces the people with the evidence of their infidelity. The *angel of the Lord* is regularly used in the Old Testament to denote the manifestation of the Lord Himself in a theophany. Some scholars find the idea of an angel journeying from one place to another a difficult concept and suggest that the word should be translated literally as *messenger* (RV mg.) and interpreted as a prominent leader amongst the Israelites, possibly Phinehas. This difficulty is removed when the movement is related to the change in site of the amphictyonic shrine, with its tabernacle and the ark of the covenant. Throughout the wilderness period the Shekinah Glory, the evidence of the Lord's presence in their midst, had been associated with the tabernacle. Now, after the closing of the initial stages of the occupation of the land, the central sanctuary was moved from *Gilgal*, between the river Jordan and Jericho, to a more suitable location. *Bochim* means 'weepers' and its position is unknown. The LXX at this point reads *to Bochim and to Bethel and to the house of Israel*, a reading not without its difficulties but one which does suggest the connection of Bethel and Bochim, a conjecture strengthened by the fact that the sanctuary is found at Bethel elsewhere in Judges (20:18-28; 21:1-4). The offering of sacrifice (5b) would normally be at the central shrine. Another indication of the connection between the two may be found in Genesis 35:8 where Deborah, Rebekah's nurse, was buried beneath 'the oak of weeping' in the vicinity of Bethel. Such a play on place-names was typically Hebrew.

Our appreciation of the covenant-idea has been immeasurably deepened in recent years by archaeological evidence of Mesopotamian treaty forms and, in particular, of

Hittite suzerainty treaties.[1] In these a set pattern is apparent. The great Hittite king first declares his name, his splendid character and his mighty works on behalf of the subject peoples. Then, in the main body of the treaty, the various stipulations to be observed are set forth, one of the chief of these being loyal obedience to the great king. The gods are then invoked as witnesses, and blessings and curses are invoked upon the obedient and disobedient respectively to complete the treaty. Many scholars have seen certain parallels to this form in Exodus 20, Deuteronomy 1-28 and Joshua 24.

The emphasis here is on the broken covenant. The Lord had been faithful in the fulfilment of His promise to the patriarchs (*cf.* Ex. 33:1; Nu. 14:23; 32:11; Dt. 1:35; 10:11; 31:20, 21, 23; 34:4; Jos. 1:6). He had brought them up out of Egypt and into the Promised Land. In this and every situation no blame could be attached to the Almighty, who could not act in a way inconsistent with His own righteous nature. But the covenant was not unconditional. Israel was required to be loyal to her Saviour-God and obedient to His commandments, 'by loving the Lord your God, by walking in his ways, and by keeping his commandments and his statutes and his ordinances, then you shall live and multiply, and the Lord your God will bless you in the land which you are entering to take possession of it' (Dt. 30:16). Israel was, in particular, to make no covenant with the Canaanites and no compromise with its debased religion (Ex. 23:32,33; 34:10-16). The nation, in its failure to obey these injunctions, showed itself, not for the first or the last time, unfaithful to the Lord and it suffered as a consequence. The prevalence of mixed marriages with the Canaanites inevitably compromised the purity of the worship of Yahweh, and in the generally low spiritual atmosphere a superstitious deference was paid to the local gods deemed responsible for the fertility of the land.

The Canaanites were eventually to disappear as a people.[2]

---

[1] See J. A. Thompson, *The Ancient Near Eastern Treaties and the Old Testament* (Tyndale Press, 1964).

[2] *Cf.* J. Gray, *The Canaanites* (Thames & Hudson, 1964). The author points out (p. 16) that the word 'Canaanite' denotes a *culture* rather than a

They became assimilated into the nation of Israel which thereby showed its superior virility, but the leaven of Canaan eventually permeated the whole nation. Nowhere else in the sacred record, perhaps, are the disastrous effects of compromise seen so clearly as in this chapter of Israel's history. Absolute loyalty and obedience and the rejection of the claims of expediency and selfishness are required of those who would follow the Lord. But the graciousness of God became the more apparent through this sad chapter of events. He did not cast off the nation irrevocably because it had broken the covenant. Rather He raised up judges and, later on, prophets, to woo and to win the nation back from its infidelity. And even when His final judgment fell upon the nation in the catastrophes of 721 and 587 BC He did not abandon His redemptive purposes, but, working through a purified remnant, prepared the way for the New Covenant, sealed by Christ's death, with a new and inward dynamic making for that filial obedience so sadly lacking in Israel's chequered history. Truly it can be said of our God, *I will never break my covenant with you* (1).

Confronted with their sin the children of Israel wept, but in the light of their subsequent history it may not be unjust to regard their tears as superficial. Certainly there was no evidence of a true and abiding repentance. The Lord is not deceived by the external expressions of repentance; He looks for the rent heart, not the rent garments (Joel 2:12–14; *cf.* Ps. 51:17).

**3.** The Hebrew text reads 'they shall be as sides to you' and most scholars favour a minor emendation of the word 'sides' (*ṣiddîm*) and read 'they shall be adversaries (*ṣarîm*) to you', linking the text more directly to the earlier warning in Numbers 33:55 and Joshua 23:13. Another view compares *ṣiddîm* with the Assyrian *ṣaddu* meaning 'net', 'snare' or 'trap' and makes the whole section a sustained metaphor, in other words the inhabitants will be traps into which the Israelites will stumble by being led astray to worship the gods of the country,

---

distinct ethnic group, and covers the mainly Semitic population of Syria and Palestine in the second millennium BC.

and the gods will be the striker which pins them down so that
they cannot escape.[1] Here the reference is to a type of bird
snare still familiar in Palestine in which the victim, flying into a
trap, actuates a spring which causes it to be knocked down or
pierced.

## II. ISRAEL IN THE PERIOD OF THE JUDGES
### (2:6 – 16:31)

### a. Introduction to the period (2:6 – 3:6)

**2:6–10. The death of Joshua.** These verses are paralleled
in Joshua 24:28–31, strengthening the view noted in the Introduction that 1:1–2:5 comes from a separate source but was
possibly introduced by the original editor to provide the background for the main part of his book. In Joshua the section concludes the book and the account of the Conquest, here it really
introduces the period of the judges, and the minor differences
are easily accounted for when this is borne in mind. For
instance, in verse 7 the adjective *great* qualifies the *work of the
Lord*, but this is not found in Joshua 24:31. The addition is
significant, for the apostasy of the period of the judges is all
the more reprehensible when set against the *great work of the
Lord*. Great privileges do involve great responsibilities.

Verse 6 helps us to understand the nature of the Conquest.
The united campaigns under Joshua's leadership had broken
the back of the Canaanite resistance, but much of the local
campaigning was left to the individual tribes. So after the
covenant-renewal ceremony at Shechem the tribes, having
been dismissed by Joshua, set about completing the occupation of their own allotted territory. Joshua 23, dating from the
period when 'Joshua was old and well advanced in years', *i.e.*
from approximately the same time as chapter 24, makes it
clear that the tribes had a considerable amount of hard
fighting to do before the land could properly be said to be
conquered. Some of the problems associated with the Conquest
are eased when it is borne in mind that there were these two
phases.

[1] Driver, p. 6.

The influence of Joshua is revealed in Israel's loyalty to the Lord during his lifetime and that of the elders who were associated with him. In the biblical records stress is laid upon the soldierly qualities and exploits of Joshua. Underlying these, however, there was obviously a deep loyalty to the Lord and an integrity of conduct akin to that of his great predecessor, Moses. Joshua, and true men of God of all the ages, are the salt of the earth, staying corruption and ensuring purity. But each generation must enter into its own living religious experience; it cannot continue in the spiritual strength of its past heroes. It is clear that paganism was never very far from the surface during this early period of Israel's history and, when Joshua and his close contemporaries died, the new generation shared neither their faith nor their recollections of the great deliverance wrought for them by the Lord (2:10).

In the Introduction 30 years was suggested for the period of Joshua, and the elders who survived him. This must be regarded as a minimum, since Joshua, 110 years old at his death, was a young man at the time of the Exodus (*cf.* Ex. 33:11). He is described here as *the servant of the Lord* (8), a designation frequently used of Moses and also applied to other outstanding leaders in Israel's history, such as David and the prophets. It implies a vocation to a special mission. There is no higher and more honoured position than that of a faithful servant of the Lord (*cf.* Heb. 3:5). *Timnath-heres*(9) should be read as 'Timnath-serah', as in Joshua 19:50; 24:30; a scribe has obviously reversed the consonants. The site of Joshua's burial has been fairly certainly identified as the modern Tibneh, 10 miles north-west of Bethel.

**2:11–19. God's judgment on Israel's apostasy.** The history of almost two centuries is here summarized, indicating the principles behind the Lord's dealings with Israel. During this period there was a recurring cycle of four phases: apostasy, servitude, supplication and deliverance. It is this pattern which is illustrated in the succeeding chapters. The nation forsook the Lord, a crime which involved disloyalty to their forefathers and a wilful overlooking of the mighty works of the

Lord on their behalf, especially the deliverance from Egypt. All the evidence of their traditions ought to have ensured their faithfulness, but instead they turned to the gods of the people into whose midst they had come, whose religion seemed more directly concerned with their own prosperity.

**13.** *Baal*, the son of El in the Canaanite pantheon, was the god of the storm and the rains and therefore the controller of vegetation. He was the great active god, El being a somewhat nebulous figure, and Baal worship was widely diffused in the Ancient Near East. Several local variants are noted in the Old Testament, for example Baal-berith (Jdg. 9:4), Baal-peor (Nu. 25:3), Baal-gad (Jos. 11:17), and Baal-zebub, or more probably Baal-zebul (2 Ki. 1:2). Jezebel introduced into Israel the worship of Baal-melqart, the Phoenician variety. Hadad was the name of the Syrian counterpart of the Canaanite Baal. It is for this reason that the Old Testament writers, somewhat contemptuously, lump the various forms together as *Baalim*, the plural form. The fact that Baalim may also mean 'husbands', 'owners' or 'lords' gives point to the metaphor of adultery (*cf.* verse 17) so frequently employed by the prophets (*e.g.* Ho. 2:1ff.; 3:1ff.; Je. 3:6ff., *etc.*).

*Ashtaroth*, the consort of Baal, is the plural form of Astarte, the goddess of war and fertility, who was worshipped as Ishtar in Babylonia and as Anath in North Syria. In the Ugaritic texts Anath, often styled as 'the Virgin', is the sister of Baal and the great active goddess. There is a certain fluidity in the inter-relationships of the nature gods of the Fertile Crescent. The religion of these fertility gods was accompanied by all kinds of lascivious practices, especially in Canaan, where it was found in a degraded form which even incorporated child sacrifice.

**14, 15.** Israel's failure to exterminate the Canaanites automatically allowed for the continued worship of the Canaanite gods. Thus the nation which had defeated the inhabitants of the land in battle succumbed to the enervating influences of the gods of the land. The historian, however, was keenly aware that the gods of the land had no existence except in the imaginations of their worshippers. Only one god *was* God and His sovereign displeasure at Israel's infidelity was shown in the way He used the surrounding nations as a rod of chastisement to His own people. Israel was harried, enslaved and enfeebled, and, through the operation of the law of cause and effect (the sapping of its spiritual strength by the sensuous Baal cult being accompanied by a corresponding decline in its moral and physical vitality), the nation was brought into deep distress. Their forsaking of the Lord had one further consequence. Since the bond which united the nation was primarily a religious one, centred in the covenant and expressed in worship at the amphictyonic shrine, the weakening of the bond led to a weakening of their unity and they became disorganized and divided.

**16.** No express mention is made here that in their distress the Israelites turned to the God whom they had forsaken, but the regularity with which this is noted subsequently (3:9, *etc.*) allows us to assume it here. When the nation *did* cry to the Lord He, in His mercy and longsuffering, *raised up judges* to save them from their oppressors. We have already observed in the Introduction[1] that these men were conceived to have been divinely endowed with supernatural powers, which they manifested in delivering the people and in their subsequent rule. But even their influence was short-lived. The Israelites had short memories and when the immediate crisis was over they forgot both their earlier misery and the state of temporary repentance which it had induced. Their 'turning to the Lord' was thus revealed as a superficial expedient. It may be that we can recall something similar in our own lifetime, either in the life of our nation (witness the days of national prayer during the world wars of this century) or, more pertinently, in our own experience. How easy it is to use Almighty God as a kind of emergency, crash-aid service! Gratitude for deliverance, both for Israel of old and the spiritual Israel of today, ought to be expressed in lifelong dedication (*cf.* Rom. 12:1ff.).

**17.** Imperfect obedience was shown even during the lifetime of the judges themselves, a process which is described as

[1] See pp. 15ff.

spiritual adultery, *they went a whoring after other gods* (AV, RV), or *they played the harlot after other gods* (RSV). Israel, called to be the bride of the Lord, had forsaken Him to follow other lovers, *i.e.* the fertility gods of Canaan. This graphic imagery of the violated covenant of marriage provides the background for the entire book of the eighth-century prophet to Israel, Hosea, and is also applied by Jeremiah to the equally desperate situation in Judah a century and a half later (Je. 3:1ff.).

**19.** A progressive deterioration is revealed, each successive cycle being characterized by a greater descent into apostasy and corruption, and by a more superficial repentance, than the one preceding. This process is consistent with our modern understanding of the psychology of man. Terminology changes with the passing of the years, but the profound insights into human nature which the Old Testament gives us cannot be denied. The voice of conscience can become dulled by successive acts of sin, and repentance can become more and more superficial until, ensnared in the character formed by a multitude of thoughts and actions, a miracle is needed to produce a genuine repentance and a seeking of the Lord with the whole heart.

**2:20–23. The result of continued apostasy.** Israel's obligation within the Sinaitic covenant was to give loyalty and unswerving obedience to the Lord who had wrought such mighty works for them. This could not be considered onerous in view of their unique relationship to their Saviour-God (Dt. 4:32–40), who had kept His side of the compact in fulfilling the promise made to the patriarchs concerning the Promised Land. Israel's disobedience, however, was followed inevitably by the divine chastisement. To the modern reader it seems somewhat incongruous that God should leave the foreign elements within Israel's borders as a punishment for apostasy, and to test the future faithfulness of the nation, when the very reason for the nation's defection is attributed to the failure to drive out this alien population.

There was no such difficulty to the Israelite historian, whose view of the Lord's sovereignty ruled out all secondary causes, everything being directly attributable to His overruling will. In the changed situation caused by Israel's disobedience this sovereignty was still manifested: the Canaanites were allowed to remain so that the loyalty of the covenant-people might be adequately tested. It was a searching examination which the nation, in the main, failed to pass.

**3:1–6. Israel and her neighbours.** Another supplementary reason for the presence of a considerable alien element is introduced here. It was not only a punishment, or an opportunity to test the nation's fidelity; it was also to provide them with experience in the art of warfare. These reasons must not be regarded as contradictory, for it was the manifold result, related directly to the Lord, which occupied the attention of the historian, rather than a single, all-embracing purpose. Israel was to be in a hostile environment for the major part of her history, due either to the pressures of the petty kingdoms which surrounded her or, at a later stage, due to her strategic position between the successive world-powers of Assyria, Babylonia, Persia and Greece on the one hand and Egypt on the other hand. Military prowess was a necessary accomplishment, humanly speaking, if she was to survive. And yet the attainment of this prowess only rarely obscured the fact that the victory was not the result of their own might but of the Lord's working for them (*e.g.* 2 Sa. 8:6,14).

It is likely that the original historian included the lists of verses 3 and 5. The former lists four nations compared with the latter's six, the *Canaanites* and *Hivites* being common to both, suggesting that the two sources were available to the writer who made no attempt at conflation. The *Philistines* were established in their five-city state of Gaza, Ashkelon, Ashdod, Ekron and Gath. Their rulers are always referred to by the designation *seren* (*lord*), a word which is probably connected with the Greek *koiranos* or *tyrannos*, the tyrant familiar in Greek classical history. The Aegean ancestry of the Philistines has already been noted.[1] *Canaanites* sometimes designates all the original inhabitants of the land, sometimes those who dwelt in the valleys

[1] See p. 58.

and coastal areas. The *Sidonians* were the Canaanite inhabitants of the area around the port of Sidon. These were to be known as the Phoenicians in a later age. Sidon at this early date was of greater importance than Tyre. The *Hivites* are usually identified with the Horites (Gn. 36:2; *cf.* 36:20,29) who established the flourishing kingdom of Mitanni in Upper Mesopotamia in the middle of the second millennium BC and encroached south-westwards into the Hermon and Lebanon ranges, and as far as the tetrapolis of the Gibeonites north-west of Jerusalem (Jos. 9:7,17). Two suggestions have been made regarding *the entering in of Hamath* (AV, RV). It could mean either the point of access between the Lebanon and the Anti-Lebanon ranges to the great Syrian valley in which Hamath stands, or, as contemporary scholarship suggests, 'Labo of Hamath', the modern Lebweh, 14 miles north-north-east of Baalbek. A less likely identification links the Hivites with the Hebrew word for 'tent village' and regards them as a rural community. The *Hittites, Amorites, Perizzites* and *Jebusites* have been described in the exegesis of 1:4,21,26,34. Surrounded by all these diverse elements Israel was unable to maintain her purity of race and religion; instead of remaining faithful to the Lord there was a facile acceptance of the nature gods of the land, and the corrupt practices associated with them. Israel's resolutions and protestations of loyalty to her covenant-God disappeared swiftly when confronted with the forces of expediency and sensual attraction.

## b. Othniel and Cushan-rishathaim of Aram (3:7-11)

The pattern into which the editor has arranged the narratives with which he deals is well illustrated in this description of Israel's sin and the Lord's anger; of their bondage to an oppressor and the length of such servitude; of their prayer for deliverance and the emergence of a saviour, anointed with the divine spirit; and finally, of the duration of the period of peace. But there is little supplementary information beyond these bare details, and even these are not free of difficulties of interpretation.

*Mesopotamia* (8) is in Hebrew *'ªram nah°rayim* which was 'the fertile land east of the river Orontes covering the upper and middle Euphrates and the lands watered by the rivers Habur and Tigris, *i.e.* modern E Syria – N Iraq'.[1] Only after the fourth century BC was the term extended to describe the whole Tigris-Euphrates valley. But as an attack from this area would come from the north it is not easy to see how Othniel, associated with the tribe of Judah in the extreme south, should be chosen as the deliverer. The difference is eased only fractionally if 'Aram of the two rivers' be regarded as a reference to the Euphrates and one of its tributaries. The name does occur in Egyptian and Assyrian inscriptions, generally indicating a region in North Mesopotamia but occasionally referring to the area to the westward as far as the river Orontes. The fact of an attack from the north has occasioned some extreme hypotheses, even to the suggestion that originally the name of the deliverer had not been preserved and that the editor supplied the name of one who was already familiar (1:13ff.) to complete his scheme.[2] Such drastic conjectures are invariably unwise.

The name of *Cushan-rishathaim* is also suspect, for it reads literally 'Cushan of double-wickedness', not a likely personal name, and it would appear that the historian has made a deliberate distortion to cast ridicule upon this oppressor. Various emendations have been suggested, the most plausible being *Cushan rosh Teman* ('Cushan chief of Teman', a town or region in northern Edom). If this be accepted then Aram-naharaim could be read as Edom-naharaim; the two words are often confused in the Old Testament. Othniel would then fit more readily into the picture if the invasion came from Edom, whose territory bordered on that of Judah. But there is considerable evidence to support the more difficult view that there is here preserved a memory of an attack from the Mesopotamian area. Cush (Gn. 10:8) was the father of Nimrod who established the Babylonian civilization. It is known that the Kassites overran Babylon and ruled for four centuries until

[1] D. J. Wiseman, 'Mesopotamia', in *NBD*, p. 811. See also J. J. Finkelstein, *Journal of Near Eastern Studies*, XXI, 1962, pp. 73–92.
[2] Burney, p. 64.

the twelfth century BC (Othniel may be dated *c.* 1200 BC[1]). Archaeology has revealed possible further links with Cushan-rishathaim in the name of a woman, Kashsha-rishat, and the name borne by two Kassite kings, Kashtiliash, which could easily be modified to the form found in our text. A name Kassi occurs at Alalakh. We may surmise tentatively that here we may have a witness to a westward movement of the Kassite dynasty, a movement which found the tribes of Israel sufficiently united to allow for Othniel, the southern hero, to act on their behalf.

**7.** *The groves* (AV) should be translated *the Asheroth* (RV, RSV), the mistake, which occurs regularly throughout the AV, having been perpetuated from the LXX. Asheroth is the plural form of Asherah, which indicates both a female goddess, the consort of Baal and also a cult object. The latter was probably a wooden pillar, the formal substitute for a sacred tree, representing the female element in the debased Canaanite religion. As the plural of Asherah is usually Asherim it is likely that the original here was Ashtaroth (*cf.* 2:13). Asherah and Ashtaroth may be viewed as interchangeable forms.

**10.** The supernatural empowering of the judges of Israel is here revealed for the first time. The same expression is used of Jephthah (11:29), but there is no stereotyped formula. It is noted that the Spirit of the Lord 'took possession of' (RSV) or 'clothed itself' with (RV mg.) Gideon (6:34); that it 'began to stir' or 'impel' or 'rush upon' Samson (13:25; 14:6,19; 15:14). These individuals are styled 'charismatic' since the divine grace (*charisma*) was bestowed upon them, a phenomenon which continued into the period of the monarchy (1 Sa. 10:10; 11:6; 16:13). Since Pentecost (Acts 2) a more general and permanent endowment of the Holy Spirit has been the privilege of every disciple. It is likely that Othniel was already regarded as a judge on the basis of his earlier spectacular achievement (1:12ff.).

## c. Ehud and Eglon of Moab (3:12-30)
**3:12-14. The Moabite oppression.** The sovereignty of

[1] See Introduction p. 32.

the Lord is indicated in the way in which He used *Moab* to
chastise His wayward people. A similar thought occurs in
Isaiah 10:5ff. where the arrogant Assyrian king, ruler of a great
world-power, is described as 'the rod of mine anger' (*cf.* His use
of Cyrus of Persia, Is. 45:1ff.). The king of Moab is said to be
*strengthened* against Israel, a verb which is used in Ezekiel 30:24,
where the Lord strengthens the arms of the king of Babylon.
It is a comforting thought in these days of nuclear power to
realize that God still orders and controls the destinies of nations
and overrules the decisions of world rulers, including the
most arrogant and atheistic among them. *Moab*, situated to the
east of the Dead Sea between the Arnon and the Zered, was
settled as a kingdom some fifty years before the Israelite
invasion. *Ammon*, to the north-east of Moab, was established
about the same time as Israel in the late thirteenth century BC.
The Amalekites, who were akin to the Edomites, were a
nomadic race occupying the considerable area south of Judah,
and were possibly Israel's bitterest enemy (Ex. 17:8–16; *cf.*
1 Sa. 15:2,3).

It is clear that the coalition under Eglon crossed the Jordan
in approximately the same area as Israel and took the city of
Jericho (*the city of palms*). The allusion to Jericho here is surprising, since Joshua had pronounced a curse upon anyone
attempting to rebuild it (Jos. 6:26). Some scholars have been
disposed to treat lightly the account of the fulfilment of this
curse in the time of Ahab (1 Ki. 16:34) but excavation in
1952–8 showed that the Late Bronze Age city of Jericho (*i.e.*
the one conquered by Joshua) was almost completely eroded,
indicating strongly a considerable period when the area was
unoccupied. The site, however, would retain many of its
advantages, for it possessed an adequate water-supply and it
dominated the lower Jordan valley. The Moabite occupation,
using the abundant supply of building material from the
ruined city, was of a temporary character in any case.

**3:15–22. The assassination of Eglon.** *Gera* (15) is noted
as the son of Benjamin in Genesis 46:21, but the relationship
of our text cannot be taken literally; it simply implies that

Ehud was a descendant of Gera. As the tribal portion of Benjamin was particularly affected it is not surprising that Ehud, the deliverer, was raised up from that tribe. He is described as a *left-handed* man, lit. 'restricted as to his right hand'. In the eyes of an Israelite, this was regarded as a physical defect and it appears often in connection with the Benjamites, without affecting their prowess in battle (*cf.* 20:16). 1 Chronicles 12:2 suggests that they were ambidextrous. The *present* (AV, RV) which Ehud took to Eglon is a euphemism for *tribute* (RSV), probably in the form of agricultural produce, hence the need for a number of porters (18). Ehud had carefully planned the assassination of the oppressing king, making a two-edged sword or dagger about fourteen inches long (the Hebrew word for *cubit* is not found elsewhere in the Old Testament and it is usually interpreted as a short cubit, *i.e.* the distance between the elbow and the knuckles of the closed fist). The ease with which the dagger penetrated the king's body, hilt and all (22), suggests that it had no cross-piece and thus would be the more readily concealable under the long, flowing outer-garment. Such incidental details as the length of the murder weapon and the fact of Eglon's corpulence (mentioned only because the dagger was completely buried in his body) attest the historicity of the event. Ehud's return after the dutiful presentation of the tribute would not occasion the king's suspicions.

**19–22.** There is some ambiguity about the *quarries that were by Gilgal* (AV, RV). The Hebrew word (*peṣîlîm*) means 'sculptured stones' (RSV) or 'graven images' (RV mg.). As they are mentioned again in verse 26 it is apparent that they were a prominent landmark. In the latter reference they seem to mark the point where Ehud could consider himself safe, and for this reason it has been conjectured that they were boundary stones which marked the limits of Moabite influence. A parallel has been drawn with Babylonian boundary stones, but this cannot be sustained, since these were always placed in the centre of property as title-deeds. A better parallel might be found in the stones marking city-state boundaries mentioned in Ugaritic Akkadian texts. But any suggestion that the reference is to boundary stones seems hardly plausible in the historical situation of actual Moabite aggression and faces us with the added problem of accounting for the Moabite possession of Jericho, 3 miles west-north-west of Gilgal. An easier and more likely explanation is that they were the actual stones set up by Joshua to commemorate the miraculous crossing of the Jordan (Jos. 4:19–24) and thus were a well-known landmark.

Ehud's stratagem was carried out with considerable skill and courage. Pretending to have a secret message to the king from God (notice how he used the general word for God, *Elohim*, widely used throughout the region, rather than *Yahweh*, the particular name of Israel's deity), he excited the king's curiosity and secured a private audience. It is possible that the king left his audience-chamber and went to his *summer parlour* (AV, RV) to ensure privacy, thus accounting for Ehud's coming to him again (20). The summer parlour (lit. 'roof-chamber of coolness'; *cf.* RSV) was a room erected on the flat roof-top, provided with many windows to catch the breeze and thus well suited as a place for meditation or interviews of a personal nature. When Ehud announced that he had a message from God the king rose reverently from his seat to receive the divine oracle. No suspicions were aroused by the movement of Ehud's left hand; there was no cry which would undoubtedly have alerted Eglon's attendants; he died swiftly as the dagger of his assailant was buried completely in his body. The corpulence of the king is noted (17) to show how this was possible.

The phrase *and the dirt came out* (22, AV, RSV) has caused considerable conjecture. One of the words used (*pars͏ᵉdona*) occurs nowhere else. The reading of the AV and RSV infers that the intestines were pierced. But a study of the cognate languages, particularly Assyrian and Sumerian, suggests that the *hapax legomena* refers to some kind of cavity or opening, which has led some scholars to suggest that a vestibule is indicated (*cf.* RV mg.), which is not easy to relate to the porch of verse 23. The most plausible, if gruesome, suggestion is that it refers to the opening of the king's body, the downward motion of the dagger being with such force that it passed completely through the abdomen and projected from the vent (*cf.* RV, *it came out behind*). Such sensational details have a habit of impressing themselves indelibly upon the human memory.

**3:23-26. The escape of Ehud.** There is some uncertainty concerning the escape-route of Ehud, for the word translated *porch* (AV, RV) occurs nowhere else. Probably the roof-chamber of a king was more elaborate than the simple type of structure found elsewhere. Most likely it was some form of colonnade. To delay the detection of his crime Ehud drew the double doors of the roof-chamber together and locked them before making good his escape undetected. When the servants of Eglon observed the locked doors they drew the obvious conclusion that their master was *covering his feet* (AV, RV), a euphemism for the performance of the offices of nature (*cf.* 1 Sa. 24:3). But the passing of the time eventually overcame their acute embarrassment (Heb. 'they tarried till the point of confusion') and they came with the key to investigate. The *key* was a flat piece of wood fitted with pins which corresponded to holes in a hollow bolt. A hole in the door gave access to the bolt, which was on the inside. The insertion of the key in the bolt pushed out the pins of the lock and enabled the bolt to be withdrawn from its socket in the doorpost. The door could be locked without a key, but not unlocked. When the servants discovered the grisly fate which had overtaken the king the alarm was raised, but by this time Ehud was well clear. The two words rendered *tarried* (AV, RV) in verses 25 and 26 are dissimilar, the latter, containing an element of reproach, could be translated *delayed* (RSV). The location of *Seirath* (AV) has not been identified.

**3:27-30. Victory over the Moabites.** The death of the Moabite king would create an atmosphere of uncertainty and consternation in Moab which would be favourable to an attacker. The astute Ehud, who had doubtless seen that this would be the propitious moment to consolidate his advantage and cast off completely the yoke of Moab, gathered together an army. The need for speed in this operation would restrict the recruitment of volunteers to the immediate area of the Ephraimites, a mountainous region which had probably felt the pressure of the Moabites. The capture of *the fords of the Jordan* enabled the Israelites to wipe out the demoralized Moabites so that ten thousand of them, all *strong, able-bodied men* (RSV), perished. The Moabite domination was broken, and the territory of Israel was freed, but verse 30 does not necessarily imply that Ehud followed up his victory by an invasion of Moab. The situation had been saved by his resolution and cunning, but we are not called to admire his cold-blooded assassination of Eglon, although tyranny and oppression are themselves ugly things and are not lightly removed.[1] After this deliverance the land enjoyed relative security for eighty years, which probably represents two generations.

**29.** Objections have been raised concerning the large number (*about ten thousand*) of Moabites involved in this encounter. Not only does it represent a huge slaughter; it was a vast army for the Moabites to have on the west side of Jordan. The 10,000 may designate an army force (*cf.* 4:6,10; and see commentary on 20:2, where the uncertainty attaching to the Hebrew word *'elep̄*, 'thousand', is discussed).

### d. Shamgar and the Philistines (3:31)

Certain characteristic features of the narratives concerning the judges are missing in connection with Shamgar. There is no mention that Israel did evil in the sight of the Lord, nor is there any direct mention of a Philistine oppression or its duration. The length of the time when the land enjoyed rest is also absent. Another peculiarity is that Ehud, not Shamgar, is mentioned, in 4:1, although the historicity of Shamgar and the chronological order of events is attested by the reference in the Song of Deborah (5:6). The reference to Ehud in 4:1 could be easily explained on the assumption that Shamgar's isolated exploit was during his lifetime. Certain Greek and other recensions set the Shamgar episode after 16:31, although this appears to be an attempt to connect it with the Philistine

[1] See Introduction, section v. *c.*, pp. 41ff.

menace reflected in the Samson stories rather than an indication of its original position. It has been conjectured by some
that the story of Shamgar was not included in the original
selection of the exploits of Judges, but was added by a redactor
who, wanting to eliminate the usurper Abimelech from the
list of twelve judges and yet wanting to retain the number
(corresponding to the twelve tribes), inserted this verse concerning Shamgar on the basis of 5:6, supposing him to have
been an Israelite hero.[1] Such a view is without any real foundation. Moreover, if such inventiveness on the part of editors or
redactors be allowed, can the Old Testament, or Old Testament scholarship, ever be taken seriously? Surely a redactor
inserting an extra character into the book would take care to
conform to the pattern of the book? It seems better to allow the
difficulties to remain unresolved rather than to accept an
unlikely solution for them. However, the significant omissions
may indicate that there *was* something unusual about Shamgar; he may not have been a judge after the usual pattern but
just a warrior who effected this one local stroke of valour
against a nation who afterwards became Israel's principal
oppressor. So the original editor may well have included him,
and yet excluded him from the regular pattern.

The name of *Shamgar* is non-Israelite and may have been of
Hittite or Hurrian origin. This does not automatically infer
that he was a Canaanite, although this is possible; it may
witness to the intermingling of the Israelites with the native
population. In any case his action benefited Israel. *Son of Anath*
has been taken as a reference to Beth-anath in Galilee, and
this would explain the mention of him in the Song of Deborah
(5:6) which recounts a victory in which the northern tribes
predominated. But sanctuaries of Anath, the Canaanite
goddess, were not uncommon at this time. Probably his
exploit over the Philistines was performed at an early stage
of their settlement on the coastal plain, but the exact circumstances cannot be determined. The weapon of Shamgar,
an *ox goad*, was a formidable one in the hands of a determined
man. It was a long-handled (between 8 and 10 feet), pointed

[1] *Cf.* Burney, p. 76.

instrument tipped with metal, and when freshly sharpened it would have many of the qualities of a spear. The use of such an impromptu weapon is paralleled elsewhere in Judges: Ehud had to make his own weapon (3:16); Samson improvised with the jawbone of an ass (15:16). This, in conjunction with the statement in 5:8, may indicate that the Philistines were already carrying out their policy (1 Sa. 13:19-22) of disarming their subject peoples.

### e. Deborah and Barak against Jabin and Sisera of Canaan (4:1-24)

**4:1-3. The oppression of Jabin.** The focus of attention now switches from the southern to the northern tribes, and the threat from Jabin and Sisera, far from concerning relatively small tracts of territory, involved six of the tribes in actual conflict. It was the first major threat of the period of the judges.

Mention is made of a *Jabin, king of Hazor* in Joshua 11:1-11, where the capture and destruction of the city by Joshua's army is noted. Many scholars have suggested that the accounts of Joshua 11 and Judges 4,5 have been confused by the historian, or that the great name of Joshua attracted to itself a sweeping victory gained a century later mainly by the tribes of Zebulun and Naphtali. There are, however, no insoluble difficulties in the narrative as it stands. The name of Jabin may be a hereditary title adopted by the successive kings of Hazor. *Hazor* itself, burnt by fire by Joshua's army almost a century before but presumably not occupied by the Israelites, had been rebuilt by the Canaanites and had regained its old dominance. This is hardly surprising, for Hazor was in a strategic position about 4 miles south-west of Lake Huleh and, like Megiddo in the Esdraelon valley, commanded the principal route between Egypt and the Western Asian Empires. The site, identified by John Garstang in 1927, but not excavated until 1955-8, covered over 200 acres, compared with Megiddo's less than 20 acres. Its population has been estimated at *c.* 40,000, compared with Jericho's 1,500. These facts account for its being called 'the head of all those kingdoms' (Jos. 11:10) and may indicate why Jabin was called the *king of Canaan* (4:2,23,24; cf. 4:17, 'king of Hazor')[1]. *Harosheth of the Gentiles* (AV, RV), the city of Sisera, has not been positively identified; Tell el-Habarj, south-east of Haifa,[2] and Tell 'Amr, 12 miles north-west of Megiddo,[3] have been suggested. The movement of the battle makes the latter the more likely. Either alternative is some distance from Hazor and it is probable that there was a coalition of Canaanite city-states, under the nominal leadership of the king of the most important city, Hazor, but under the military leadership of Sisera, its most able captain.[4] *Sisera* may have been the petty king of Harosheth, but his principal role in the narrative is that of the military leader of the combined armies. These facts explain the infrequency with which Jabin, who may have been an old man, is mentioned (not at all in chapter 5 nor in connection with the actual combat) and the prominence of Sisera in these records.

The superior equipment of the Canaanites is shown in their deployment of *nine hundred chariots of iron* which would give them complete control of the valleys and plains, unless some unusual occurrence should immobilize this powerful striking-force. Such an event, viewed as a miracle of divine intervention, was to transfer the advantage to the Israelites in the decisive encounter.

**4:4–9. Deborah and Barak.** At this point we are introduced to *Deborah*, the saviour of her people and the only woman in the distinguished company of the judges. In the tribal structure of Israel women normally occupied a subordinate position, but they could and did on rare occasions rise to prominence and the Old Testament witnesses to the qualities of prominent women like Miriam (Ex. 15:20) and Huldah (2 Ki. 22:14). Nothing is known of *Lappidoth*, the husband of Deborah, apart from the mere mention of his name, but he was not the only

---

[1] See also K. A. Kitchen, *Ancient Orient and Old Testament* (Tyndale Press, 1966), pp. 67f.
[2] J. P. U. Lilley, 'Harosheth', in *NBD*, p. 505.
[3] Myers, p. 712.
[4] Such coalitions are found frequently in this period, *e.g.* Jos. 9:17; 10:3; and the instance including Hazor itself in Jos. 11:1 ff.

one to be outshone, for Barak himself played a secondary part to this great and gifted woman and drew courage and inspiration from her presence. The view that Lappidoth, meaning 'torches', and Barak, whose name means 'lightning', are one and the same person, and that Barak the deliverer was the husband of Deborah, rests upon very flimsy evidence.

A difficulty in these chapters is the specific mention of only the two tribes of Naphtali and Zebulun in 4:7,10 compared with the list of participating tribes in the poetic account, which also includes the tribes of Ephraim, Benjamin, Machir and Issachar. One suggestion to account for this is that there were two phases of the campaign, an initial one in which only two tribes took part, and a second one when they were joined by contingents from neighbouring tribes (fuller consideration is given to this problem later in this section[1]).

The geographical allusions of the chapter may indicate the magnitude of the task confronting a would-be deliverer. Deborah herself came from *between Ramah and Bethel* in the south of Ephraim, about 50 miles from the scene of the decisive conflict; the depradations of the Canaanite confederacy under Jabin may have extended this far south. On the other hand there may be an illustration of a greater unity of the tribes in this period than is commonly assumed. The plight of the northern tribes was clearly known to Deborah and, conversely, they were not only aware of her reputation but came to her in their predicament with their request for help (5b). The suggestion of such a basic unity and inter-knowledge is made more plausible by Deborah's choice of *Barak* as the military commander of the tribes, for he was an inhabitant of *Kedesh-naphtali*, about 5 miles to the north-west of Lake Huleh in an area particularly affected by the Canaanite oppression. The Canaanite domination of the principal valleys and trade routes does not seem to have prevented free movement of the Israelite tribes in the highlands to the north and south of the Esdraelon and Jezreel valleys.

At the time of the crisis Deborah was already established as a prophetess and a judge in the non-military sphere; indeed.

[1] See p. 84.

it was the demonstration of charismatic qualities in this realm which, in all probability, led the tribes to seek her assistance. Her summons and challenge to Barak was in the name of Yahweh, the distinctive name for the God of Israel. Barak was commanded *'Go, gather your men at Mount Tabor'* (RSV); the verb means 'to draw out' or 'extend', suggesting a very loose formation such as might be adopted by lightly-armed soldiers, anxious to escape detection, moving through hostile territory to a central meeting-point. *Mount Tabor*, at the junction of the tribal portions of Issachar, Naphtali and Zebulun, was chosen as the rallying-point. It was a conical shaped mountain rising a little over 1,300 feet from the north-eastern corner of the Esdraelon valley, and was such a prominent landmark that any confusion on the part of the assembling Israelites would be avoided.

The initial summons was to the men of Naphtali and Zebulun, two of the tribes principally concerned, although chapter 5 makes it clear that four other tribes took an active part, possibly in a later phase of the operation. The suggestion that there were two major battles, or, at least, two stages in the one campaign, is strengthened by the fact that in chapter 4 the conflict is waged between Mount Tabor and the river Kishon, whereas in chapter 5, while the river Kishon is still prominent (5:21), another site a few miles southward is also mentioned as the battle-ground, 'in Taanach, by the waters of Megiddo' (5:19). Others have conjectured that Naphtali and Zebulun took part in a battle at *Kedesh* (4:9,10,11), identified as Kedesh-naphtali, Barak's home-town (see note on verse 10), with Jabin of Hazor, before a second battle by the Kishon against Sisera in which a larger and more representative Israelite force took part. Perhaps it is hardly fair to expect military precision in the exultant poem of Deborah and it is always wise to remember that the Israelites, in preserving their traditions, were concerned to celebrate the saving power of Yahweh rather than to preserve the minute detail to enable later historians to make a precise reconstruction of each battle! We may, at times, regret the lack of fuller information, but we must not deny the right of the Hebrew historian to his point of view, which gave the principal credit to Yahweh (*cf.* 4:7b, 'I will deliver him into thine hand'; *cf.* also 2 Sa. 8:6,14).

**7.** *The river Kishon* has its source in the hill-country to the south of the Esdraelon valley, after which it is the principal river of the valley itself, flowing in a north-westerly direction until it empties itself in the bay of Acre, northwards of the Carmel ridge. The whole of the upper section of the river is seasonal, depending on the rainfall, so that in the dry summer it is little more than a wadi, but when swollen by the rains of winter and early spring it could become a raging torrent. In such conditions the low-lying areas surrounding the river would be completely waterlogged and the deployment of chariots would be impossible.

**8, 9.** The lack of alacrity with which Barak responded to the challenge is understandable, humanly speaking, for the disparity between the opposing forces was considerable. It may be observed that, in his hesitation, Barak is in excellent company in the Old Testament period. Moses, even at the end of the encounter with God at the burning bush, displayed remarkably little enthusiasm to accept the divine call (Ex. 4:13); Gideon felt himself to be the worst possible choice (Jdg. 6:15); and Jeremiah protested on account of his youthfulness (Je. 1:6). A great man realizes his own inadequacy when called by the Lord to some great task, but the divine call is never alone, it is accompanied by the divine provision. Paul's words refer to all those who are called to God's service, 'Not that we are sufficient of ourselves to claim anything as coming from us; our sufficiency is from God, who has qualified us to be ministers . . .' (2 Cor. 3:5,6, RSV). Barak made the presence of Deborah the condition of his acceptance, and in her acceptance there is a hint of her displeasure at his attitude as she announced that the deed of a woman would eclipse any honour due to him. It is natural to ascribe this position to Deborah herself, for the hind-sight of posterity has seen her as the commanding force behind Israel's deliverance. The prophecy, however, was fulfilled in Jael's callous act of treachery to the vanquished Sisera, who trusted in the security of her hospitality. We would regard this as a despicable act, but to a people suffering under a cruel and prolonged bondage it would be regarded in a completely different light, and the details of the murder have been gloatingly preserved for us, as were those in the case of Eglon. Perhaps it is too facile, for those who have not endured extreme persecution or bondage, to pass judgment on the Israelites of old, or the survivors of the Nazi prison camps in our own generation. But, nevertheless, the Christian attitude is opposed to an exultant spirit of revenge.

**4:10–16. The assembly and defeat of the Canaanite host.** The *ten thousand men* of Barak are mentioned again (*cf.* verse 6) to underline the disparity between the Israelite army and the massive, well-equipped army of Sisera. *Kedesh* is hardly to be identified with Kedesh-naphtali, but to another place nearer the scene of the battle. The name, meaning 'sanctuary', is an exceedingly common one.

**11.** The note concerning *Heber the Kenite* is parenthetical, serving as an introduction to the family group to which Jael (17) belonged. The Kenites were a nomadic group associated with Judah, so an explanation was required regarding the presence of this family group so far north (see note on 1:16). The *plain of Zaanaim* (AV) should be read as 'the oak or terebinth of Zaanaim', a district noted in Joshua 19:33 as on the border of Naphtali. Apart from this information, and the obvious fact that it lay on Sisera's escape-route, there is no certain knowledge of its position.

**12–14.** Sisera, the leader of the Canaanite coalition, was doubtless informed of the movements of the Israelites, although the method of their deployment may have concealed their actual numbers. To meet this threat he gathered a massive army, including his complete chariot force, doubtless intending a decisive blow against the rebellious Israelites. It is unlikely that he would be so foolish as to attempt to use his chariots in the rainy-season; 5:4,5,20,21 suggest an unusual torrential downpour, possibly a thunderstorm, which came after the normal season of the latter rains in April and early May. Possibly Deborah gave the order to attack (14) as she saw the storm approaching, knowing that a heavy downpour would nullify the numerical advantage and the superior equipment of the Canaanites and thus make this the propitious moment to strike. The Lord was often depicted as the God of the thunderstorm, moving in awful splendour and power to the help of His people (*cf.* Jos. 10:11; 1 Sa. 7:10; Ps. 18:9–15), and this belief may be implied in the words of Deborah: *. . . is not the Lord gone out before thee?* (AV, RV). It must be realized, however, that the Israelites did not have a monopoly of this conception, for recent discoveries at Ras Shamra (the ancient Ugarit) have shown that the Canaanites looked upon Baal in much the same way. He was the storm-god, the rider upon the clouds (*cf.* Is. 19:1). He is uniformly depicted as wielding a club in one hand and a stylized spear in the other, representing thunder and lightning respectively. A storm at this juncture, however, favoured the Israelites and enabled them to extend their advantage from the hill-country (where chariots could not operate effectively) to the valley, where the Canaanites had hitherto been supreme.

**15, 16.** The verb *discomfited* (AV, RV) does not convey to the modern reader the completeness of the Lord's action. The origin of the word is the Mediaeval Latin verb *disconfigere*, meaning 'to unloose' or 'to part asunder', and it indicates a complete and utter rout (*cf.* RSV, *routed*). The scene may be reconstructed in the imagination. The ten thousand Israelites, lightly armed and highly mobile, poured down into the valley and joined battle with a chariot force which was unable to manoeuvre on the softened ground. Escape, with the possibility of fighting under better conditions on another day, was the only wise course, so Sisera attempted to fall back on his base camp at Harosheth of the Gentiles. To the south was the central hill-country; to the north, beyond the swollen river, was the hill-country of Galilee. But as they made their way in a general north-westerly direction, with the Israelites in hot pursuit, the valley narrowed, decreasing the space available for deployment. This caused chariot to jostle with chariot, churning up the surface of the ground and making it even more difficult for those in the rear of the panic-stricken army.

Meanwhile the river would continue to rise as it was fed by innumerable small tributaries, rushing down from the surrounding hills. The words of Deborah (5:21) must have formed the epitaph of many, 'the river of Kishon swept them away'. Nor did the jubilant Israelites relent, for their advantage was pressed right to the walls of Harosheth of the Gentiles. It was a sweeping victory, completely decisive in its effects, for there was no other major engagement between the Israelites and the Canaanites, although isolated pockets of resistance were not overcome until the time of David. Sisera deserted his position, probably when he realized that the chaotic situation made escape by chariot impossible, and attempted to escape on foot, probably in a northerly direction, since Heber the Kenite was encamped at Zaanaim, on the borders of Naphtali (see the note on 4:11).

**4:17-22. The flight and death of Sisera.** The captain of the shattered army, utterly exhausted from his strenuous and terrifying ordeal, was glad to avail himself of the offer of sanctuary in the tent of a woman. His ultimate destination was almost certainly the city of Hazor, in whose proximity the nomadic group of the Kenites had settled. The assurance of Jael that he need not fear, the hesitancy and courtesy of his address, the precautions he advised and the immediacy of sleep, all indicate a man at the end of his tether, shattered in mind and morale as well as weary of body. According to the conventions of the day he had every reason not to be suspicious; Jael herself appeared the personification of friendliness and consideration and, of even greater assurance, the offering and acceptance of hospitality in a nomad's tent was, traditionally, a guarantee of protection. Moreover, any pursuer would hardly think to look in a woman's tent for any man, let alone a weary fugitive, for this would be a breach of etiquette.

**19.** So Sisera was lulled into a false sense of security by this treacherous woman. Accepting her invitation he allowed her to cover him with a *mantle* (AV), a word which occurs only here and the meaning of which has caused conjecture. The most likely explanation is that it was a 'fly-net' rather than a *rug*

(RV, RSV), the former being much more essential to a man in Sisera's condition, dirty, caked with perspiration after his exertions, and seeking sleep. The request for water was answered generously, *a skin of milk* (RSV) being opened. The skins of animals were frequently used to store liquids, particularly milk, which could then be easily churned to produce curds. That this was the drink offered to Sisera is shown in the second half of 5:25 where 'butter' (AV, RV) is best rendered as 'curds' (RSV). Known generally as yoghurt, it is commonly given by modern-day Arabs (as *leben* or *shensan*) to those who are tired and it is usually the only sustenance when one of their number is ill. They also drink a kind of fermented milk which has soporific qualities, but it is not necessary to suggest that this was the refreshment proffered to Sisera. In his case there was no need to induce sleep; it came naturally and readily.

Jael then acted with callous efficiency. Sisera was not to know that the woman sheltering him was a member of a tribe which had strong ties with the Israelites and that he was, in fact, in the tent of an enemy. Her dexterity with the *tent peg* (RSV) and *hammer*, or wooden mallet, is explained by the fact that the erection and taking down of tents was the work of a woman. Stealthily she approached her sleeping, unsuspecting guest and with a few swift blows drove the tent peg into his temple and through his head, completely transfixing him. So violent were her movements that the peg itself went through *into the ground*. So Israel's persecutor met a treacherous but swift death at the hands of a woman, itself a disgrace in the view of that age (*cf.* 9:54).

**22.** It is difficult to estimate the lapse of time before Barak appeared in pursuit of Sisera. It may have been several hours after the captain of the Canaanite army had first appeared at Jael's tent. When he did arrive it was to find that the prophecy of Deborah had been fulfilled (*cf.* verse 9) and that the principal honour, of slaying Sisera, was not to be his.

**4:23, 24. The end of Jabin.** The historian, in completing the prose narrative, does not make extreme claims. The immediate capture of Hazor is not claimed any more than that of Harosheth of the Gentiles. What is asserted is that the back of the Canaanite domination was broken, and that the Israelites continued their pressure (*the hand of the children of Israel prospered, and prevailed*, AV, indicates that unabated pressure; *cf. bore harder and harder*, RSV) until Jabin and his kingdom were no more, a process which may have taken many years.

We have already alluded to the act of Jael as one of treachery and no attempt need be made to condone or whitewash either her or her action. We have, however, attempted to enter into the feelings of a downtrodden, cruelly oppressed people and to understand the very human reaction of savage delight in the death of their arch-enemy, and the gloating preservation of the gruesome details. We look back upon the incident through the eyes of Christ who taught us to love our enemies, to bless them that curse us, to do good to them that hate us and to pray for them who despitefully use us, and persecute us (Mt. 5:44). And, lest we think that this would be an impossible demand upon anyone in a comparable situation to that of the oppressed Israelites, let us remember that Christ, who gave us an example of longsuffering in His endurance of the mockery of a trial and a cruel death, is able by His indwelling to transform our weak, human natures into His own likeness.

### f. The Song of Deborah (5:1–31)

The Song of Deborah is one of the finest examples of an ode of triumph preserved in Israelite literature and it is generally agreed that it is contemporary with the events it describes. Whilst the poem has undoubtedly suffered in transmission, as indicated by the large number of marginal notes in the English versions, the Hebrew still retains a vividness, an almost staccato effect of action and a spirit of sheer exultation that indicates a participant, or at least an eyewitness. It is beyond question one of the oldest elements in our present book of Judges and is therefore of great importance in its witness to the economic, social, political and religious conditions of the period. In all probability it was included in one of the anthologies of poetry which existed in ancient Israel. Two of these collections are mentioned specifically in the Old Testament. In Numbers 21:14 there is a reference to 'the Book of the Wars of the Lord', which presumably was an anthology of poems celebrating victory, always conceived as the work of the Lord Himself. In Joshua 10:13 and 2 Samuel 1:18 'the Book of Jashar' is mentioned. The derivation of the title is uncertain; generally it is translated 'upright', in which case the title would be a prototype 'Book of Golden Deeds'. But it has also been suggested that 'Jashar' is a shortened form of Israel, or a corruption of the word 'song'.

The authorship of the poem is also a matter of conjecture. The first verse describes it as the song of Deborah and Barak, but in verse 12 both of the principals are addressed directly. This fact is not decisive, however, since direct allusions to the author by name occur in other Ancient Near Eastern texts. Verse 7 (AV, RV), in which Deborah speaks in the first person, appears conclusive, but most modern scholars (*cf*. RSV) render the verb as a second singular feminine, which is grammatically allowable. The matter is unimportant, but who better than Deborah would be fitted to describe the event, to pass judgment on the non-participating tribes and to express praise to the Lord for His intervention?

The poetic form is completely obscured in the AV and for this reason the RV, RSV and other modern translations are greatly to be preferred. A complete account of the features of Hebrew poetry would be out of place in a commentary of these dimensions but the main characteristics may be observed. Two principal devices were employed:

*i. Parallelism.* The unit of Hebrew poetry is normally not the single line but the couplet, with a short pause at the end of the first line and a longer pause at the end of the second. Occasionally a triplet, still as a well-defined unit, is substituted. This means that the association is one of thought not of sound, as in traditional English poetry; a mental picture is produced which is answered by another supplementary word-picture. Parallelism takes various forms, two of which appear prominently in the Song of Deborah. The first is synonymous or identical parallelism, where the thought of the first line is reproduced in the second with no marked variation, so that the lines reinforce each other. The second is climactic or stair-like parallelism, where part of the line is repeated and then a fresh detail added, thus carrying the movement of thought forward. The reader may care to look for examples of these in the poem.

*ii. A system of rhythm or metre.* In traditional English poetry there is a careful balance of the number of feet in each line, this balance being achieved in a number of possible combinations. In Hebrew each separate thought is expressed in a strongly accented word, which, with prefixes and suffixes, may be equivalent to a short sentence. Each of these words has a tone-syllable, which is particularly stressed and is itself determinative of the accent which falls upon all other syllables in the word. In over half of the Song of Deborah there are three of these words or beats to a line, with a little over a quarter employing a four-beat measure. Occasional variations are introduced, such as a four-word measure followed by a three-word measure, or the reverse. There is no suggestion that the poem is composed from different sources; such variations are a feature of ancient poetry, a fact amply attested by the Ugaritic texts. The general effect of this system, which unfortunately cannot be adequately reproduced in a translation, is to create an impression of vigour and movement.

Reference has been made to the alleged points of difference between the accounts in chapters 4 and 5. These include the absence of any reference to Jabin king of Hazor, or to Mount Tabor, in chapter 5; the inclusion of four other tribes besides Zebulun and Naphtali, the tribes who, alone, are mentioned in chapter 4; the location of the battle of chapter 5 south-west-wards to Taanach and the waters of Megiddo, and the slight dissimilarities in the accounts of Sisera's death. These differences are probably due to the incompleteness of the record. Possibly, as we have already suggested, there were two stages in the campaign, with a concerted action on the part of the tribes of the Esdraelon area following an initial success by the tribes of Zebulun and Naphtali. It must also be remembered that the language of poetry is not always precise; elaborations and hyperbole are employed to increase the effect. Our pre-occupation with historical details must not be allowed to cloud our appreciation of either account.

Before we begin our examination of the poem itself attention must be drawn to the view of God and His relationship to His people which is witnessed here. It was formerly thought that the religion of Israel evolved gradually over many centuries, culminating in the insights of the eighth-century prophets, Amos, Hosea, Isaiah and Micah. Scant attention was paid to the literature purporting to have come from an earlier period and the idea of the covenant-relationship existing in this early period was regarded as unlikely. The Song of Deborah, originating from the last decades of the twelfth century BC, is important because of its incidental allusions to the relationship between the nation and its God. The kings and princes of the surrounding nations are invited to take heed of the greatness of the God of Israel (3). The Lord (note the use of the name of the God of the covenant) is shown intervening on behalf of His people and fighting their battles, a theme which may be paralleled in the Pentateuch, the Historical Books and the Psalms. And despite the almost savage spirit of exultation that obtrudes itself, the writer is concerned for His glory. The covenant-relationship was clearly in existence at this time, and within that relationship the tribes have responsibilities to each other. Those not responding to the summons of Deborah were censured in terms that suggest an *ought* rather than a *must*. The principal point of the censure is not that they failed to come to the help of the other tribes, but that they failed to come to the assistance of the Lord Himself (23), the covenant God. There are many indications of apostasy and moral laxity in Judges, but the evidence of a strong faith in God, a realization of His almighty power, His involvement in Israel's situation and the existence of the covenant-bond, all of which may be seen in the Song of Deborah, do something to redress the situation.

**5:1, 2. Invitation to praise.** The opening verse of the chapter, in prose, was probably introduced by the editor when he incorporated the Song into his account of the judges. The original title may be preserved in verse 2, *bless the Lord* (RV, RSV), indicating that it was a song of praise. The remainder of the verse gives the setting of the occasion and records the spontaneous response of the people. Considerable discussion has centred on the first part of verse 2, which reads literally 'in the breaking forth of the breakers in Israel'. One possible interpretation is that it refers to the response of the rulers of the people (RV, RSV), which restores the parallelism with the second part of the couplet. Another alternative translation is 'When long locks of hair hung loose in Israel', an allusion to the custom of allowing the hair, which was considered sacred, to grow during the period of fulfilment of a vow to the Lord (*cf.* Nu. 6:5,18; Acts 18:18). It was the practice of soldiers going out to battle to leave their hair uncut, which may suggest that they were engaged in a holy war. The custom speaks of complete dedication and in this sense also restores the parallelism of the verse, complementing the ready offering of the people.

**5:3-5. The intervention of the Almighty.** The *kings* and all persons of consequence (the meaning of *princes*) are invited to pay attention to the hymn of praise addressed to Israel's God. Other nations surrounding Israel will fear and marvel when they hear of the mighty acts wrought for His people. The ascription of praise to the Lord is of great interest, since it appears to connect *Sinai*, the mount of the covenant, with *Edom*, an identification found elsewhere in the Old Testament (*e.g.* Dt. 33:2; Ps. 68:7ff.; Hab. 3:3ff.). There is, of course, nothing sacrosanct in the traditional site of Sinai, Jebel Mûsâ, in the Sinai Peninsula, and either site can be equated with the evidence of the wanderings in the wilderness. In poetic language the Song links the present deliverance with the past revelation at Sinai, when at the covenant-ceremony, God spoke to the accompaniment of a great storm and, possibly, an earthquake. The same Almighty God had gone before them on the present occasion and the singer attempts to convey something of the exceeding greatness of His power. The vividness and significance of the picture is increased if it be accepted that an unusually severe storm caused consternation and confusion in the army of the Canaanites. The whole of creation appeared to array itself on the side of the puny, ill-equipped Israelite force.

**5:6-8. The effect of the Canaanite oppression.** The theme of these verses is the impoverished, pitiful condition of Israel under the Canaanite yoke. The linking together of the names of *Shamgar* and *Jael* is surprising. We have already considered the unusual features of the former's deliverance of the Israelites (see exegesis on 3:31). The point seems to be that, although these two were living, neither of them effected any really permanent release from the Canaanites. Various emendations have been made to remove the name of Jael from the poem, but none is really satisfactory.

In this turbulent period communications were disrupted. A slight change in vocalization allows *highways* (AV, RV) to be read as 'caravans' and this preserves the true meaning of the verb, *caravans ceased* (RSV), *i.e.* commercial trading was impossible and those who had to travel did so on the less-frequented routes, to avoid being molested. Agriculture was similarly affected by the depredations of the Canaanites, the small, unwalled villages of the Israelites being no protection against the forays of their aggressive neighbours. This desperate situation obtained until Deborah arose to effect the deliverance of the nation. Verse 8 gives a summary and a judgment upon Israel. They had forsaken the Lord and had chosen themselves new gods (*cf.* Dt. 32:17; Jdg. 2:12,17). The result of this was war, weakness and servitude. It has been objected that the situation immediately prior to Deborah's deliverance was one of abject submission to a cruel bondage, not one of war in the gates. This objection has little weight, for in these chapters we see not the process but the end, when Israelite opposition had been effectively crushed. They had been deprived of their weapons (*cf.* 1 Sa. 13:22), although it may be unwise to accept this as an absolute statement. If it were, the battle at the Kishon could hardly have been undertaken. Probably the meaning is that these weapons dared not be displayed publicly. *Forty thousand* may be an indication of the available manpower of the tribes at that time. Certainly the miracle of the victory over Sisera's well-equipped host is enhanced by these details, as is also the complete change in Israelite morale as a result of Deborah's inspired leadership. These abject specimens, cowering under the cruel bondage, were the same men who plunged headlong into the valley to attack a vastly superior force. The difference made by a living faith in the living God is nothing less than sensational, and the words of Joshua, 'One man of you puts to flight a thousand, since it is the Lord your God who fights for you' (Jos. 23:10), were literally fulfilled on this occasion.

**5:9–11. Invitation to testify.** The thought of verse 2 is taken up again here, for the campaign could not have been undertaken without the support of the rulers; hence the prominence given to them throughout the poem. The words are most natural in the mouth of Deborah. With dramatic effect the transformed situation is depicted. No longer did the wayfarer travel furtively along the lesser-known tracks: there was a freedom of movement and a natural congregating at the wells, the obvious meeting-places of travellers. The whole population was exhorted to join in a hymn of praise to the Lord for the great deliverance. All classes were to participate: those who rode on white asses, *i.e.* the ruling classes (*cf.* 10:4; 12:14), as well as their less fortunate brethren who travelled on foot. The word translated *rich carpets* (*judgment*, AV, is quite misleading) means anything which is stretched out, possibly carpets or saddle-cloths, which may indicate yet another class, somewhat vaguely defined, but perhaps those who remained at home, in contrast to the two classes of travellers. The townsfolk were to assemble at *the gates*, the traditional place of assembly for judgment and discussion, but now the occasion of their gathering was a thanksgiving service.

Two points in verse 11 call for comment. The words (usually italicized) with which the sentence opens in the AV, *They that are delivered*, show that the translators have resorted to conjecture. The meaning of the Hebrew word translated *archers*

(AV, RV) is uncertain, but most probably it has to do with some kind of *musicians* (RSV), most likely that class of wandering musicians who played the lyre. These minstrels were back at their accustomed places, but with a new song! Another point of interest concerns *the triumphs of his peasantry in Israel* (RSV), where the reference is to the sturdy yeomen (*cf.* verse 7), who formed the backbone of the army. The deeds of these heroic men were set alongside the *righteous acts* (AV, RV) or *triumphs* (RSV) of the Lord. Glory is given where it is due, but the contribution of the lesser participants is not overlooked.

**5:12–18. The roll-call of the tribes.** Inspired by the example of their leaders, the prompt response of many of the tribes is traced in this section, the absence of others being the more reprehensible in the light of such spontaneous support. The direct address to Deborah is not necessarily incompatible with her authorship of the poem.[1] Before the tribes could be aroused to action she herself, at the word of the Lord (4:6), must be awakened from an apathetic acceptance of the situation. Similarly Barak, who fought so valiantly and gave such outstanding leadership, had to be shaken out of his weak acquiescence in the Canaanite bondage. Before the mass of the people could be revived there had to be a stirring in the hearts of those with the qualities of leadership. Verse 13, which appears so obscure in the AV, notes the general response of the people to the summons, the response of the particular tribes being listed in the succeeding verses:

*Then down marched the remnant of the noble;*
*the people of the Lord marched down for him against the mighty*
(RSV).

The response was magnificent, and yet such were the effects of the twenty years of cruel oppression that the numbers were pathetically low, a fraction of the manpower available in the days of Israel's supremacy.

**14.** The first part of the verse reads literally 'From Ephraim their root in Amalek', which has the obvious meaning 'From

[1] See p. 91.

Ephraim came those whose root was in Amalek'. The reference to *Amalek* is surprising and it has been held that it indicates a group of Amalekites, a semi-nomadic group like the Kenites, who had settled amongst the Ephraimites, as did Heber the Kenite a little further to the north. Since the Amalekites were the sworn enemies of Israel (see note on 3:13), this is unlikely. No more acceptable is the suggestion that Ephraim occupied the area once occupied by the Amalekites, there being no evidence of such a northward penetration by this group. A slight emendation makes sense of the line and preserves the unity of thought in verses 13-15, 'From Ephraim they sprang forth into the valley' (*cf.* RSV). The general picture is of the precipitous descent of the Israelites into the valley to engage the host of Sisera, with Benjamin in the lead, followed by Ephraim, Machir, Zebulun and Issachar. *Machir* normally refers to the settlement of the half-tribe of Manasseh eastward of the Jordan, but here it refers more naturally to the western section, with the territory of the six allied tribes giving some idea of the range of the Canaanite depredations. The primacy of the Benjamites is noteworthy, although reference has already been made to their prowess in battle (see note on 3:15-22; *cf.* note on 20:12-17). A comparison of verse 14 and Hosea 5:8 suggests that their war-cry may have expressed this ascendancy, 'After thee, Benjamin!' Naphtali is not mentioned until verse 18 where, in conjunction with Zebulun, it is given an especially honoured place in the record.

**15b-17.** But if there was a ready acknowledgment of the participating tribes, there was also a stern rebuke for those who set their own safety before the claims of their brethren. The four tribes mentioned had their tribal portions well away from the battlefield and were probably not directly affected by the Canaanite oppression, but it is clear that the appeal made for their assistance fell upon deaf ears, for not even a token force was sent. The circumstances of these tribes may have made it impossible for them to respond to the appeal of their distressed brethren. The reference to *Dan* suggests that they had not yet migrated northward, and if this was correct they were probably already enduring the pressures from the Amorites and 'the

98

Peoples of the Sea' which eventually made their original tribal portion untenable (see note on 1:34,35). The plight of *Asher* was noted in 1:31,32. Concerning *Reuben* and *Gilead*, two tribes whose holdings were in Transjordania, very little is known except that this area was itself subject to encroachments from the Moabites and Ammonites. Criticism of those who do not come to our aid in a time of distress can often be a condemnation of our own lack of alacrity in coming to the help of our brethren.

Before leaving this section, it must again be observed that this appeal to four tribes not immediately affected witnesses strongly to the essential unity of the tribes. Only Judah and Simeon are not mentioned. Their geographical remoteness was accentuated by political factors, notably the barrier caused by an unreduced Jerusalem and other towns on their northern frontier and, possibly, pressure by the Philistines on their western frontier.

**5:19-22. The overwhelming of the Canaanites.** The course of the battle has been dealt with in detail in the commentary on chapter 4 and no repetition is called for. The massed armies of the kings of the Canaanite city-states were met by the might of the forces of nature, operating at the behest of Israel's God. The violent storm and the turbulence of the swollen Kishon were the chief architects of victory and the gallant ten thousand Israelites receive no mention in this section. The Canaanite kings came looking for the spoil of battle (19) but fled empty-handed, trusting to the speed of their galloping horses (22) which proved inadequate to save them.

The engagement moved westwards as the Israelites pursued the retreating Canaanites, but the decisive moment was *at Taanach, by the waters of Megiddo*. It has been suggested that Megiddo and Taanach, being only 5 miles apart, were too close to flourish at the same time and that the reference in verse 19 implies that Megiddo was not occupied at this particular time. Archaeological research indicates that Megiddo (Stratum VII) was destroyed in the period 1150–

99

1125 BC, which allows the dating of Deborah's victory *c.* 1125 BC.[1]

**21.** One brief exultant cry of victory punctuates this vivid description of an army's annihilation. 'March on, my soul, in strength!' is more accurate than the reading of the AV, *O my soul, thou hast trodden down strength.*

**5:23–27. Treachery and patriotism.** The treachery ot *Meroz* is deliberately contrasted with the patriotic action of Jael. A bitter curse was called upon Meroz for its lack of support, not simply to the Israelite army but to the Lord Himself. Meroz may be the modern Khirbet Maurus, 7 miles south of Kedesh-naphtali. But whether this identification is accepted or not, it is clear that Meroz proved a notable exception to the ready response of the other tribes. Most likely it was in the area directly affected (unlike the four tribes whose rebuke is mild in comparison), and therefore its cowardly non-participation, possibly for fear of reprisals, was the more reprehensible. *Jael,* on the other hand, had shown no hesitation in murdering in cold blood the principal enemy of the Israelites, regardless of the consequences. The seemingly generous action of offering Sisera curds instead of milk, thus lulling him into a false sense of security, was the prelude to an act that, as has been noted,[2] broke every accepted standard of hospitality. Every detail is dealt with with relish, and finer feelings vanished in the savage delight occasioned by Sisera's death. The repetition in the poetical account, together with the uncertainty in translating several of the verbs in this description, account for most of the differences between this and the prose account.

**5:28–30. The scene in Sisera's household.** There is an equally dramatic and vindictive note in this delineation of the apprehension of *the mother of Sisera.* It may be that the attention devoted to Jael and the state of a mother's heart betokens the authorship of a woman. If so, the savage exultation in the gruesome or harrowing details illustrate Rudyard Kipling's

[1] Albright, p. 117.
[2] See p. 88.

semi-humorous dictum that 'the female of the species is more deadly than the male'! But allowing for this element, the description is vivid and moving. The delay in the loved one's return has an underlying question, an agonized uncertainty, '*Will* he return?' With anxious gaze Sisera's mother stands at the window-lattice, looking for the chariot, or the reassuring beat of the horses' hooves. The author of the poem knows that Sisera will never return; but imagination supplies a plausible explanation which could be advanced by the attendants and by Sisera's mother herself. The captain of the host must superintend the division of the spoil so the very delay is suggestive of a rich booty. The ill-treatment which awaited the women-folk of a defeated army is passed over without any twinge of conscience or pity. The word translated *damsel* (AV, RV) is contemptuous. Elsewhere in the Old Testament it means 'womb', and in the Moabite Stone it has the meaning 'girl-slaves'. The nearest English equivalent is 'wench', and it is clear that these unfortunate captives would be used to gratify the lusts of their captors. War brings many vile effects in its train. The mother of Sisera would be much more interested in the richly embroidered dyed cloth which, as one of the principal indications of wealth and position, would be most likely reserved for the commanding officer; in imagination she would anticipate the use which she could make of it. At this point the poem ends, leaving to the imagination the thought that, instead of *dyed work embroidered* (RSV), there would be the sackcloth and ashes of mourning.

**5:31. Final chorus.** Many scholars regard this verse as a liturgical addition to the Song, expressing the sentiments of a later age and with distinct parallels in the Psalms (*cf.* Ps. 68:2b,3). It may be objected to this that, if this verse is removed, the Song is left without its logical conclusion. The writer is concerned to stress the Lord's intervention on their behalf and the inevitable corollary of this is that those who oppose Him must perish, but those who love Him and co-operate with Him will prosper.

## g. Gideon and the Midianites (6:1 – 8:28)

Gideon and Samson are dealt with in greater detail than any other of the judges. Three chapters (100 verses) are devoted to Gideon and four chapters (96 verses) to Samson. Most scholars accept the view that the Gideon narrative is composed of two strands, although it is generally admitted that it is impossible to distinguish them. There can be no fundamental objection to this, as composition and editorship are as much the province of inspiration as actual authorship. If the editor of Judges had two accounts of the same events he would probably allow complementary elements to lay side by side, although he would hardly be so undiscerning as to admit actual contradictions. Yet the acceptance of duplicate narratives must not be made lightly simply because of marked differences from our accepted conventions of literature. In the poem of Deborah attention has been drawn to the tendency to elaboration which is the consequence of the device of parallelism; a statement is made, then repeated in similar language or with significant additions before the thought is carried on. The basic attitude of mind expressed thus in poetry was inevitably revealed also in prose, and this may account for some of the alleged doublets. It is a matter of regret that much of the critical investigation of the structure of the Old Testament literature has been carried on in a vacuum, confining itself to the Scriptures, instead of including within its scope the contemporary literature of other adjacent peoples, to see whether similar phenomena are apparent there.

**6:1-6. The oppression of Midian.** The victory over Sisera and the Canaanite host, so manifestly the work of the Lord, would doubtless lead to a resurgence of Israel's faith. But the passing of the years blurred the memory of the great deliverance and the next generation reverted to an easy-going syncretistic religion that again threatened to obliterate Israel's distinctive religion. The historian saw the chastening hand of the Lord in a new and formidable oppression, spearheaded by the Midianites, who were traditionally related to the Israelites (Gn. 25:2). *Midian* was located south of Edom at the northern extremity of the Gulf of Aqaba. A semi-nomadic group, they were joined in their raids of Israel by *the Amalekites*, who occupied the area to the south of Judah, and *the children of the east*, a nomadic group from the Syrian desert. A new 'secret weapon' was employed in these forays in the use of the *camel*, and in this chapter there is the first documentation of the large-scale use of this animal in a military campaign. It gave the Midianites and their allies the immense advantage of a speedy, long-range fighting force and it is clear that the use of this angular and imposing beast struck terror in the hearts of the Israelites. The extent of these raids can be observed with the aid of an atlas: the tribe of Manasseh was principally affected, but the territories of Asher, Zebulun, Naphtali and Ephraim were also involved (6:35; 8:1), and penetration was made as far as Gaza, at the southern end of Philistia. The final battle took place in the valley of Jezreel (6:33). The non-mention of Issachar is surprising, since its territory must have been affected. This invasion appears to have been an annual event during the seven years of the Midianite oppression and in typically nomadic style the invaders came *with their cattle and their tents* (5), living off the land. The simile of *locusts* (RV, RSV) is an appropriate one, indicating the absolute devastation of these rapacious hordes as they moved from one area to another. The cumulative effect of these raids would be considerable: all agriculture would be affected and the plundering of Israel's herds, crops and fruits would make for long, lean winters. Moreover, it was unsafe to dwell in open villages or even towns, the natural targets of an attacker seeking supplies or plunder; so the Israelites were forced into a primitive existence in the inaccessible mountainous regions (2).

**6:7-10. The prophetic condemnation.** The children of Israel appear to have turned to the Lord in their extremity as a last resort, which hardly indicates a vital religious faith. The reason for their misfortune was brought home to them by an unnamed prophet whose words were similar to those of the angel of the Lord at Bochim (2:1ff.) The fundamental failure of the Israelites was their forgetfulness of the implications of the covenant-relationship, the God who had done great things for them required loyal obedience, which they failed conspicuously to give. The reference to *the gods of the Amorites* (10; *cf.* note on 1:4) may confirm the locale of this persecution as the central hill-country.

**6:11-24. The call of Gideon.** The alternation of the phrases used to describe Gideon's divine visitor shows that *the angel of the Lord* was used synonymously with *the Lord*. The theophany was in human form, as was usual in the earlier part of the Old Testament period, and the language was strongly anthropomorphic, which allowed full personality to the Deity. The site of *Ophrah* (11) is not definitely known, but the detail given serves to distinguish it from the Benjamite Ophrah (Jos. 18:23; 1 Sa. 13:17). The *oak*, or sacred tree, was the site where the oracles of God were traditionally given (*cf.* 4:5). Gideon's father, Joash, was descended from Abiezer, the son of Manasseh, whose tribal portion was west of the Jordan (Jos. 17:2). Some extent of the influence of the Midianite raids can be gained by the reference to Gideon beating out wheat in *the winepress*, which was normally a hollow carved out of the rock with a channel connecting it to a lower trough. The grapes were placed in this depression and trodden out by foot, the juice running down into the lower receptacle. Threshing was normally carried out with a threshing-sledge drawn by oxen, in an exposed place so that the wind could carry away the chaff, but Gideon was improvising in the winepress, away from the sight of marauding bands. The same reference indicates the smallness of the harvest. It could be beaten out with a rod or staff in a confined place.

The dialogue between the angel of the Lord and Gideon is not without its humorous undertones, as Gideon, described as a *mighty man of valour*[1] (12) and as the prospective saviour of his people, protests, in contrast, his utter inadequacy and

[1] Heb. *gibbôr ḥayil.* Since Jephthah (11:1) and Boaz (Ru. 2:1) are similarly described, this expression has been regarded as the designation of a military aristocracy 'who owned and operated large plantations in time of peace, quite like the Homeric heroes' (C. H. Gordon in a review, *JSS*, VIII, 1963, p. 93). But is there any evidence of vast estates until the time of the eighth-

weakness. However, it is when a man is fully conscious of his own weakness and the difficulties of the situation that the Lord can take and use him. The man who relies upon his own innate strength is not likely to draw upon the Lord's grace, nor give Him the glory for anything that is achieved. It is also equally true that the Lord saw not only the man that was – weak and timorous, but the man that could be – strong, resolute and courageous.

**13–16.** The complaint of Gideon was doubtless shared by most of his contemporaries: the Lord had forsaken them; His mighty exploits were in the past, not the present. Nor was Gideon convinced by the assurance in the Lord's reply (14) that deliverance was at hand. Instead he described himself as the least likely person for such an assignment. The words may indicate his natural humility, but may also be based on the hard facts of experience. Gideon knew just how poor his father was at this time of crisis. The second assurance of the Lord (16) seems to have had a greater effect upon Gideon. In passing, it should be observed that there are timeless assurances in verses 14 and 16 for all those who are called to the work of the Lord. There is might in the consciousness of the Lord's commission (14); there is a greater might in the consciousness of divine companionship (16). *Have not I sent thee?* and *Surely I will be with thee* have their New Testament parallel in Matthew 28: 19, 20 and they have been a source of strength and inspiration to many who, like Gideon, have been called to the Lord's service.

**17–24.** Gideon was not fully aware of the identity of the One who was commissioning him, but he did realize that there was something unique about Him, hence his request for a sign and his offering of a *present* (Heb. *minḥâ*), a word which was often used of the freewill offering in Israel's sacrificial system, but was also used of the tribute brought to a king or a superior (*cf.* note on 3:15). The leisureliness of the East is reflected in the time it must have taken to prepare such a meal (*cf.* Gn.

century prophets? Their condemnation of 'land-grabbing' rested upon the fact that Yahweh was the real landlord, with the individual Israelites holding their allotted portion as a sacred trust from Him.

18:6ff.). The *ephah of flour* (19) alone weighed between 34 and 45 pounds, which, in a time of scarcity, was a not inconsiderable gift. The food was disposed of in accordance with the instructions of the angel of the Lord (20), the rock upon which the food was placed being probably a part of the winepress itself. It has been suggested that it was an ancient rock-altar with cup-shaped hollows for receiving libations; but such an altar, while well known in antiquity, is not necessarily indicated. It was when the meal was consumed with fire at the touch of the angel's rod, followed immediately by the disappearance of the angel himself (21), that Gideon realized with terror the nature of his heavenly visitor (22). It was widely believed in Israel that no man could see God face to face and live (Gn. 16:13; 32:30; Ex. 20:19; 33:20; Jdg. 13:22; Is. 6:5). Gideon, assured that no harm would befall him, immediately erected an altar, the name of which, *The Lord is peace* (RSV), reflected the opening words of the divine promise. That altar, which doubtless became a centre of interest and worship following the sweeping victory of Gideon, still existed in the editor's day, which indicates a considerable lapse of time, otherwise there would be no point in the observation.

**6:25–32. Gideon's first assignment.** No lengthy period intervened between Gideon's call and the assignment of his first task, which was, significantly, near at hand. The man who was to throw off the yoke of Midian and bring his people back to a true faith in the Lord must first of all set things right in his own home. There are strange inconsistencies in the narrative which reflect the syncretistic tendencies of the age and suggest strongly that, for Joash, Yahweh was regarded as one of the Baal gods. His own name is compounded with the name of Yahweh (lit. 'Yahweh has given') but the alternative name of his son, Jerubbaal (meaning 'may Baal give increase'), incorporates the name of Baal. Later on the name was deliberately emended to Jerubbesheth (2 Sa. 11:21), the Hebrew word *bosheth*, meaning 'shame', being substituted for Baal, the Canaanite god whose worship had led Israel astray (other examples of this tendency may be seen in the names Ish-baal

= Ishbosheth; Merib-baal = Mephibosheth). The sacred oak is contrasted with the Asherah (*grove*, AV, see note on 3:7), a wooden pillar representing the sacred tree, which was regularly associated with the Canaanite cultus, and the altar which Gideon built contrasts with the Baal altar of his father. Even the reference to the bull which Gideon employed and then sacrificed may fit into this pattern, for the bull was the sacred animal of the fertility cults. El himself, the head of the Canaanite pantheon, was often distinguished by the epithet 'Bull'. This particular animal may already have been designated for sacrifice to Baal.

The altar which Gideon had constructed at the place of the theophany (24) was in no way connected with the one which he was now commanded to erect *upon the top of this rock, in the ordered place* (26, AV). The rock was not the rock of the winepress, but a *stronghold* (RV, RSV) or fortress, perhaps a natural strong-point like an inaccessible crag, which formed a place of retreat and refuge for Joash and his neighbours when the Midianites were in the vicinity. The phrase *in the ordered place* refers to the construction of an altar, *i.e., with stones laid in due order* (RSV). The references to the bullock and especially to the ten menservants suggest that the family of Gideon was not so insignificant as he had inferred in verse 15. Indeed, Joash appears as the custodian of the Baal-sanctuary which served the whole community. Gideon carried out his orders to the letter, but not in the broad light of day, for such was the reverence paid to Baal that he feared not only the other inhabitants of the city but even the members of his own household (27). That his fears were well founded appears in the prompt reaction of the townsfolk when they saw the devastation wrought in their sanctuary (28). Their enquiries soon implicated Gideon (a secret known to ten men is no secret) and this led to the demand for his death, a suggestion which was met by the sound common sense of Joash. *If* Baal was a real god it was an insult worthy of death to intervene on his behalf (31); a god who was really God could vindicate Himself, without the necessity for human interference. If this advice had been followed by the devotees of the world's religions, not excepting many who claimed to be Christians, the world would have been spared a great deal of torture, bloodshed and untold misery. Joash's defence of his son was possibly the first step in his own spiritual rehabilitation.

**6:33-35. Gideon's response to the Midianite invasion.** The annual invasion of the Midianites and their allies is indicated here. For the eighth year in succession they crossed the Jordan and encamped in the valley of Jezreel at the eastern end of Esdraelon, which was not only a particularly fertile area, but also provided a convenient point for raids on the surrounding areas. It is known that Gideon's brothers were slain at Tabor, in this area (8:18), but it is by no means certain that it was on this particular occasion. Gideon became a typical, charismatic judge when *the Spirit of the Lord came upon him* (34). The verb is suggestive, meaning 'to clothe with' (*cf.* RV mg.): 'the Spirit of the Lord clothed itself with Gideon' betokening complete possession (*cf.* 1 Ch. 12:18; 2 Ch. 24:20, where the same verb occurs, and see note on 3:10). Jacob M. Myers observes, 'The spirit of the Lord became incarnate in Gideon, who then became the extension of the Lord.'[1] Thus equipped, Gideon was ready for the immense task that awaited him and the summons went out to the tribes (35). The fact that the men of *Abiezer*, Gideon's home town, were the first to respond, must have been an encouragement to him and shows that his earlier resolute action had caused no lasting rift. *Manasseh*, his own tribe, likewise rallied to his support, quickly followed by representatives from Asher, Zebulun and Naphtali (see the note on 6:1-6), although the full contingents from these tribes may not have participated in the battle until after the initial success (*cf.* 7:23). The omission of Ephraim, the most powerful of the tribes, may reveal the timidity of Gideon even at this stage. Perhaps he feared the reaction of the Ephraimite rulers if he, a member of a less-powerful tribe, should be presumptuous enough to set himself up as a leader. In view of the sequel (7:24; *cf.* 8:1ff.) the failure to summon the Ephraimites was significant.

[1] Myers, p. 736.

**6:36–40. The sign of the fleece.** Gideon's faith was not constant; it knew moments of uncertainty as well as heights of greatness. The patience of the Lord is remarkably shown in this section, in which Gideon twice sought confirmation of the challenge presented to him. The Lord very graciously accommodated Himself to Gideon's request, understanding fully the frailty of human nature (*cf*. Ps. 103:14). The reason for the change in the detail of the sign was probably Gideon's realization that the fleece would absorb a heavy dew much more readily than the rock of the threshing-floor and would therefore dry much less quickly when the sun arose. The reverse would be the greater miracle and Gideon asked for this, conscious that he was coming very close to angering God by his lack of trust and yet searching desperately for confirmation of the divine promise. This was readily forthcoming, for the Lord deals more tenderly and graciously with His children than any earthly father.

**7:1–8. Strange generalship.** Gideon and his army took up their positions at the spring of *Harod*, which has been identified with the modern 'Ain Jalud, at the foot of Mount Gilboa. Just northwards across the valley of Jezreel, less than 5 miles from the Israelite force, was the Midianite encampment by the hill of Moreh. The Midianites were obviously aware of the presence of the Israelite army and their intelligence service knew the name of its leader (7:14), but it does not seem to have been regarded as a serious threat; probably they felt secure in their greatly superior numerical strength and the confidence engendered by the success of the seven preceding years.

Before the engagement in the conflict Gideon was commanded to reduce his army from 32,000 men to a paltry 300, the number appearing the more insignificant in view of the strength of the opposing army (described in hyperbolic language in verse 12). The point is often stressed in the Old Testament that mere numbers themselves are no guarantee of success; it is the presence of the Lord that ensures victory and He is able to work through a handful of dedicated men. The glory of that victory was to be manifestly the Lord's, not men's (2; *cf.* Dt. 8:17; Ps. 115:1).

There were two stages in the reduction of Gideon's army. First, in accordance with the provision of Deuteronomy 20:8, all those who had no real heart for the battle were to be released. Fear is contagious and could have disastrous effects upon an army, even reaching panic proportions, as in the case of the Midianite host. Nevertheless it is a somewhat shattering discovery to find that more than two-thirds of Gideon's army melted away when given such an opportunity! The reference to *mount Gilead* (3, AV, RV) is enigmatic, as Gilead was across the Jordan, and there is no other known place with the same name. Most likely the reference is to Mount Gilboa, the site of Gideon's camp. Whilst the first stage in the reduction of the number was concerned with the morale of the army, the reason for the second step is not immediately apparent, as is witnessed by the diverse explanations of commentators. It may be that we are not to look for any explanation other than the desire to reduce the number by one means or another. However, it may be that the second test placed a premium upon alertness and the display of a soldierly spirit that took care not to be caught off-guard. Those who were rejected were those who, casting caution to the winds, dropped to their knees to drink. Those who were retained were those who lapped *as a dog laps*, a description that has perplexed many. Obviously it cannot mean that the 300 used their tongues to lap up the water from the spring, since this would involve falling upon their knees like the others and, in any case, the use of the hand is specifically indicated (6). The best explanation appears to be that the 300 used their hands as a dog uses its tongue to scoop up the water while they remained on their feet, watchful and prepared for any emergency. Such was the confidence in victory that the rejected 9,700 were allowed to return home!

The earlier part of verse 8 (AV) needs clarification. It cannot have been the 300 men who were supplied with *victuals*, for their lack of provisions is expressly noted in 8:4,5, and, moreover, the nature of the projected campaign required them to be unencumbered. Most likely the reference to victuals refers to the earthenware vessels (*jars*, RSV) in which the provisions were stored, a suggestion strengthened by the mention of *trumpets*. Three hundred men would not all possess trumpets, nor would there be a sufficient number of pitchers or jars to effect the ruse employed to terrify the Midianites, so before the larger company departed any deficiency in these items was made good. This, of course, anticipates verses 16–18 and shows that Gideon was planning at an early stage for the surprise attack. How else could 300 men take on a multitude?

**7:9-15. Confirmation of victory.** The summons to attack the Midianites, although accompanied by an absolute assurance of victory, provided for a further strengthening of Gideon's faith, and it is noteworthy that he availed himself of the opportunity. The witness to the underlying qualms of Gideon is true to human nature, for the general who appears strong and resolute before his men is often subject to fears within. It is also indicative of the veracity of the narrative, for such hesitancy on the part of one of Israel's heroes is not likely in a fabrication. Gideon and his servant Phurah went down into the valley and crossed to the encampment of the enemy where, in spite of their superior strength, a watch was being maintained. *The armed men that were in the host* (11, AV) may be a reference to the main striking force of the Midianites, which would carry out the plundering raids whilst the base camp was guarded by less able forces. This élite group, better equipped and disciplined, may have been disposed around the perimeter of the *camp* (RV, RSV) to afford maximum protection. The sheer weight of numbers of the invaders is again stressed (12) to indicate the magnitude of Gideon's task.

The two men overheard a couple of the Midianite sentries conversing about a *dream* which one had had. Dreams were considered of great importance in ancient times, especially if the dreamer was a man of rank or authority, for the gods were conceived to make known their will or desires by this means. Every dream was believed to be capable of interpretation, although this was, of course, the point where difficulties arose. It is generally maintained that the *cake of barley bread* (13) represented the poor yeoman farmer of Israel, whose staple crop was barley, whilst the *tent* was the natural symbol for a nomadic community like the Midianites. The Hebrew word for *cake*, found nowhere else in Scripture, is quite appropriate, as the context demands something circular. G. R. Driver suggests a connection with an Arabic verb meaning 'dry and crackled', or 'putrid', and observes 'a stale loaf, going bad and hard, would be much more likely than a soft and crumbly loaf of new bread to go bouncing into the camp'.[1] The meaning of the dream was apparent to the second soldier (14) and such an interpretation, coming from a Midianite source, provided Gideon with the final assurance which he sought. With gratitude in his heart for such an encouraging sign he first worshipped the One who had dealt so graciously with him and then returned to his own small company to share with them the conviction of a complete triumph (15; *cf.* verse 9).

**7:16–22. The rout of the Midianites.** The Israelites were divided into *three companies*, a stratagem adopted on many occasions in the Old Testament period (*cf.* 1 Sa. 11:11; 2 Sa. 18:2), but never did an army advance with such a motley assortment of equipment! It seems unnecessarily pedantic to suggest that verse 16 is a clear indication of duplication on the assumption that it would take three hands to hold a trumpet, a flaming torch and a pitcher to conceal the light of the torch, and to protect it from the wind. The *trumpets* at this early stage were usually made of the horns of rams or cattle, attached to the wearer in such a way that, when they were not in use, the hands were free to wield weapons. At the moment when the trumpets were blown the torch and the pitcher could be held temporarily in the one hand without undue difficulty. Gideon's instructions (17, 18) were that the Israelites were to imitate his action, and his reference to the blowing of trumpets is given as an illustration of this. It does not mean that this strand in the narrative had no knowledge of the use of pitchers and torches. Nor need it be assumed that the trumpets were blown once only and that verses 20 and 22 are therefore witnesses to the

[1] Driver, p. 13.

duplicate accounts. It is expressly stated that the Israelites maintained their positions in the early part of the proceedings (21) and it can be imagined that they would continue to make as much noise as possible, under Gideon's direction, to add to the atmosphere of confusion. The general order of events seems to have been, first a loud concerted blast on the trumpets, then the shattering of 300 pitchers followed by a thunderous battle-cry, after which the trumpets sounded forth again. Until such time as they pursued after the fleeing remnants of a once-proud army, it is probable that trumpet-blasts and battle-cries alternated.

The effect of such a clamour, with 300 waving torches creating the impression of a great host, must have been shattering. The time is noted precisely as *the beginning of the middle watch* (19), *i.e.* 10 p.m. on the assumption that the hours of darkness were divided into three and not four watches. Those not involved in the first or second watches would be in the deep sleep of the earlier part of the night, whilst those who had just been relieved would still be moving about the camp, thus increasing the fear of those awakened by the din, that the enemy had already penetrated the camp. The clamour would also cause unrest among the large numbers of camels (12), possibly leading to a stampede. It is not surprising that in the resultant confusion soldiers lashed out at everyone who loomed up in the darkness, not knowing who was friend or foe: *all the host ran, and cried, and fled* (21, AV). The verbs in this verse describe graphically the process of panic which struck the Midianites: *ran*, which appears tautologous to *fled*, is never found in the Old Testament with the meaning of running away in flight. Its meaning here undoubtedly suggests the first reaction of the Midianites when their slumber was so rudely shattered; 'they leapt up', in alarm, uttered a loud cry of alarm and fled precipitately.

**22.** The natural line of flight for the Midianites was eastwards down the valley and over the Jordan into the region from which they had attacked Israel, and that they took this route is confirmed by the instructions to the Ephraimites to secure the fords of the Jordan (24). All three towns mentioned were in Transjordania and each may be located with reference to Jabesh-gilead: *Zererath* (or Zaretan) was 10 miles due south; *Abel-meholah* was about 6 miles east and *Tabbath* about 7 miles south-south-east. The mention of Succoth and Penuel at a later stage of the flight (8:5,8; see also 8:11) indicates the general south-easterly direction the Midianites took. A wide dispersion of the survivors is likely in such a situation.

**7:23-25. Reinforcements for Gideon.** No doubt the inhabitants of the hill-country to the north and south of the valley of Jezreel were keeping a close watch on the situation, so it would not take long to bring them into action following the rout of the Midianites. The initial summons (6:35) had gone to the tribes of Manasseh, Asher, Zebulun and Naphtali. Now it appears that a fresh call for assistance was issued. Those who had formerly been so fearful would take courage on hearing of Gideon's success and it is probable that most of the members of his augmented army were among the original 32,000. Gideon now found the necessary confidence to approach the Ephraimites, whose tribal position south of Manasseh would enable them to intercept the remnants of the fleeing Midianite army. Specific instructions were given to them to secure the fords. The location of *the waters unto Beth-barah* (AV) is completely unknown, but the reference shows that it must be distinguished from the Jordan. Most likely they were asked to take the fords of the minor tributaries of the Jordan, thus sealing off the escape route along the western bank of the river. The Ephraimites carried out their commission and slew two of the Midianite princes, *Oreb* (Raven) and *Zeeb* (Wolf), at places which are referred to elsewhere only in Isaiah 10:26, and which cannot be identified. The arrangements for the secondary phases of the campaign must have taken some time, so that by the time the Ephraimites had taken up their positions some detachments of the enemy had already crossed the Jordan, pursued by Gideon and the original army (8:4). It was in Transjordania, therefore, that the heads of the two princes were presented to Gideon.

**8:1–3. Resentment and appeasement.** The tribe of Ephraim appears to have enjoyed a supremacy over the other tribes during the earlier period of the settlement. Its territory in the central highlands was one of the few areas where the Conquest was in any way complete and the Ephraimites, preserved by their central position from many of the incursions of Israel's hostile neighbours, experienced a far greater freedom to consolidate themselves than did the other tribes. The two most prominent sanctuaries of the judges' period, Bethel and Shiloh, which functioned as the rallying-point of the tribes, were situated within its boundaries and this fact undoubtedly further increased its prestige. The similarities between the incident noted here and that concerning Jephthah (12:1–6) are apparent, but the sequels are so diverse that no confusion of each need be postulated. Both incidents are completely in accord with the temper of the Ephraimites, of whom Gideon obviously stood in some awe. It has already been suggested that his hesitation to call upon the Ephraimites for help was caused by his reluctance to appear to be assuming the leadership; now this omission called forth a sharp rebuke from them. Perhaps this was not altogether disinterested, since there was obviously a prospect of considerable booty following Gideon's victory. The answer of Gideon is an excellent illustration of the maxim that 'a soft answer turneth away wrath' (Pr. 15:1). No mention was made of his own prowess, or of his position at the head of a group of tribes which excluded Ephraim. Instead he conveyed the impression that his own contribution was insignificant in comparison to that of the Ephraimites, and that the operation of his own contingent (*the vintage of Abiezer*, 2) was a somewhat small-scale effort. Mollified by this flattery the Ephraimites calmed down, Gideon's tactful action having averted a potentially dangerous situation. This is in marked contrast to the response of Jephthah in a similar crisis.

**8:4–9. The refusal of hospitality.** It is probable that 8:1–3 are out of chronological order in their present position, having been set there following the recording of Ephraim's intervention in 7:24,25. The adventures of the original 300 are now resumed. Some indication of the disorderliness of the precipitate flight of the Midianites can be gained by reference to the Israelite forces taking part in the mopping-up operations. Gideon appears to have made no attempt to integrate his force with that of the men of Naphtali, Asher and Manasseh (7:23). The lack of an effective rearguard action by the Midianites allowed his puny force to forge ahead as fast as possible, whilst the hastily-assembled, allied supporting force made its own way in pursuit of the widely-separated stragglers. Somewhere in this confused chapter of events came the sealing-off of the fords by the Ephraimites.

The army of Gideon had been equipped for a surprise attack, not a lengthy pursuit of a routed army, but Gideon doubtless expected to obtain supplies from the Israelite tribes situated eastward of the Jordan. In this he was disappointed, for the citizens of Succoth and Penuel refused to assist him, considering it expedient not to lay themselves open to reprisals from the Midianites. Gideon *may* have won a great victory, but Zebah and Zalmunna were still at liberty. The reply of the officials of Succoth (6) showed that they gave Gideon's minute peasant-army little chance of capturing the leaders of an elusive and still numerous semi-nomadic group operating in conditions favourable to them. The recollection of at least seven years' domination was not dimmed by what could prove to be a passing victory. This unpatriotic action indicates the breakdown of the tribal unity which led to the virtual separation of the eastern tribes from their brethren west of the Jordan. Gideon's harsh words (7,9), compared with the mild answer to the Ephraimites (2,3), reveal his reaction to such treachery. The exact meaning of the punishment in store for the men of Succoth (7) is not clear, but as the word *tear* (AV, RV) means 'to thresh' or *flail* (RSV), it may have been a threat to drag them over thorns as a threshing-sledge is dragged over grain, or to lay them upon thorns and thresh *them* by drawing threshing-sledges over them. In any case an unpleasant fate is indicated by these words and one that was destined to end in certain death.

**5.** *Succoth* was in the tribal portion of Gad, on the eastern edge of the Jordan valley just northwards of the Jabbok. *Penuel* (8) lay by the Jabbok about 5 miles to the east of Succoth. It was the scene of Jacob's supernatural encounter (Gn. 32) and its importance is shown by the fact that a *tower* was built there, into which the inhabitants could retreat in an emergency (*cf.* 9:47,51). The distance of these towns from the scene of the initial battle must have been at least 50 miles.

**6.** *Zebah* (meaning 'sacrifice') and *Zalmunna* ('withheld its hospitality') have significant names in the context of the narrative, and it has been suggested that they are not original but were given in jest by the victorious Israelites. However, recent research on Midianite proper names, based on archaeological evidence, suggests that they may be genuinely Midianite.

**8:10–12. The final rout of the Midianites.** The remnants of the once-mighty Midianite army must have considered themselves safe when they reached *Karkor*, by the Wadi Sirhan, well to the east of the Dead Sea, but they reckoned without the tenacity of Gideon and his men, who must have secured provisions en route. Not all the cities east of Jordan were as boorishly self-interested as Succoth and Penuel. The site of *Nobah* is not known, but *Jogbehah* was situated between 15 and 16 miles south-east of Penuel. Gideon, following *by the way of them that dwelt in tents* (AV, RV), *i.e.* along the caravan-routes (*cf.* RSV), fell upon the Midianites who, secure in this remote area, had apparently neglected to set a watch. This second appearance of Gideon and his men, so far from the hill of Moreh, struck further terror into their demoralized antagonists and led to further headlong flight. To say that Gideon *discomfited* (12, AV, RV) the host appears tautologous after the smiting of the host and the capture of its kings had been noted. C. F. Burney, by altering the final letter of the Hebrew word, emends it to read 'he devoted to destruction'.[1] More plausible is G. R. Driver's association with an Arabic verb meaning 'to part', 'scatter' or 'disperse', indicating the final dispersion

[1] Burney, p. 231.

of an army which had lost all morale and cohesion.[1] The capture of the Midianite kings would make it difficult for the surviving Midianites to regroup and reassert themselves, but Gideon wisely withdrew before his own position became vulnerable. A great and decisive victory had been consolidated by the dogged and courageous persistence of Gideon and his men, always outnumbered by their enemies.

**8:13–17. Vengeance upon Succoth and Penuel.** *Before the sun was up* (13, AV) should be read *by the ascent of Heres* (RSV), a place which has not been identified. The sweeping victory and the consequent spoils that fell into the hands of the victorious 300 did not lessen Gideon's determination to show to others that the deplorable conduct of the men of Succoth and Penuel could not escape unpunished. There is a certain rough justice in his concern that all the guilty men of Succoth should suffer, and the names of the city officials were written down by the captured youth. It is particularly unfortunate that the translation of the AV and RV, *described* (14), should obscure this last fact, which is a vital witness to the wide dissemination of the arts of writing and reading (*cf.* RSV, *wrote down*). The development of the alphabetical script, with its limited number of letters compared to the multitude of elements in ideographic or syllabic writing, was one of the great steps forward in civilization, and brought writing within the compass of this young man of Succoth, as well as of Gideon himself. Possibly the youth used a sharp-pointed instrument to scratch the words upon a fragment of pottery or a piece of shale, a method frequently employed for much of the Old Testament period. Armed with this list Gideon reminded the rulers of Succoth of their taunt (15; *cf.* verse 6), the presence of the captured kings indicating that he had power to carry out his intention. He then proceeded to show equal resolution in carrying out his threat and these inhospitable men were subjected to a form of torture which almost certainly ended in their death (*cf.* the fate which befell a similar group in Penuel, where Gideon again showed himself to be a man of his

[1] Driver, p. 14.

word). The punishment was drastic and it witnesses to the heinousness of the offence in Gideon's eyes.

**8:18–21. The slaughter of the Midianite kings.** It may be assumed that the scene had now reverted to Ophrah, since Jether, Gideon's first-born son, would not have accompanied the 300 warriors in their exacting campaign through Transjordania. Up to this point Gideon's main concern had been the deliverance of his downtrodden countrymen from the Midianite menace; but now a secondary concern is introduced, the exaction of blood revenge for the death of his brothers at the hands of the Midianites. The question of verse 18 is literally, 'Where are the men . . .?' (*cf.* RSV), and this is best rendered idiomatically, 'What about the men you slew at Tabor?' Having dealt with the national crisis, Gideon was now free to settle his own private account with Zebah and Zalmunna. There is no means of establishing the time or the circumstances of the death of his brothers. It could have been in a preliminary skirmish when Gideon's army was assembling, or in a Midianite campaign of a previous year. If it was the latter case Gideon was clearly lacking in courage to avenge his brothers' deaths before the divine intervention. Verse 19 may suggest that his brothers had been captured by the Midianites and subsequently put to death, not killed in the heat and anonymity of battle, and that the two kings were therefore directly responsible. Gideon's basically humane nature is revealed in the latter part of the verse, but, according to the harsh standards of his day, he had no alternative but to exact vengeance. The reply of the two kings (18), who knew full well that they were marked out for death, hardly answers Gideon's question. It is clear that they recalled the incident and Gideon's words probably made them aware of the likeness between the men they had slain and the man who now confronted them. There is also an incidental witness to the imposing appearance of Gideon. The command of a father to his son to slay two kings in cold blood is indicative of the general standards of the age, which were not those of the New Testament.[1] It would be

[1] See Introduction, section v. *c.*, pp. 41ff.

accounted an honour for a youth to slay such important prisoners of war, and a corresponding disgrace for the captives themselves.

The Midianite kings showed considerable courage in the way they faced death. It was no shame to die by the hand of a warrior like Gideon, but a youth unskilled in warfare would hack and bungle the execution, and even these brave men flinched at such a prospect (the pronoun *thou* in verse 21 is emphatic; *cf.* RSV, *Rise yourself*). The situation was saved by Jether's inability to carry out the distasteful assignment, so the end came swiftly at the hand of Gideon. The *ornaments* (AV; the word indicates that they were crescent-shaped, RV, RSV) which adorned their camels became part of the spoils of war. Such crescents are mentioned in the Bible only in this chapter and Isaiah 3:18, but crescent-moon-shaped ornaments have been found at many excavated sites in Palestine. They are widely used by the Arab peoples up to the present day.

**8:22, 23. Invitation to kingship.** It is not clear how representative was the delegation from *the men of Israel* who requested Gideon to establish a dynastic rule. It could have been limited to a relatively small area (*cf.* the extent of Abimelech's rule in chapter 9), and it is not easy to envisage the powerful and proud tribe of Ephraim accepting a king from another tribe. However, this section is of great importance in any consideration of the period of the judges. In an acute crisis involving a number of the tribes the courageous action of an individual had integrated the resources of the tribes and had averted disaster. Such was the sense of gratitude that the throne was offered to the deliverer. It was not accepted, but it was only a matter of time before an even greater emergency, involving a majority of the tribes, precipitated a similar situation and led to a demand for a single ruler to co-ordinate the forces of the tribes. It was the Philistine pressure which provided such a stimulus and led to the demand to 'make us a king to judge us like all the nations' (1 Sa. 8:5). Gideon's reply was a model of noble unselfishness which recognized the essential fact that the nation *had* a king if they would only acknowledge Him.

Their king was Yahweh, who was all to them and more than the kings of other nations were to their subjects (*cf.* 1 Sa. 10:19). The government in Israel was essentially a theocracy, not a monarchy, and even when the monarchy was introduced it was qualified by this consideration. Gideon's action in resolutely thrusting from him the prospect of personal advancement was exemplary and merits the highest praise.

However, not all scholars have accepted the transparent meaning of verse 23 that Gideon refused the monarchy. G. Henton-Davies suggests that his refusal was, in reality, 'an acceptance couched in the form of a pious refusal with the motive of expressing piety and of gaining favour with his would be subjects'.[1] This he supports by an examination of three other incidents, the 'anonymous refusal' of Exodus 4:13ff. and the transactions of Genesis 23 and 2 Samuel 24, where property ostensibly offered as a gift passes hands for a considerable price. That Gideon exercised many of the privileges of a typical monarch of the Ancient Near East has often been pointed out: his use of the ephod-oracle (see note on 8:27); his use of jewellery and royal raiment (8:26); the creation of a harem (8:30); the name given to one of his sons, Abimelech meaning 'my father a king' (8:31); the assumption that his sons would succeed him (9:2); the wrangling between Abimelech and Jotham over the succession; even the reference to the kingly stature of Gideon and his brothers (8:18), all these have been held to indicate the position which Gideon, in fact, held. But against this view, verse 29 suggests strongly that Gideon, having refused the monarchy, retired into private life, albeit with a considerable reputation and private fortune. The nation was not yet ready for a monarchy and Gideon's deference to the Ephraimites (see note on 8:1-3) may have had a part in his refusal of this honour.

**8:24-28. Gideon's ephod.** The final chapter of Gideon's life appears as a distinct anticlimax to the heroic actions of the earlier section, and the man who had given such a magnificent

[1] G. Henton Davies, 'Judges viii. 22-23', in *VT*, XIII. 2, 1963, pp. 151-157.

lead to his fellows now sets a deplorable example of self-indulgence in which he, his family and the whole nation were involved. Perhaps it is easier to honour God in some courageous action in the limelight of a time of national emergency than it is to honour Him consistently in the ordinary, everyday life, which requires a different kind of courage. Gideon, who came through the test of adversity with flying colours, was not the first nor the last to be less successful in the test of prosperity. The request of the people to him is countered by his request for *earrings* captured from their foes; the possible alternative, 'noserings', is less likely since these appear to have been used only by women in the Old Testament period (as in Gn. 24:22; Is. 3:21; Ezk. 16:12). These Midianites are described as *Ishmaelites*, an unusual reference since the Midianites traced their descent through Keturah (Gn. 25:2), the Ishmaelites through Hagar (Gn. 16:15). The probable explanation is that the term Ishmaelites had come to be used very loosely to describe any trading nomadic group (*cf.* Gn. 37:25,27,28; 39:1).[1] The amount of *gold* (26) collected in this spontaneous offering was incredible, amounting to between 40 and 75 pounds' weight, depending on whether the light or heavy shekel was employed. It illustrates both the extent of the victory and the esteem in which Gideon was held. A further indication of the vast amount of booty gained is found in the reference to the crescents (see note on verse 21), pendants (AV, *collars*), purple garments and camel ornaments, which had nothing to do with the matter in hand (*i.e.* the construction of an ephod), but reflected the generous response of Gideon's men, who gave more than was requested of them.

**27.** The nature of the *ephod* has been a matter of conjecture. The ephod of the high priest (Ex. 39:1–26) was made of costly material worked with gold, blue, purple, scarlet and precious stones; it reached from the breast down to the hips and was secured by two shoulder-bands and a waist-band. With it were associated the Urim and Thummin (Ex. 28:30; Lv. 8:8) which were used for oracular purposes. But whilst the oracular con-

[1] See F. D. Kidner, *Genesis* (Tyndale Press, 1967), pp. 182f.; K. A. Kitchen, *Ancient Orient and Old Testament* (Tyndale Press, 1966), p. 119.

nection remained, the nature of the ephod itself appears to have changed over the years and at times the reference appears to be to a free-standing image, or to the receptacle containing the oracle, for in the period of the monarchy the priest was said to bear the ephod, not to wear it (1 Sa. 2:28; 14:3; where the verb *nāśā'* means to 'bear' or 'lift up'). Another possible reference is to a piece of cloth which was used to cover the eyes when the oracle was consulted. In all these instances there was the desire to ascertain the will of God by means of the sacred lot, but the situation is further complicated by the fact that the ephod commonly designated an ordinary article of everyday dress. In the case of Gideon there are three possible alternatives: that it was a garment after the pattern of the high-priestly ephod but with an unusual degree of gold ornamentation; that it was a replica of the high-priestly garment made of pure gold; or that it was a free-standing image. Its very preciousness became *a snare*, for it became an object of worship to a people only one stage removed from polytheism (*cf.* Jos. 24:15) and obliterated one of the characteristics of Israel's faith, namely the entire prohibition of images. It may be assumed that Gideon had no intention of departing from the Lord, any more than Aaron or Jeroboam intended apostasy by their creation of calf-images (Ex. 32:4; 1 Ki. 12:28). But the expression *and all Israel played the harlot after it there* (RSV) suggests that the form of worship inspired by his ephod was Canaanite in origin.

The editorial note in verse 28 completes the account of the subjugation of Midian, and notes the peace which the following generation enjoyed.

## h. Gideon's later years (8:29-35)

**8:29-31. The family of Gideon.** Gideon's retirement from public life following his rejection of the invitation to become king, and the establishment of a large family, serve as a necessary introduction to the events of chapter 9. The *many wives* of Gideon show that he lived in considerable prosperity, a far cry from the day when he described his family as 'poor in Manasseh' (6:15). A large harem was the usual appendage of the monarchy in the Fertile Crescent (*cf.* 2 Sa. 5:13ff.; 1 Ki. 11:1–4), but the effects of such a situation in the history of Israel's kings appears uniformly disastrous. There is a marked contrast between the seventy sons and Abimelech. The former 'came out of his loins' (so the meaning of the Hebrew), the seat of procreative power, the meaning being that they were reckoned by male descent to his own tribe. *Abimelech*, on the other hand, was the son of a concubine who probably remained with her own family group in Shechem, being visited by her husband from time to time. A similar situation may be observed in the case of Samson (15:1; 16:4ff.). It is important to observe that any offspring of such a union belonged to the wife's family. Thus the seventy legitimate sons traced their descent through Gideon and Abiezer, but Abimelech's lineage was reckoned through his Shechemite mother. As there is evidence to show that Shechem was a Canaanite city incorporated by alliance into Israel (see introductory note to chapter 9), she may have been a Canaanite woman. The name given to Abimelech ('my father a king', or 'the king is father') may show that Gideon still hankered after the honour he had refused, although names compounded with *melech* were common in Israel.

**8:32–35. The death of Gideon.** The death of a judge once more led to the removal of restraint and a movement towards the Baal-worship of their neighbours. The particular variant of Baal-worship which was followed was that of *Baal-berith* ('Baal or lord of the covenant') or 'El-berith' (9:46, 'god of the covenant'), which appeared to have centred in Shechem. The covenant may have been that between Israel and the incorporated Canaanite cities, or between the cities themselves and their own native deity. There is further evidence here of the Canaanization of Israel's worship, in which the nature of Yahweh was obscured and His mighty acts were forgotten. Yahweh might well be the God for a time of crisis, but the fertility gods appeared to offer more for the everyday life. For, as well as the sensual appeal of their worship, there was the preoccupation of these gods with the 'bread and butter' of existence. Less surprising was the failure of the Israelites to hold the remembrance of Gideon in honour. Many years had passed since his magnificent exploit (all his sons had grown to manhood in that time) and the opulence of his family life may have aroused jealousy in the new generation, and the feeling that he had been rewarded sufficiently.

## i. The rise and fall of Abimelech (9:1–57)

This chapter is of outstanding interest, for it offers clear evidence of the influence of a Canaanite community existing within the tribal structure of Israel. The city of *Shechem* was marked out by nature to play an important part in the history of its day. It was situated in a fertile valley between Mounts Ebal and Gerizim, which formed a natural link between the coastal plain and the Jordan valley. Many of the trade-routes converged on Shechem, which, standing at one of the crossroads of Palestine, dominated a considerable area of the surrounding countryside. It was hallowed in Israelite tradition as the place where Yahweh first revealed Himself to Abraham after his arrival from Haran (Gn. 12:6,7). Jacob had lived on friendly terms with the children of Hamor at Shechem until the vindictive action of Simeon and Levi had disrupted this harmony (Gn. 33:18–34:31), but at a later date the patriarchs are again found in the vicinity (Gn. 37:13, 14). The Tell el-Amarna letters show that Shechem fell into the hands of the Habiru in the fourteenth century BC and this group is believed to have been related to the Hebrews. The relationship was probably not an ethnic one, however, since the Habiru are mentioned in periods and places which can have no connection with the Hebrews. 'Habiru' possibly designates all semi-nomads of a particular type.[1]

The capture of Shechem by Joshua is nowhere hinted at nor mentioned in passing and yet at a very early date a covenant-renewal ceremony was held between Mounts Ebal and Gerizim (Jos. 8:30–35). This would have been impossible unless Shechem had been either captured or else

[1] See W. F. Albright, *The Biblical Period from Abraham to Ezra* (Harper Torchbooks, 1963).

been on friendly terms with the invaders. The evidence points to this latter as being the more probable.

The fact that the Shechemites were still described as 'the men of Hamor' (9:28), together with their allegiance to the Canaanite deity Baal-berith, and the obvious point of the appeal made by Abimelech at the end of verse 2, make it clear that the population of Shechem was dominantly Canaanite. It had probably been incorporated into Israel by treaty at the time of the Conquest. Here, then, is a witness to the friction which existed between the Israelites and the original inhabitants of the land. This was probably the reason why Shechem, although it was hallowed as the resting-place of the bones of Joseph (Jos. 24:32), maintained its place as the central sanctuary for a limited period only, being replaced by Bethel and then Shiloh.[1]

**9:1-5. The massacre of the sons of Gideon.** The reference to *the men of Shechem* (2) is literally 'the baals of Shechem', the word having here its original meaning of 'lord' or 'owner' (as in Jos. 24:11; Jdg. 20:5; 1 Sa. 23:11,12; 2 Sa. 21:12). The fear implanted in the minds of the Shechemites by Abimelech may have had little foundation in fact, his own personal ambition and, possibly, a jealous hatred of his brethren (who probably regarded him as inferior; *cf.* verse 18) being the real motives. The fact that the family of Gideon was still in residence at Ophrah (5), and not in one of the more important centres, indicates that the influence of Gideon himself was limited. Shechem, one of the old city-states of Canaan, may have been more inclined to accept a king than the Israelites, and the son of the great Gideon, who was one of them by the ties of flesh and blood, was an obvious candidate. Abimelech's plan met with a ready acceptance and he acted with a vigour characteristic of his father, but without any of his father's scruples. The resources of the sanctuary were used to finance the operation (4; *cf.* 1 Ki. 15:18; 2 Ki. 18:15,16) and the hired assassins appear to have met with little opposition at Ophrah,

[1] A. E. Cundall, 'Sanctuaries in Pre-Exilic Israel', in *Vox Evangelica*, IV (Epworth, 1965), pp. 12–17.

which may indicate that the family of Gideon maintained a very modest establishment without armed retainers. The precise reference to the place of execution as *upon one stone* (5, 18) may be a significant parallel to the sacrificial slaughtering of animals in the open (*cf.* 1 Sa. 14:33–35). The disposal of the blood of slaughtered beasts was a matter of great consequence, for 'the life of the flesh is in the blood' (Lv. 17:11), and in this ritual slaughter of his half-brothers Abimelech may have been seeking to avoid adverse repercussions by punctilious care in disposing of the blood of his victims.

**9:6. Abimelech made king.** The bloody deed accomplished, Abimelech was proclaimed king by the Shechemites. With them were associated *all the house of Millo* (6, AV, RV), which is best regarded as a proper name, *Beth-millo* (RSV). The word *millo* derives from a verb meaning 'to be filled', and originally referred to a rampart or earthwork; but its association with fortifications may have developed into a reference to fortresses generally. Thus *Beth-millo* may be identical with *the tower of Shechem* (46ff.). The site of the coronation was hallowed by tradition, the mention of an *oak* (RV, RSV) or 'terebinth' (AV, *plain*) and a *pillar* connecting with Joshua 24:26 where Joshua, in the covenant-renewal ceremony at Shechem, set up a memorial stone by the oak which was adjacent to the sanctuary (see also Gn. 35:4). The associations of such sites were very tenacious and it is of interest to note that Rehoboam went to Shechem, following the death of Solomon, to secure the acclamation of the Israelites although the city itself was in ruins at this time (1 Ki. 12:1,25).

The extent of Abimelech's kingdom was very limited; only Shechem, Beth-millo, Arumah (41) and Thebez (50) are mentioned as under his jurisdiction and it is unlikely that it extended beyond a portion of western Manasseh. The reference in verse 22 must be understood in this limited sense. His turbulent three-year rule, secured by guile and maintained by force, was hardly more than an incident in the development of the monarchy, for the kingdom itself did not survive his death. In the same way Abimelech, the opportunist, must not be given a place amongst the judges of Israel who owed their position to their character and achievements in delivering the people.

**9:7–21. The fable of Jotham.** The sole survivor of the blood-bath at Ophrah was *Jotham*, the youngest son of Gideon, whose hope of safety lay in putting the greatest possible distance between himself and Abimelech. Before his flight, however, he uttered his famous parable, which was both a protest against the shameful treatment meted out to the house of Gideon and a prophecy of the effect of Abimelech's rule. Approximately a century and a half before, six of the tribes had stood on the slopes of Mount Gerizim and thundered out their 'Amens' to the blessings of the law, pronounced by the Levites (Dt. 27:12; 28). Now Jotham stood on the same mountain, using it as a pulpit from which to denounce the shameful action of the Shechemites. It is unlikely that he was on the summit of the mountain, 1,000 feet above the city; a convenient crag is indicated, from which he could be heard by at least some of its citizens and from which he could beat a hasty retreat. Voices can carry a long way in the atmosphere of the Near East and Gerizim itself was used as an open-air pulpit in the great religious ceremony of Joshua 8:30–35, which itself was a fulfilment of the provisions of Deuteronomy 27 noted above. Similarly, our Lord could address thousands without apparent difficulty (Mk. 4:1; 6:34–44).

The parable deals with their choice of a king and it is interesting to observe that the principle of the monarchy itself is not condemned. The main point is that a worthless person, Abimelech, has been chosen. The implication is that the sons of Gideon, including Jotham himself, would have been a more desirable choice, although this is not specifically stated.

**8–15.** The fable itself is of importance as an ancient illustration of a story with a moral, and it bears comparison with Nathan's parable to David (2 Sa. 12:1–4) and the message of Jehoash, king of Israel, to Amaziah of Judah (2 Ki. 14:9,10). The *olive tree* was the first to reject the position of ruler over the trees, for the reason that the oil which he provided was used to honour God and man. Oil was used to anoint priests and to feed the lamp which illuminated the sanctuary. At a later date the kings of Israel were anointed with oil, but amongst Israel's neighbours there is evidence to show that the great kings were not anointed but their vassals only, which fact suggests that in Israel the king may have been regarded as the vassal of the Lord. The *fig tree* was equally reluctant to accept the honour of kingship because of its important position in the agricultural economy, the fig being the staple fruit of the whole area. The *vine* similarly declined the offer *to sway over the trees* (RSV), symbolizing the exercise of authority. The produce of the vine, like that of the olive, was used for both religious and secular purposes; it was used in libations offered to God (*e.g.* Ex. 29:40) and it was the principal beverage in every home. The rabbis of a later age suggested that the olive, fig and vine of Jotham's fable were representations of Othniel, Deborah and Gideon respectively, but a more general application is likely; men of dignity and influence within the community were not anxious to forsake their spheres of usefulness for the dubious honour of the monarchy.

Finally, the position was offered to the *bramble*, which not only produced nothing of value and was quite worthless as timber, but was a positive menace to the farmer who had to wage continual war against its encroachments. Its carpet-like growth was an especial menace in the heat of summer when scrub fires, fanned by the wind, could travel at incredible speeds along the tinder of dried brambles. The giant cedars of Lebanon were indeed threatened by this fire that came *out of the bramble* (15). This threat was accompanied by an absurd invitation *to put your trust in my shadow*, for the bramble, clinging closely to the ground, cast almost no shadow and offered no protection to the forest giants at whose feet it lay. Jotham's point had been graphically made; Abimelech could offer no real security to the men of Shechem; instead, he would be the means of their destruction.

**16–20.** The meaning of the parable was self-evident and the words of Jotham were only a loose application. In the fable the focus of attention was the worthless Abimelech. Here the emphasis was upon the *men of Shechem* who had shamefully treated the family of one who was completely worthy of their honour because of the great deliverance which, at the risk of his own life, he had wrought for them. The expression *adventured his life far* (AV) is a graphic one. Literally it reads 'he cast his life in front', and the thought is of a complete disregard of his personal safety. The contrast is the more pointed by the reference to Abimelech as the son of Gideon's *maidservant*, or slave-concubine, a deliberate slur on Jotham's part since the mother of Abimelech was, in fact, a free-woman of Shechem. Such was the man they had acknowledged as their brother! Jotham then stated that time would reveal the wisdom or folly of their action. *If* their action was honourable their relationship with Abimelech would be mutually cordial, but *if* the situation was otherwise they could expect mutual destruction, a word which was grimly prophetic. Bramble and cedars alike would perish in the conflagration that would develop between the newly crowned king and his subjects.

**21.** There is no record of the reaction of the Shechemites, but it may be gauged by the precipitate flight of Jotham to a retreat beyond the reach of Abimelech. *Beer*, meaning 'well', was exceedingly common as a place-name in ancient Israel and the site of Jotham's refuge is quite unknown.

**9:22-25. Friction between Abimelech and the Shechemites.** Self-seeking opportunists and those capable of treacherous murder never make easy companions, and it was not long before a breach occurred between Abimelech and the men of Shechem. Perhaps it is of significance that Abimelech does not seem to have resided in the principal city of his domain but delegated the oversight thereof to Zebul (30). The nature of his rule (*reigned*, AV, is too strong; the word is literally 'princed') was that of a local chieftain or petty-king over a limited area, and there was no question of a general acceptance of his role by all the tribes. The overruling action of God, sovereign in history, is indicated in verse 23 (*cf.* 1 Sa. 16:14; 18:10; 1 Ki. 22:19-23). The point which precipitated the dispute was the action of the Shechemites in setting armed bands in ambush beside the trade-routes in the vicinity of Shechem, thus depriving Abimelech of the dues which he would normally exact from the caravans which passed through his territory. This would have the effect of reducing the number of travellers and caravans in such a troubled area, thus emptying the pockets of Abimelech as well as hitting at his pride, for he could not guarantee safety of travel in his domain.

**9:26-29. The rebellion of Gaal.** Abimelech appears to have taken no action against the marauding bands which were terrorizing the countryside and it was not until there was a direct challenge to his authority that he was stirred to action. Nothing is known of *Gaal the son of Ebed* apart from the information given in this chapter. The men of Shechem were apparently easily swayed and Gaal gained their confidence by his slick talk, just as Abimelech had done previously. The time of this change of allegiance was the season of the vintage harvest at the end of summer. The great New Year Festival of Israel's immediate neighbours, the chief event in their cultus, was associated with the ingathering of the summer fruits. Its counterpart in Israel was the Feast of Tabernacles, which, under the influence of the Canaanite religion, displaced the Passover Festival as the great popular festival until the reformations of Hezekiah and Josiah (2 Ki. 23:21ff.; 2 Ch. 30:1ff.; 35:1ff.). Grapes were gathered and trodden out in the wine-presses to produce wine at this season, which became a time of merry-making, over-indulgence and licentiousness, hardly compatible with the spirit of truly religious thanksgiving.

Verse 27 illustrates the possibilities for evil in such a situation. Gaal, taking advantage of Abimelech's absence, took the opportunity of addressing the crowds which assembled for this celebration, denigrating Abimelech and urging the Shechemites to return to an earlier allegiance. The first part of his address is capable of two interpretations. Either '*Who is Abimelech, and* (in contrast) *who are we of Shechem, that we should serve him?*' (RSV). Or, with the LXX, 'Who is Abimelech, this (self-styled) son of Shechem that we should serve him?' The first alternative is the more likely, but in either case there was the challenge to cast off their loyalty to Abimelech. Gaal then craftily traced the parentage of Abimelech through his father, not his Shechemite mother, in direct contrast to the earlier appeal of Abimelech himself (verses 1–3). Next, he appealed to them to serve *the men of Hamor the father of Shechem* rather than Abimelech. *Hamor* means 'ass' and W. F. Albright maintains that the expression 'the sons of Hamor' is equivalent to 'the sons of the treaty', since the sacrifice of an ass was an essential feature in the ratification of a treaty amongst the Amorites.[1] There is probably a further allusion in the name of the local deity of Shechem, *Baal-berith*, 'the lord of the covenant or treaty'. Gaal thus set himself up as the upholder of the ancient faith and the old ways, a conservative appeal often made by demagogues like him. Finally, having undermined their confidence in Abimelech and having made this emotional appeal, he hinted how different things would be if he were made the leader of the Shechemites. How quickly would he drive out this upstart Abimelech! With empty bravado he flung out his challenge to the absent king to set his army in array to meet him. The tone and the methods of Gaal have their parallel in the speech and actions of Absalom (2 Sa. 15:1–6).

**9:30–41. Zebul's decisive action.** The insurrection was nipped in the bud by the prompt action of *Zebul*, whose anger was prompted by the derogatory remark made concerning him, inferring that he was just Abimelech's lieutenant and no more (28). A message was hastily despatched to Abimelech to acquaint him of the situation. The AV notes that this message was sent *privily*, a word which is emended by the RSV to read *at Arumah* (*cf.* verse 41), although, if this is accepted, the attached preposition would also need to be changed from 'in' to 'to'. The root of the word is *ramah* which in the *Pi'ēl* means 'to deceive', and the most likely meaning here is 'by a ruse', to avoid arousing the suspicions of Gaal and the men of Shechem who, if rebellion were contemplated, would be con-

[1] W. F. Albright, *Archaeology and the Religion of Israel* (John Hopkins Press, 1953), p. 113.

cerned to intercept any warning message to Abimelech. Zebul not only warned of the potentially dangerous situation, he urged a certain course of action upon Abimelech, no doubt reasoning that it would be preferable to take the initiative rather than to allow Gaal time to consolidate his position. The freedom which Zebul himself enjoyed in the remainder of the story does suggest that the uprising was still in an early stage. Abimelech followed the advice of his deputy and deployed his forces by night in four companies, thus lessening the risk of detection. F. F. Bruce observes, 'So the contingent in the city under Zebul was literally a "fifth column".'[1]

Zebul's own part was played with conspicuous skill. Coming alongside Gaal near the city gates he first lulled his suspicions, when the force in ambush was first observed, by attributing it to Gaal's imagination. When concealment was no longer possible he flung Gaal's boastful taunt back to him, thus allowing him no alternative but to fight or lose face. The advantages of initiative and surprise lay with Abimelech, and the valuable time gained meant that Gaal was unable to give adequate attention to either the defences of the city or his own assault force. His hastily marshalled force, pressed into a combat for which it was unprepared, was soon dispersed and the survivors fled back into the city. All the heart had gone from the rebellious party and Abimelech was able to retire to *Arumah*, the site of which is unknown, although it is clear from the context that it was in the vicinity of Shechem. Zebul was able to mop up the disaffected elements and to expel the trouble-maker in chief, Gaal, and his supporters from the city. He is not mentioned again in the narrative, but his prompt and astute action saved the day temporarily for Abimelech.

**37.** *The middle of the land* is literally 'the navel of the land', a reference to some prominent landmark, probably a mountain-top. *The plain of Meonenim* (AV) should be read as 'the oak of the diviners' (*cf.* RSV), *i.e.* a sacred tree where divination was practised, possibly, but not necessarily, the one mentioned in verse 6.

---

[1] Bruce, p. 248.

**9:42-45. The destruction of Shechem.** Abimelech, by his action in destroying Shechem, abandoned all pretence of ruling over a kingdom, for the sphere of his influence was truncated without this important city. It appears as an act of revenge against those who had questioned his leadership. Men like Abimelech, who rise from an inferior status to a position of authority, are often capable of vengeful actions which destroy the basis of their own power. Zebul's action had brought the situation under control, but his master was concerned to teach Shechem a lesson. The people, apparently confident that the matter was concluded, *went out into the fields* as usual to engage in their daily occupations, although it has been suggested that the reference is to the marauding bands leaving the city on their errand of brigandage, in which case a different construction must be set upon Abimelech's action. However, this second alternative is not well supported by the context. Another ambush was set and at the opportune moment one company captured the gate, thus cutting off the retreat of the Shechemites in the fields. These were butchered by the remaining two companies, who were later able to reinforce their companions in the city and exact a similar, terrible vengeance there. The sowing of the city *with salt* does not mean that all cultivatable soil was made unfruitful; this would have required an operation of impossible magnitude. Rather, it indicates a symbolic ritual action in which the destroyed city was condemned to perpetual desolation (*cf.* Dt. 29:23; Ps. 107:34; Je. 17:6). Shechem was rebuilt during the reign of Jeroboam I, more than a century and a half after the campaign of Abimelech (1 Ki. 12:25).

**9:46-49. The destruction of the tower of Shechem.** Normally the stronghold of a walled city would be within the walls, but the impression gained from this narrative is that the tower of Shechem was outside the city, possibly on some adjacent outcrop of rock. But the impression may be more apparent than real, due to the narrator's method of dealing with one subject at a time. Having dealt exhaustively with the destruction of the city itself, he now deals with the destruction of its stronghold. It may be observed that no reference is made to the stronghold in connection with the two ambushments, which would be seriously threatened if a manned fortress was in the vicinity. The *house of El-berith* (46, RV, RSV) may be equated with the 'house of Baal-berith' (4; see note on 8:32–35). El was the nominal head of the Canaanite pantheon, but his position was virtually taken over by Baal, the great, active god, in a process taking many generations. El or Baal, therefore, was the deity invoked by the Shechemites in ratifying their covenant. The 'hold of El-berith' appears to be synonymous with the tower of Shechem itself. Here the remnants of the population gathered to make their final resistance. Abimelech adopted a stratagem which has been employed many times since by a besieging army. Leading his men to *mount Zalmon* (*cf.* Ps. 68:14), a heavily-wooded hill popularly located to the south of Gerizim (Jebel Suleimân), he and they lopped branches from the trees and piled them against the fortress walls. The intense heat generated by the conflagration that was kindled destroyed the tower and all its occupants. So perished the men of Shechem and another Canaanite enclave was obliterated.

**9:50–57. The death of Abimelech.** *Thebez* lay approximately 10 miles north-north-east of Shechem, on the road leading to Beth-shean, and whilst there is no record of its implication in the revolt against Abimelech the narrative suggests that this was the case. The city itself fell easily into the hands of Abimelech, but the defenders retreated into their fortress, which in this case was certainly within the city walls (*cf.* 8:8,9; 9:46). The method of reducing the fortress by fire, which had been so successful at the tower of Shechem, was again applied, but Abimelech, possibly lacking in caution, was mortally wounded when his skull was fractured by a portion of a *millstone* thrown by a woman. The Hebrew word (*pelaḥ rekeb*, lit. 'a stone of riding') shows that it was probably the upper millstone, which was normally about two or three inches thick and eighteen inches in diameter, with a hole in the centre. Less likely is the suggestion that it was the roller used for replastering the mud-roof. The grinding of corn was delegated to women, and it was considered a humiliation for a man to do it (*cf.* 16:21). This woman, in her desperation, had brought up this upper millstone (grinding was not normally done on the roof) as a defensive weapon. As was noted in the case of Sisera (4:21), it was accounted a dishonour to die at the hands of a woman, so Abimelech, realizing the nature of his injury, urged his attendant to run him through with his sword. Within a hundred years the first official king of Israel made a similar request to his armour-bearer on Mount Gilboa, within a few miles of Thebez, to spare him the disgrace of being captured alive by the Philistines (1 Sa. 31). With the death of Abimelech this vicious episode came to an end. *The men of Israel* (55), who had supported him in his campaign against the dominantly Canaanite population of Shechem and its allies, in spite of his treacherous action in engineering the deaths of the sons of Gideon, dispersed to their homes at the death of their leader.

**56, 57.** The moral of the incident is pressed home. Whilst we may be indebted to the final editor for this particular version, it is certain that the moral would have been drawn and applied in the earliest accounts. The Hebrews overlooked what might be called secondary causes and saw in these events the direct action of *God*, the evidence of His sovereignty within history, in the judgment upon Abimelech and the fulfilment of the curse of Jotham upon the Shechemites.

### j. Tola (10:1, 2)

With Tola we are introduced to the second of the minor judges, the others being Shamgar (3:31), Jair (10:3–5), Ibzan, Elon and Abdon (12:8–15). Scant detail concerning these men has been preserved, with the inevitable consequence that they appear as very nebulous characters in comparison with Gideon, Deborah, Abimelech, Jephthah and Samuel. Sometimes they are regarded as being concerned with judicial affairs, the arbiters of disputes within or between the tribes, or the custodians and interpreters of the casuistic laws. It may be that they were the leaders in Israel during the periods of rest when no foreign domination threatened. But the statement concerning Tola, that he *arose to defend Israel* (AV), warns against reading too much into the little extant information concerning these men. The likelihood is that if spectacular deeds had been performed by these men some traces of them would have survived, but we cannot go beyond this and say that, in fact, no such exploits were wrought. In the case of Tola little has survived apart from his name and a few essential facts. In Genesis 46:13 and Numbers 26:23 Tola and Puah are connected with the tribe of Issachar. The location of *Shamir* is uncertain; an identification with Samaria is hazardous, since the latter was in the tribal portion of Manasseh, not Ephraim, and its establishment is noted in the reign of Omri, king of Israel (1 Ki. 16:24).

**k. Jair (10:3-5)**
The record concerning Jair appears to connect with the conquest of Gilead, when a predecessor with the same name captured a group of towns in Bashan and renamed them *Havvoth-jair, i.e.* 'the tent-villages of Jair' (Nu. 32:39-42; Dt. 3:14, *etc.*). In this same area, about 12 miles south-east of the Sea of Galilee, Jair exercised his authority, supported by his thirty sons. The mention that they rode on thirty ass-colts (*cf.* the similar reference to the sons and grandsons of Abdon, 12:14) was a mark of prestige as well as a sign of prosperity.

*Camon* (AV; or *Kamon*, RV, RSV), the burial-place of Jair, has been identified with some ruins about one mile north-west of the modern village Qumên.

**l. Jephthah and the Ammonites (10:6 – 11:40)**
**10:6-16. The effect of apostasy.** This section forms the second extensive commentary (*cf.* 2:6-3:6) by the editor and provides the introduction to the oppressions of the Philistines and Ammonites. These, as was noted in the Introduction, were almost certainly contemporaneous. The Ammonite attack was the lesser menace and is dealt with first, before the account of Samson's private war with the Philistines (chapters 13-16),

which has a minimum of editorial comment, and the Danite migration in the first of the two appendices (chapters 17, 18). The editor is always concerned to impress upon Israel the consequences of apostasy and the structure of this section bears the unmistakable impression of this policy; for instance, the sevenfold idolatry of verse 6 is balanced by the sevenfold oppression of verses 11 and 12. Thus, while most of the facts here noted deal with the period immediately connected with the Ammonite and Philistine oppressions, verse 6 is a more general comment covering the apostasy of the whole period of the judges. The worship of the Baalim and the Ashtaroth has already been dealt with (see notes on 2:11–19; 3:7, *etc.*) and the worship of the gods of Syria and Zidon was of a similar pattern, with local variations. The evidence suggests that *the gods of the Philistines* were also of the same type, as the Philistines rapidly adopted the customs and the culture of the peoples over whom they ruled. The three gods mentioned elsewhere in connection with the Philistines, Dagon, Ashtoreth and Baal-zebul, were all Canaanite deities. The gods of Moab and Ammon, two kingdoms which came into existence within fifty years of the Israelite settlement, were Chemosh and Malcam (with its associated forms Milcom, Molech and Moloch) respectively. The only kingdom contiguous to Israel which did not make any religious impact upon the Israelites was, significantly, the profane kingdom of Edom. The subtle attractions of these heathen religions, with their material and sensuous satisfactions, proved too much for Israel.

Now the Philistines and the Ammonites became the rod of God's anger (*cf.* Is. 10:5) just as He had used Cushan-rishathaim (3:8), Eglon (3:12), Jabin and Sisera (4:2) and the Midianites (6:1) on earlier occasions. The main weight of the Ammonite attacks fell on Gilead in Transjordania, *i.e.* on the Israelite territory adjacent to their kingdom, but there were also forays against the west-Jordan tribes of Judah, Benjamin and Ephraim. As there was undoubtedly pressure from the Philistines against the western frontiers of these tribes their predicament can be imagined. The acuter pressure at this stage came from the Ammonites who were crueller in nature and more predatory in their methods than the Philistines (*cf.* 1 Sa. 11:1,2).

**10–16.** The extremity of the plight of the Israelites led to a recognition of their waywardness and an appeal to God. This met with no easy response, for the cycle of deliverance followed by forgetfulness, ingratitude and apostasy had occurred too often for a facile overlooking of their sin. God required, and requires still, the steadfast love, loyalty and obedience of His subjects, in which He can operate continually on their behalf, rather than a relationship, lightly severed, in which He is used in times of emergency only. He reminded them therefore of His former deliverances. The reference to the *Egyptians* concerns the Exodus and its associated events, there being no historical evidence of any oppression subsequent to the settlement in Canaan; the *Amorite* deliverance relates to the great victories over Sihon and Og (Nu. 21:21–24,33–35); the *Ammonites* were associated with the Moabites (3:13); Shamgar had saved Israel by his exploit against the *Philistines* (3:31). There is no specific reference to the *Zidonians*, but they may have been allied with Jabin and Sisera, which would account for the non-mention of Asher in the battle at the Kishon; the *Amalekites* appear as the allies of both the Moabites (3:13) and the Midianites (6:3). The reference to the *Maonites* is possibly a scribal error for Midianites, which is found in the LXX, the Maonites themselves appearing as Judah's adversaries at a later date (1 Ch. 4:41; 2 Ch. 20:1; 26:7). There can be no certainty on this point, for the name is a common one: there is a Maʿan south of Petra, a Maʿîn south of Hebron, whilst a Maʿon is listed among the descendants of Caleb (1 Ch. 2:45). No complete catalogue is intended, however, as the Moabites and Canaanites are not mentioned; probably the number seven, as in the case of the sevenfold idolatory (6), is significant, with its religious association of completeness.

God declared that by their absolute apostasy and their ingratitude for His deliverances the people have no legitimate claim upon Him (13). Let the gods they have accepted instead of Him deliver them, if they could! But this apparent rejection, and the apparent indifference to the pleas of His people, was designed to test the sincerity of their response. Action was required, not words which can be no more than a shallow profession. But God is gracious and merciful, slow to anger, and He met the limited response of Israel. He knew that it would be of short duration and that the old familiar pattern would be repeated many a time before the nation finally learned the folly of forsaking Him. Perhaps before we condemn Israel for its slowness of heart we would do well to acknowledge *our* dependence upon the patience of a long-suffering God. In the case of Israel the gods which could neither save nor satisfy were put away as the people sought the Lord in penitence.

**10:17, 18. Renewed Ammonite pressure.** This particular invasion of the Ammonites, Israel's eastern neighbour, whose capital was at Rabbah, was presumably at the end of the eighteen years' oppression noted in verse 8. *Gilead* is normally used to designate the central of the three main divisions of the Israelite settlement east of the Jordan, between Bashan in the north and the southern tableland, but the term is used somewhat loosely. To meet this emergency the people of the Israelite tribes involved assembled themselves together, with possibly a new morale and a will to resist following their repentance and return to the Lord. All they lacked was a suitable commander to marshal their forces. *Mizpeh* (AV) or *Mizpah* (RV, RSV), which means 'watchtower', was a common place-name in a country often subjected to attack by marauding bands, and any identification is hazardous. The Mizpah associated with Jacob's covenant with Laban (Gn. 31:46ff.) and Ramoth-mizpeh (usually identified with Ramoth-gilead, Jos. 13:26; *cf.* Jos. 20:8; Dt. 4:43; 1 Ki. 22:3) have been suggested as possible sites, but there can be no certainty. The frequent mention of the *leaders of Gilead* (RSV) in the narrative indicates that this was the area principally threatened at this time and that the deliverance of Jephthah was achieved without any general appeal to the tribes.

**11:1–3. The rejection of Jephthah.** Here we are introduced to Jephthah, in a parenthetical section, the main narrative being resumed at 11:4. The cloud upon his birth appears greater than that of Abimelech. He was the son of Gilead, whose name is identical with the grandson of Manasseh who was the founder of the clan, but his mother was a *harlot* (1), a *strange woman* (2, AV) who may have been a non-Israelite. Living in his father's house Jephthah was deprived of his family rights by his illegitimacy and, unlike Abimelech, he had no share in his mother's clan. Eventually he was thrust out by his stepbrothers, an event which determined his whole future, for he became a brigand-chief over a group of outcasts and social misfits. There is some correspondence with the factors that shaped the career of David who, driven into the wilderness by Saul's jealousy, gathered to himself those who were in distress or debt, or who were discontented (1 Sa. 22:2), and welded them into a formidable force. At a later stage, still pursued by Saul and unsure of the loyalty of his own countrymen, David went over to the Philistines as a mercenary captain, learning the arts of warfare which were to serve him in good stead in the course of his long reign. So Jephthah the despised, through dire misfortune, was prepared for the task of saving the very people who had thrust him out. *Tob* has been tentatively identified with the modern el-Taiyibeh, about 15 miles east-north-east of Ramoth-gilead, in the desolate area which lay just outside the eastern boundary of Israel and the northern frontier of Ammon.

**11:4-11. The recall of Jephthah.** The encroachments of the Ammonites made the elders of Gilead desperate enough to seek help from Jephthah, who must have built up a considerable reputation for leadership in the course of his brigandage. His answer to their request implies that they were as blameworthy as his own brethren in his expulsion from the family, but in spite of the sting in his words, there is not the vindictiveness that is revealed in 12:1-6. Jephthah probably realized that the conventions of society left them no alternative but to acquiesce in the harsh action of his brethren. Illegitimacy remains a stigma upon the innocent, who are compelled to suffer for the sin of their parents. The elders of Gilead had

swallowed their pride in approaching him and he was opportunist enough not to let his pride stand in the way, not only of
advancement, but of acceptance into normal society. His
reluctance was soon overcome after he had established the
fact that he would be accepted as their leader after, and not
only during, the Ammonite war. The word for *captain* (AV;
*leader*, RSV) (Heb. *qāṣîn*) has an Arabic equivalent, which indicates one who discharges a judicial function. The invitation
to Jephthah was virtually that he should become a local
dictator for the rest of his life. But while his self-seeking
impulse is evident, his strong faith in Yahweh is evident. It
was *the Lord* who would be the real deliverer (9). The compact
between Jephthah and the elders was sealed in a solemn
ceremony, almost a coronation, at the local sanctuary of
Mizpeh (see note on 10:17). It will be observed that Yahweh,
the covenant-God of Israel, was invoked as the witness to this
agreement (10, 11).

**11:12-28. Charge and countercharge.** Wrangling over
frontiers and claims to prior possession of areas have been
commonplace in relationships between countries since time
immemorial, and almost invariably there has been no settlement short of war. Jephthah, in his first act as a statesman,
accused Ammon of violating his territory (12). His accusation
was countered by the Ammonites who claimed that the region
had originally belonged to them and that they were therefore
within their rights in acting to restore the situation (13). This
was matched in turn by a detailed statement of history,
defending Israel's right to its territory east of Jordan, and
attempting to show that there was no violation of the land of
the Moabites or the Ammonites (15). The reference to the
Moabites is explained by the fact that they had a better claim
to the disputed area than did the Ammonites, since the region
between the Arnon and the Jabbok had been wrested from
them by the Amorite king Sihon (Nu. 21:23ff.). There is, of
course, the possibility that Sihon had enlarged *his* kingdom at
the expense of the Ammonites as well as the Moabites, since
some of the region allocated to the east-Jordan tribes is stated

to have been taken from Ammon (Jos. 13:24-26; but note Nu. 21:24, which appears to exclude any Israelite violation of Ammonite territory). At the end of his message Jephthah pointed out that the Moabite king at the time of the occupation had not laid claim to the territory which was formerly his, the inference being that as he had remained silent when he had greater justification for intervening, the Ammonites were completely without justification for their intervention at this stage (25).

But, as we shall observe, the reply of Jephthah was not entirely based on sweet reason! The first point which he emphasized was that Israel, on the journey from Egypt, had behaved with restraint and propriety in its relationships with Edom and Moab. The two kingdoms were established about fifty years before the Israelites entered Canaan, but during this period their frontiers had become well established and secured by a series of fortresses. Israel had not violated their land although this involved a long detour around their frontiers. The reference to the *Red Sea* (16) indicates the Gulf of Aqaba. *Kadesh* is Kadesh-barnea, where the Israelites spent the major period of their sojourn in the wilderness. A glance at the map will show how greatly Edomite approval of a passage through her territory would have shortened the journey of Israel. A similar request to Sihon, the Amorite king, was met with downright hostility as well as refusal. There being no kinship between the Israelites and the Amorites, as there was between Israel, Edom and Moab (*cf.* Dt. 2:4-9), Israel dealt resolutely with this barrier to their access to the Promised Land. *Jahaz* (20) has been tentatively identified as either the modern Jālûl or Khirbet et-Teim, both of which are about 7 miles south of Heshbon. The victory over Sihon was the first major military success in the conquest of Canaan. Jephthah stressed that the country was taken from the *Amorites* (not the Ammonites, witness the reference at the end of verse 21; *cf.* 23; and the delineation of the frontiers in verse 22, which corresponds to the accusation of the Ammonite king in verse 13). The real point at issue was the eastern frontier, defined as *the wilderness* (22), and where this was in relation to the Ammonite kingdom; but statesmen rarely confine themselves to such points. Jephthah confined himself to the assertion that the disputed territory never belonged to the Ammonites but was wrested from the Amorites and no others.

The reference to *Chemosh* (24) is perplexing in the context, since Chemosh was the god of the Moabites, Malcam being the deity of the Ammonites (*cf.* 1 Ki. 11:5). On the basis of this verse, together with the prominence given to Moabite cities and kings elsewhere in the chapter, it has been conjectured that Jephthah's campaign was directed against the Moabites, not the Ammonites, but such utter confusion appears improbable. Less objectionable, but still conjectural, is the view that the Moabites were associated with the Ammonites in this campaign. Alternatively, it has been argued that there was a wide diffusion of the worship of the various deities, but this is extremely unlikely at such an early period in the history of these petty kingdoms. In the seventh century BC parts of Moab and Gilead were occupied by the Ammonites which resulted in a merging of religions, but by this time the territories affected had lost their former virility. A fourth possibility is that verses 21–28 date from the seventh century BC, in which such an interchange of religions was likely, and that a later writer is here asserting the claim of his country to this east-Jordan territory, but there is little in favour of this view.

A fifth alternative is that Jephthah himself was confused, which raises the question as to whether we should look for precision and accuracy in the realms of history and comparative religion from such a man. Jephthah was the captain of a robber-band whose depredations probably took him impartially into Israelite, Moabite and Ammonite territory. His actions subsequent to this show how unfamiliar he was with the requirements of the God of his own people, and it is possible that he was in error at this point. We must avoid the tendency to view Jephthah's message to the Ammonite king as we would a statement from a great, modern world-power to a neighbouring power on some controversial issue. The doctrine of inspiration does not necessitate the elimination of all inaccuracies in the statements of a man of the character and background of Jephthah.

The reference to Chemosh does not indicate that Jephthah or the editor placed Chemosh and Yahweh on exactly the same level, as merely the national deities of the two countries, although Jephthah's apprehension of Yahweh may have reached no higher level than monolatry. On the other hand it may be an *argumentum ad hominem*. In either case it represented a change of attack. Formerly the argument had rested on Israel's vastly superior claim to the disputed region; now it rested on the superiority of Israel's God. His argument was clinched by two further points. Firstly Balak, the Moabite king at the time of the Israelite conquest, when any adjustments ought to have been made, had made no effort to regain the territory which once pertained to his country. Secondly, the Israelites had enjoyed a very long period of undisputed occupation of this region, so there was hardly a case at such a late stage for questioning her right to do so. *Heshbon* and *Aroer* (26) were both in the territory of Reuben and were both on the 'King's Highway', the main north-south trade route, between 12 and 15 miles east of the Dead Sea. But Heshbon was in the extreme north of Reuben and Aroer was by the river Arnon, the southern boundary. Both cities were captured by Sihon, who made Heshbon his capital (Nu. 21:26) but at a later date they reverted to Moab (Is. 15:4; Je. 48:2,19, *etc.*).

The *three hundred years* (26) is remarkably close to the total of the various figures for the judges and the periods of oppression given up to this point. The exact figure is 319 years, but since Ammon's claim could be held to have commenced at the beginning of the eighteen-year oppression (10:8) it would be reduced to 301 years. As was pointed out in the Introduction,[1] the entire period of the judges cannot be extended much beyond 180 years, and the actual interval between Israel's conquest of Transjordania and the rise of Jephthah was no more than 160 years. The reference to the 300 years may be an editorial amplification of the remainder of the verse, or it may

[1] See p. 30.

be a broad generalization for approximately seven or eight generations, or it may represent Jephthah's rough guess, since he would hardly have access to reliable historical records. Jephthah concluded that right was on his side and invoked Yahweh as the ultimate Judge, but this ancient diplomatic wrangle ended with the Ammonite king completely unimpressed and uninfluenced by Jephthah's reasoning.

**11:29-31. Jephthah's vow.** The lack of a sense of chronological sequence is illustrated here, since this account of Jephthah's recruiting campaign takes the narrative back beyond the statement of 10:17. It is, in a sense, a recapitulation of events before the account of the battle and may indicate a stage in the oral tradition where it was necessary for the narrator, having digressed, to set the scene afresh before passing on. The troops of Jephthah were drawn from the Israelites settled east of the Jordan, the base-camp being Mizpeh of Gilead (see note on 10:17). Two facts in this section stand in sharp contrast. First, Jephthah, by the coming of *the Spirit of the Lord* upon him, became a charismatic hero, empowered by God to effect the deliverance of his people. But then, in the second place, he showed his lack of appreciation of the character and requirements of the Lord, and also a lack of confidence in the divine enablement, by seeking to secure the favour of God by his rash *vow*. Attempts have been made to show that Jephthah had an animal sacrifice in mind and that he was taken by surprise when his daughter came to greet him; but these cannot be substantiated, since the designation *whoever comes forth from the doors of my house* (31, RSV) must refer to an intended human sacrifice. It is certain that this was intended as an act of devotion on Jephthah's part, a recompense for God's action through him; but had he been better versed in the traditions of Moses he would have known that God did not desire to be honoured in this way. The 'fruit of my body' (or anyone else's body) cannot be offered 'for the sin of my soul', or as a mark of devotion to the Lord (Mi. 6:6-8). The lives of others are sacred and are not to be terminated for the private end of an individual, however laudable that end may appear. As Bishop Hall observed, 'It was his zeale to vow, it was his sinne to vow rashly.'[1] On a considerably lower level may be instanced the case of the Moabite king who sacrificed his son in a desperate attempt to placate Chemosh and effect a deliverance from Israel, Judah and Edom (2 Ki. 3:27). Human sacrifice was practised amongst Israel's neighbours, although the custom was not so prevalent as is commonly supposed. But apart from this instance, which is clearly exceptional, there is little evidence of any widespread observance of this evil custom in Israel until the later period of the monarchy, notably in the reigns of Ahaz (2 Ki. 16:3) and Manasseh (2 Ki. 21:6).

**11:32, 33. Defeat of the Ammonites.** The conclusive victory over the Ammonites is recorded with very little detail, especially when compared with Gideon's encounter with the Midianites, but the credit for it is given unreservedly to the Lord. The location of *Aroer* has already been noted (see comment on 11:26). *Minnith* and *the plain of the vineyards* (AV), which is best read as a proper name, *Abel-keramim* (RSV), are both unidentified. It may be assumed that Aroer was the starting-point of the battle and that the *twenty cities* were in Ammonite territory on the line of retreat of the defeated army. The Ammonites were to re-emerge as a threat to Israel about fifty years after this defeat (1 Sa. 11:1ff.).

**11:34–40. The fulfilment of Jephthah's vow.** The victorious general returned to Mizpeh, no doubt expecting that the fulfilment of his vow would involve no more than the sacrifice of one of his many household servants. To his horror, however, he was greeted by his daughter, coming to meet her conquering father in a typically Hebrew manner (*cf.* Ex. 15:20; 1 Sa. 18:6; Ps. 68:25). The story is narrated with consummate skill. No garish details of the sacrifice itself are given but by a delicate touch here, and an understatement there, an impression of dignified tragedy is created. Great stress is placed upon the fact that Jephthah's daughter was an *only*

[1] Quoted from G. A. Cooke, *The Book of Judges* (C.U.P., 1913), p. 148.

*child* (34), the Hebrew reading literally 'and she only was an only child' (*cf.* Gn 22:2; Jn. 3:16). The fact of her *virginity* is also bewailed (38,39). Corporate personality, that sense of identification within the clan or group, was very strong at this early stage in Israel's history. The individual lost something of his identity within the group, and the concept of an individual resurrection was hardly possible in this setting. But there were compensations; the individual lived on in his descendants. He would not see the future himself but it belonged to him so long as his line was maintained; hence the power in a curse which involved a man's offspring (2 Sa. 3:28,29), and the tragedy when a family line died out (*cf.* 2 Sa. 18:18). The fact that Jephthah's daughter bore no child was more than a tragedy of a life unfulfilled (an attitude in ancient Israel which stands in contrast with that of modern western women generally). It represented the termination of the clan of Jephthah himself, since she was his only child. Thus the moment of triumph almost coincided with the moment of tragedy.

All the earlier commentators and historians accepted that Jephthah actually offered up his daughter as a burnt-offering. It was not until the Middle Ages that well-meaning but misguided attempts were made to soften down the plain meaning of the text. The susceptibilities of enlightened minds may well be shocked at such an action, particularly by one of Israel's judges; but the attempt to commute the sentence of death to one of perpetual virginity cannot be sustained. The final reference to the virginity of Jephthah's daughter is added to point the tragedy of the affair and the perfect tense is best read as a pluperfect, a use which it often has in Hebrew, 'she had known no man' (*cf.* RSV, *She had never known a man*). The plain statement, that he *did with her according to his vow which he had vowed*, must be allowed to stand. The desolation of Jephthah (35), the two-month reprieve (37, 38), and the institution of an annual four-day feast would hardly be likely if nothing more was involved than perpetual virginity.

The noble character of Jephthah's daughter has been the theme of poets down through the ages. Anticipating with feminine insight the content of her father's rash vow before he had divulged it openly, she nevertheless submitted herself immediately to what awaited her. The Lord had granted a great victory over the Ammonites and, if this involved a price, she was prepared to pay it. The pathos of such submissive nobility is enhanced for the modern reader by the realization that human sacrifice is repugnant to the Lord and a virtual contradiction of the love which is central in His character. With no hope of immortality to light the pathway to a childless death she lamented the impending tragedy, but made no attempt to avert it. The incident witnesses to the sacredness of a vow undertaken before the Lord (*cf.* Nu. 30:1ff.; Dt. 23:21,23) and we must at least respect this man and his daughter who were loyal, at such a cost, to their limited beliefs. There comes the challenge to the modern reader, whose knowledge of God is much greater than that of Jephthah, to offer to Him a comparable but enlightened loyalty.

The annual lamentation in remembrance of Jephthah's daughter is not mentioned elsewhere in the Old Testament and it may have been confined to the region of Gilead. The inference of the verb, an imperfect of frequentative action, suggests that the custom was still practised in the time of the editor. Attempts have been made to connect this incident with the worship of the deities of the underworld which was widely diffused throughout the ancient world, particularly with the custom of 'weeping for Tammuz' (Ezk. 8:14). There is no certain evidence of any such connection.

## m. Jephthah and the jealous Ephraimites (12:1-7)

The character which the Ephraimites displayed in this episode accorded with their earlier reaction to Gideon in a similar situation (8:1,2). But the similarity between the incidents ends at that point; Jephthah, the ex-bandit chief, was not a man to be trifled with and his words and actions contrast vividly with the 'soft answer which turns away wrath' of Gideon, the man to whom we were introduced when he was beating out wheat in a winepress for fear of the Midianites. The Ephraimites, undoubtedly armed, expressed their resentment to Jephthah in no uncertain terms. They, the leading tribe in central and northern Israel, had been slighted by him in not being called to the battle; now they purposed taking a summary vengeance upon this upstart. The fact that a victory had been gained over their common enemy appears to have been overlooked. Accusation and counter-accusation followed in bewildering succession; the claim that they had been passed over was met by the charge that an appeal *had* been made to them to which they had not responded. The situation is all too common in disputes and it is likely that they both shared a measure of justification. *Gilead*, in the eighteen-year Ammonite oppression before Jephthah assumed the leadership, would almost certainly have appealed to the neighbouring tribes for help, which was not forthcoming (*cf.* 1 Sa. 11:3). Jephthah, aware of this background, had not thought it worth while to invite the Ephraimites on this particular occasion, which affected Gilead alone, and had effected the deliverance with the local forces only. His words (3) point to the incongruity of the Ephraimites' attitude when it was *the Lord* who was the architect of victory. How typically human it was for Ephraim to show such indignation after the battle was over! The location of the verbal encounter between the Ephraimites and Jephthah is obscured in the AV and RV: *northward* should be read as a place-name, *Zaphon* (RSV), a small town in the Jordan valley, probably about 5 miles north of Succoth. The course of the battle makes it clear that the Ephraimites had already crossed the Jordan, so in fact their route was to the east, not the north.

It was not long before the situation worsened, fanned into a flame by the sneering aspersions of the Ephraimites (4) in which they accused the Gileadites of being renegade Ephraimites. The army of Jephthah, demobilized after the crushing of the Ammonite menace, was hastily recalled and gained as complete a victory over their fellow-countrymen as they had over the foreign invader. In Gideon's campaign with the Midianites it was the Ephraimites who had secured the fords against a defeated enemy. Now the Jordan fords were seized to cut off the retreat of their own shattered forces. Jephthah's qualities of decisive leadership are apparent throughout and the choice of the elders of Gilead (11:6) was vindicated by events. A devastatingly simple test was devised to ascertain the identity of those who sought passage over the Jordan. Those who confessed to being Ephraimites were presumably killed at once; those who denied were commanded to say a word, *Shibboleth* (meaning 'ear of corn'), which the Ephraimites were constitutionally unable to pronounce. The Ephraimite dialect appears to have been similar to that of the Amorites and Arabs, with *s* taking the place of *sh*, so their approximation of *Sibboleth* immediately revealed their identity and led to their execution. Any other word with *sh* would have sufficed, but it was the word *shibboleth* which has come into common usage to denote the watchword or catchphrase of a particular sect or group. The Ephraimites were betrayed by their speech; so was Peter many years afterward (Mt. 26:73). The number of Ephraimites slain (42,000) appears abnormally high for this period of Israel's history. The use of large numbers in the Old Testament is one of its unsolved problems; possibly an answer lies in the various meanings of the word 'thousand' (Heb. *'elep̄*; *cf.* the commentary on 20:2).

**7.** The length of Jephthah's judgeship is noted. This was probably exercised east of the Jordan, since he would be *persona non grata* west of the Jordan after the slaughter of the Ephraimites! His burial-place is not clearly indicated in the Hebrew text, which simply notes 'the cities of Gilead'. Some manuscripts of the LXX support a reading 'in his city, Mizpeh of Gilead'. The decimation of the tribe of Ephraim was decisive, for this tribe, which aspired to a position of leadership, never regained its pre-eminence. This was not without importance in the adoption of a monarchical system, for up to this point Ephraim was too strong to accept a king from another tribe. On the other hand intertribal jealousy would make it difficult for the other tribes to accept an Ephraimite king. When a king was eventually chosen it is significant that a man of Benjamin, a weak tribe (especially after the events of chapter 20), was selected. He was succeeded by David, of the powerful tribe of Judah, and it was not long before the intertribal rivalries revived.

It may be observed that there is no mention of the amphictyonic league, or of any mediation or intervention by the other tribes to prevent this act of fratricide. The decay of the intertribal structure is apparent in this period, but the lack of intervention may also be explained in part by the remoteness of the Transjordan region from the central sanctuary, and by the speed with which the crisis developed.

### n. Ibzan (12:8-10)

There is no mention of Ibzan anywhere else in the Old Testament. The number of his children indicates his wealth and position in the community. The word *abroad* (AV, RV) means no more than that his children married members of another clan (*cf.* RSV). *Beth-lehem* is not to be identified with Bethlehem in Judah, which is usually written as Bethlehemjudah. The tribe of Judah, apart from occasional references, appears to have been cut off from intertribal life during the major portion of the period of the judges. The likelihood is that this Beth-lehem was the town in western Zebulun, about 10 miles north of Megiddo (Jos. 19:15).

### o. Elon (12:11, 12)

If the identification of Beth-lehem (8) is correct, then both Ibzan and Elon were from the tribe of Zebulun. No supplementary information concerning Elon is given beyond the name of his tribe, the length of his period of office and his burial-place, *Aijalon in the country of Zebulun,* thus distinguishing it from the better-known Aijalon in Danite territory. Aijalon in Zebulun is usually located in the vicinity of Rimmon, but as the form of the word is exactly the same as Elon in the unpointed Hebrew text the name of the judge and the place of his burial may be identical, as in the LXX.

### p. Abdon (12:13-15)

*Pirathon* has been tentatively identified with the modern Far 'âtā located about 6 miles west-south-west of Shechem, in the southern fringe of the territory assigned to Manasseh, but the border may have been somewhat flexible, with Ephraim, the stronger tribe, extending its region beyond its designated portion (hence the reference in verse 15). Pirathon was the birth-place of David's captain, Benaiah (2 Sa. 23:30; 1 Ch. 11:31; 27:14). The prestige and wealth of Abdon is revealed in the number of his *sons* and *grandsons* (not *nephews* as in AV) and their mounts (*cf.* 10:4). The reference to the *mount*, or *hill country*, of the Amalekites (15) is perplexing. It has been conjectured that this reference, together with that in 5:14, supports the view that there was a small Amalekite enclave in the territory of Ephraim, a possibility which is not entirely ruled out by the inveterate hostility which existed between the Israelites and the Amalekites generally (but see the note on 5:14). The reference may be connected with one or other of the incursions into Israelite territory by hostile groups which included the Amalekites (3:13; 6:3,33; 7:12; 10:12). It should be noted that the Amalekites, because of their treacherous attack in the earlier part of the wilderness wanderings, came under permanent condemnation and were to be destroyed (Ex. 17:8–13; Dt. 25:17–19; 1 Sa. 15:2,3).

### q. Samson and the Philistines (13:1 – 16:31)

The Samson narratives have as their background the earlier part of the Philistine oppression. The editor introduced the Ammonite and Philistine threats to Israel's existence at the same point (10:7); now, having dealt with the lesser threat of shorter duration, he turns to the greater threat that was to overshadow the remainder of the period of the judges and the early monarchy up to the opening years of David's reign (2 Sa. 5:17–25). The Philistines had settled in large numbers on the coastal plain about a generation after the Israelites had entered the land (*c.* 1200 BC), although the possibility of earlier, smaller settlements of ethnically related groups is not excluded (Gn. 21:32,34; 26:1ff.; see note on 1:18,19). When they had established themselves in their pentapolis (Gaza, Ashkelon, Ashdod, Ekron and Gath) they began to penetrate the hinterland. At some point they were momentarily repulsed by Shamgar, thus affording temporary respite to the Israelites (3:31). The Philistine pressure on the Amorites led to a corresponding pressure on the Israelites (1:34–36) and this led in turn to the migration of a portion of the Danites to the extreme north of the land (18:1ff.). It is likely that this took place *before* the time of Samson, who would then be one of the remnant of the Danites in what remained their original tribal portion. The Philistine menace was the greater because it was so insidious in some of its phases. The direct and cruel aggression of the Moabites, Canaanites, Midianites and Ammonites, *etc.* was missing, to be replaced by infiltration through intermarriage and trade. Their rule over the peoples they dominated does not appear at all onerous at this early stage and the men of Judah, who like the Danites were affected by these encroachments, seem to have resented the exploits of Samson and to have accepted the Philistine yoke with docility (15:11). There was the possibility that the Philistines might have continued this movement and eventually have taken over the whole land.

It was in this situation of apathetic acceptance of a potentially dangerous situation that Samson emerged to wage a one-man war against the Philistines. With remarkably little support from his own fellow-countrymen (nowhere does he have one single soldier at his side, let alone an army), he brought the danger into the open. There is no doubt that his exploits sharpened the animosity of the Philistines against the Israelites and led to the employment of greater force in carving out their empire. This represented a greater threat to Israel than any other invasion up to that point. But at least the issues were clear and the essential conflict was on the battlefield. Israel was able to appreciate and meet this threat, whereas the earlier and greater threat had been largely unrecognized. So these narratives are of historical importance, for they document a vital stage of the Philistine threat.

It has frequently been observed that Samson was not a typical judge, although such a statement could be countered with the question, 'What *is* a typical judge?' All the judges were individualists; most of them had their flaws of character. Perhaps a 'typical judge' exists only in our imagination! Nevertheless it must be agreed that, in a group of unique individuals, Samson was in a category all of his own. Endowed with the Spirit of the Lord and dedicated to a lifelong Nazirite vow, his life seems to have revolved around illicit relationships with prostitutes and loose-living women. Whilst he is said to have judged Israel for twenty years (15:20) he effected no real deliverance from the Philistines and perished ultimately as a prisoner in their midst. It is a sad tale of a lack of discipline and true dedication, and the reader is left wondering what Samson might have achieved had his enormous potential been matched and tempered by these mental and spiritual qualities.[1] Undoubtedly the Israelites of Samson's age and, more especially, succeeding generations would revel in the tales of his exploits; in all probability they were told and retold until they were gathered up by the editor of our book. But the editor himself does not glorify Samson's exploits. He recounts them without praise or blame and with the irreducible minimum of editorial comment, perhaps allowing them to speak for themselves before the final episodes bring his account to a close with their oft-repeated comment, 'In those days there was no king in Israel; every man did what was right in his own eyes.'

In spite of the fact that the exploits of Samson read like the actions of an uncontrollable juvenile delinquent, their essential historicity, and the historicity of their perpetrator, need not be doubted and their value is unquestionable. Samson was a man of flesh and blood, linked indissolubly with a well-defined tract of country. His birth and his death are carefully documented and there is little or no correspondence with the mythical Babylonian and Greek heroes. The only thing in favour of a connection with a sun-myth is the name of Samson, derived from the word 'sun'. Attempts to equate the exploits of Samson with the 'twelve labours' of Gilgamesh or Hercules are fanciful and the direct connections with Hebrew life and thought are too strong to be broken.[2] Finally, the skill of the narrator again shows that the Israelites were incompar-

---

[1] See Introduction, section v. *c.*, pp. 41ff.
[2] Further information on the 'solar-myth' theory, which is rarely put forward today, may be found in Burney, pp. 391ff.

able story-tellers. Avoiding extravagant accretions the stories are told with vigour, an understanding of human nature and an understatement that hints rather than dictates.[1] The stories of the Bible, even as literature, will always be read and appreciated for these virtues but, above all, they will be read because, through their infinite variety, God speaks to the human heart.

**13:1. The Philistine oppression.** The forty-year oppression terminated with Samuel's resounding victory over Ebenezer (1 Sa. 7), although the Philistines again dominated Israel during Samuel's lifetime and the reign of Saul (1 Sa. 13; 14; 28-31). This domination was finally broken by David's double victory at Rephaim (2 Sa. 5:17-25).

**13:2-5. Samson's birth foretold.** The home-town of Samson's parents was *Zorah*, a small town on the border between Dan and Judah, in the Shephelah about 14 miles due west of Jerusalem. It was on the northern side of the Sorek valley, immediately opposite the town of Beth-shemesh (lit. 'house of the sun', which may have some bearing on the name of Samson). Manoah's wife, like Sarah, Hannah and Elizabeth, was *barren*, and as with the first and the third of these the birth of a son was announced by *the angel of the Lord* (see note on 2:1). The child was to be a *Nazarite* (AV) from birth. The word derives from the Hebrew *nāzîr* (hence *Nazirite*, RV, RSV, is to be preferred) meaning 'one separated' or 'consecrated'.

The Nazirite vow is delineated in Numbers 6:1-21 and contains three stipulations: the Nazirite was to abstain from all products of the vine; his hair was to be left uncut during the period of his vow; he was not to defile himself by contact with a dead body. Any breach of these stipulations nullified the period of consecration that had been covered and a fresh start had to be made. It is clear from the Samson stories that he

[1] For a view which discerns a more complex stylistic arrangement in these chapters see J. Blenkinsopp, 'Structure and Style in Judges 13-16', in *JBL*, LXXXII, 1963, pp. 65-76.

concerned himself only with the regulation concerning his hair. He is often found in contact with the dead, and that not merely accidentally (*cf.* 14:8,9); and his presence at the carousal of 14:10,17 hardly suggests abstinence from strong drink. The regulations of Numbers 6 also indicate that the Nazirite vow was personally undertaken and was for a limited period only, to be followed by well-defined rites. Samson's vow was not voluntary and it was for the whole of his life (7), so his Nazirite state must be set in a special category, perhaps paralleled by Samuel who, in a Qumran text (4Q Sam.ᵃ; *cf.* 1 Sa. 1:22), is described as 'a Nazirite for ever all the days of his life'.

In view of the unique character of the son she was to bear, Manoah's wife was to share the requirements of a Nazirite by abstaining from *wine* (made from grapes), *strong drink* (made from other fruits, honey and grain), and *unclean* food (which may be a direct reference to Numbers 6:3,4, or a more general injunction to pay particular attention to the Israelite dietary laws). The statement that Samson would *begin to deliver Israel out of the hands of the Philistines* points to the incompleteness of his life's work, which was to be followed and consummated by the activities of Samuel, Saul, Jonathan and David.

**13:6–14. The angel's second visit.** Manoah was immediately informed of this strange visitor and his incredible message, and it is indicative of the relationship existing between himself and his wife that he accepted the basic facts without question or suspicion. It will be observed that his wife made no mention of the part that her son was to play in delivering their people from the Philistines. Was this, perhaps, almost unbelievable? It is not surprising that Manoah and his wife had no real knowledge of the nature of their visitor until his supernatural disappearance (20, 21). After all, this was no ordinary event! He is described as *a man of God* (*cf.* Dt. 33:1), which often designated a prophet, but there was something strange about him which they associated with *an angel of God*. It was very natural that Manoah's wife should afterwards realize her omission in not ascertaining the identity of the one who had made such a staggering promise to her.

Manoah accepted that the visitor was a *man of God, i.e.* a prophet revealing the will of God, and prayed for a second visit, that they might be prepared for the demands of parenthood (8), an attitude which all prospective parents would do well to emulate. His request was granted, and on this second occasion the woman was sufficiently composed to take immediate steps to secure the presence of her husband. The divine messenger was treated with the respect due to a man of God, but there was still no real conception of his identity. Manoah's words (12) were a combination of prayerful gratitude and an earnest desire that they, as parents, might fulfil their responsibilities. The answer of the angel simply reiterated the instructions previously given to the woman alone.

The strongly anthropomorphic nature of this appearance has frequently been observed and it is an indication of the way in which God graciously accommodated Himself to His people of old. He communicated with this simple couple in a manner which they could comprehend. As the centuries passed such appearances became less frequent, for communion and communication became increasingly inward and spiritual. In our own day, through the ministry of the Holy Spirit, it is possible to be as sure of the will of God as when it was revealed in such a striking manner to Manoah and his wife.

**13:15–23. The sacrifice of Manoah.** Manoah's request was typical of the hospitality of the Israelites and other similar groups, and the time involved in preparing such a meal is indicative of the leisureliness of the period, a far cry from the quick-frozen, 'prepared-in-ten-minutes' meals of the modern western world! In the Middle and Far East there are still places where this kind of 'timelessness' exists. The sharing of a meal in the ancient world was a solemn act of fellowship. This incident brings to mind the hospitality proffered by Abraham (Gn. 18:3–8) and Gideon (Jdg. 6:17–23), although there are important differences as well as similarities. The suggestion advanced by St. Augustine and followed by a few modern scholars, that Manoah had in mind a sacrificial or sacramental meal with the deity, is ruled out by the considera- tion, already noted, that he had no awareness that his guest was superhuman. The angel refused to partake of such a meal but suggested instead that a sacrifice be offered to the Lord. Such a suggestion does not necessarily indicate a distinction between the angel of the Lord and the Lord Himself (*cf.* verse 22 and the note on 2:1).

The hint of the angel was not followed up at once. Instead Manoah requested the *name* of the messenger, so that he might be honoured at the fulfilment of his prophecy. In the Ancient Near East the name of a person was important as suggesting the character of the one who bore it. Jacob (Gn. 32:29) showed his desire to know the name of his divine protagonist, so that he might exercise some control by his knowledge of the character revealed in the name; but there is no suggestion of such a motive in the case of Manoah. His request was not granted. *Secret* (18, AV) does not really indicate the meaning of the Hebrew adjective, which comes from a root meaning 'separate', 'surpassing' or 'ineffable'. Most of the versions translate it as *wonderful*, which adequately conveys its meaning. Psalm 139:6, where the feminine form occurs, is an apt illus- tration of its nuance. *Wondrously* (19, AV, RV) is a participle derived from the same root. Manoah's sacrifice of a kid was accompanied by a *meat offering* (AV). The Hebrew *minḥâ* is used in a variety of forms in the Old Testament, but its greatest single use, at least ninety-seven times in all, denoted a *cereal offering* (RSV; *cf. meal offering*, RV), as in the legislation of Leviticus 2. It was often associated with the other animal sacrifices and its purpose was 'to secure or retain good-will'.[1] The *rock* upon which the sacrifice was offered was probably a rock-altar.

The participular form *did wondrously* (19) is without a sub- ject in the Hebrew. The AV and RV, which regard it as the action of the angel, connect it with the name of the angel in the

---

[1] The article 'Sacrifice and Offering', in *NBD*, pp. 1113ff., may be com- mended for further study.

preceding verse, and are to be preferred to the alternative view connecting it with the Lord *who works wonders* (RSV). In contrast with the events of chapter 6, where the staff of the angel was used to kindle the flame, Manoah appears to have offered up the sacrifice in the normal way, and the whole incredible incident came to its frightening climax when the angel ascended heavenward in the flame of the altar. Immediately full recognition flashed upon Manoah and his wife and left them prostrate and terror-stricken upon the ground. Manoah was the first to speak but the last to recover his composure, reflecting the widely held belief that if a man saw God he would die (Ex. 33:20; Jdg. 6:22,23). His wife, who had an advantage over her husband in that she had been in the presence of their divine visitor on an earlier occasion, and had survived that encounter, was more rational. With sound common sense she reasoned that the Lord would hardly have accepted an offering from them, or have revealed to them such strange things concerning the future, if He purposed their deaths.

**13:24, 25. The birth and development of Samson.** The connection of the name of Samson with the Hebrew word for sun (*šemeš*), and the improbability of any association with solar mythology, has already been noted.[1] Corresponding forms occur in the Ugaritic texts of the fourteenth and fifteenth centuries BC and the probability is that it was a common name in Canaan before it was adopted by the Israelites. The brief account of his early years is reminiscent of the narratives concerning John the Baptist (Lk. 1:80) and our Lord (Lk. 2:40,52) but in the case of Samson the early promise was not fulfilled. Like his predecessors amongst the judges of the various tribes he received his charismatic anointing of *the Spirit of the Lord*,[2] an anointing which was reflected in his unique strength and spectacular feats. The reference to the *camp of Dan* (AV; *Mahaneh-dan*, RV, RSV) is interesting for it suggests a temporary habitation, possibly caused by the pressure from the Amorites and Philistines, in which case it could

[1] See p. 155.
[2] See Introduction, pp. 15ff.

be viewed as a displaced persons' camp. 18:12, where Mahaneh-dan is set in the vicinity of Kiriath-jearim, about 8 miles north-east of Zorah, is not determinative, since the same name could apply to a number of sites at a time of tribal displacement. *Eshtaol* was within a mile and a half to the north-east of *Zorah*. Apart from visits to Ashkelon (14:19), Gaza (16:1) and his final imprisonment in Gaza, the place-names suggest that Samson did not travel more than a few miles from his birthplace. The reference in verse 25 is a general intro-duction to his career rather than a reference to exploits which have not been preserved.

**14:1–4. The first love of Samson.** *Timnah* was a little more than 4 miles to the south-west of Zorah, on the other side of the vale of Sorek. Its occupation by the Philistines demon-strates their penetration of Israelite territory and its peaceful nature, for Samson appears quite free to come and to go, and there was no barrier to his marriage from their side. But the fact of Philistine domination, however peaceful, is noted in 4b. It is also attested by archaeological evidence, for 'Philistine' ware, a distinctive type of pottery manufactured in this period, is widely distributed at sites in the Shephelah and Negeb dating from the period after *c.* 1150 BC. The proximity of Timnah and Zorah – a little more than an hour's stroll separated them – may account for the apparent confusion which some commentators have found in the narrative con-cerning the journeys to and from Timnah, *e.g.* the visit of Samson's parents to Timnah is noted in verse 5 but no account is given of their return. However, in view of the insignificant journey involved this was hardly worth mentioning.

It was at Timnah that Samson met the first of his lovers, and he was not deterred by the fact that she was a Philistine and that he was breaking the traditions of his people and the injunctions of the Law concerning mixed marriages (Ex. 34:16; Dt. 7:3; *cf.* Gn. 24:3,4; 26:34,35). The grief of his parents at this alliance can be imagined, especially with their know-ledge of his unique birth and peculiar destiny. Samson's lack of concern on such an important religious issue was matched by his lack of submission to his parents. In Israelite society the father was the head of the family and as such exercised control over all of its members, including the choice of wives for his sons (*e.g.* Gn. 24:4; 38:6). It was exceptional for a son to contravene the wishes of his parents in this or any other realm (Gn. 26:34, 35; 27:46), for the unit was the clan and personal preference was subordinated to it. The remonstrances of Samson's parents were dismissed curtly in the light of his overwhelming desire for this Philistine woman.

The likelihood that this was an inferior state of marriage, where the bride, instead of joining her husband's family, remained with her own people, being visited from time to time by her husband (15:1; *cf.* note on 8:31) is only a slight mitigation of Samson's offence. R. de Vaux observes, 'Samson's marriage has close similarities with a form found among Palestinian Arabs, in that it is a true marriage but without permanent cohabitation. The woman is mistress of her own house, and the husband, known as *joz musarrib*, "a visiting husband," comes as a guest and brings presents.'[1] There appears an element of contempt in the way in which the person of Samson's choice is described. The normal word for an unmarried girl is not employed; instead the common word for *woman* is used. Possibly she was a widow or a divorced person. Delilah is similarly described in 16:4. The epithet, *uncircumcised* (3), applied to the Philistines in many Old Testament references, is appropriate, for all Israel's neighbours with the exception of the Philistines observed this practice. There were important differences, however. For instance, circumcision outside Israel was often attached to the rites of puberty or pre-marriage, and in Egypt it appears to have been restricted to the priests and possibly the ruling class.

**4.** The explanation appears to be an editorial comment at a time when the Philistine menace was completely in the past, which suggests a date no earlier than the middle of the reign of David. The editor notes what he believes to be the overruling of the Lord in this breach of clan etiquette and the na-

[1] R. de Vaux, *Ancient Israel* (Darton, Longman & Todd, 1962), p. 43.

tional religious code. He was seeking an occasion against the Philistines.[1]

**14:5-7. Samson and the lion.** The verbs *went down* and *came* in verse 5 are in the singular and this, together with the fact that Samson did not inform his parents of his feat in slaying the lion when they were supposedly with him, has led many commentators to assume that his parents were not, in fact, with him, and that he was on his way to contract a marriage without their approval. Such a reconstruction, involving the excision of the references to his parents, is not necessary. Many circumstances could have caused a temporary separation on the way down to Timnah and, in fact, all other information in this section is secondary to the slaying of the lion, since this is linked with its sequel in the riddle which Samson put at the marriage feast. As was hinted earlier,[2] the proximity of Zorah and Timnah may account for some of the ambiguity.

Samson, attacked by a young lion, received a sudden accession of irresistible strength, attributed to *the Spirit of the Lord* coming *mightily upon him.* This manifestation of unusual physical strength appears to be the sole effect of the divine impulse upon Samson (*cf.* verse 19; 15:14; and the reference to Saul in 1 Sa. 11:6). The emphasis in the narrative is upon the ease with which he performed this exploit, not the manner itself, although the verb *rent* (AV, RV) suggests that he tore the lion down the middle, presumably by ripping the hind legs apart. The same verb is used in connection with the sacrificial act of Leviticus 1:17. There are many references to actions similar to Samson's amongst the mythical heroes of antiquity. Enkidu, the friend of Gilgamesh, is shown possibly tearing a lion apart by pulling on its hind legs; Heracles strangled the Nemean lion with his bare hands; Polydamas, imitating Heracles, slew a full-grown lion on Mount Olympus without any weapon in his hand. The reference to the unarmed condition of Samson, *he had nothing in his hand,* may indicate that the Philistines had already begun their policy of depriving

[1] See Introduction, section **v. c., p. 43.**
[2] See p. 161.

the Israelites of their weapons (1 Sa. 13:19–22); more probably, however, it is intended to draw attention to his prodigious feat. The slaughter recorded in 14:19 and 15:8 could hardly have been accomplished without weapons.

**14:8, 9. Honey from the lion's corpse.** The reference to the lapse of time is indeterminative, but since Samson shared the honey with his parents it is probable that he was on the homeward journey from Timnah to Zorah. It was almost certainly subsequent to the earlier visit, since a honeycomb had been formed. Turning aside, which suggests that his exploit was performed away from the main route, he discovered that *a swarm of bees* had settled in the carcase of the lion. In the extreme heat of a Palestinian summer a carcase becomes dehydrated very quickly, thus staying putrefaction and allowing the bees to hive, for normally bees will not approach a decomposing body. Possibly also those natural scavengers, the ants, vultures and jackals, had performed their office, thus leaving a natural cavity for the bees. Herodotus cites a comparable incident where a honeycomb was discovered in the skull of Onesilus. It will be observed that Samson, by taking the honeycomb (the verb is suggestive, indicating that he scraped it out with his hands; *cf.* RSV), broke the provisions of the normal Nazirite vow by coming into contact with a corpse; in his case, wilfully (Nu. 6:6). This may be the reason why he did not inform his parents of the source of his gift.

**14:10, 11. Samson's feast.** Again we notice an enigmatic reference to Samson's *father*; it is not clear why he journeyed to Timnah, since Samson was the one who provided the feast. This was at the bride's house, making it apparent that this was not a normal Jewish marriage. It may be that the visit of Samson's father was connected with an abortive effort to stop the marriage which he could not sanction. But we cannot be sure of this; some of the details appear to have been omitted. Marriage customs are notoriously tenacious and some of the details of this particular wedding feast appear in many subsequent celebrations, even up to the present day. The usual length of a celebration was seven days and the marriage was not consummated until the end of that period. The *thirty companions* were the 'sons of the bride-chamber' (Mt. 9:15; Mk. 2:19; Lk. 5:34, RV), who probably originated as a body-guard to prevent the wedding party being surprised by marauders seeking easy pickings. The text seems to suggest something abnormal about this particular arrangement, as though the engagement of the thirty men was an afterthought. The LXX reflects this caution by its translation 'when they feared him' (11), *i.e.* they were a body-guard to protect *against* Samson! But there was no apparent reason to fear him at this juncture, and his frequent visits to Timnah would have made them familiar with his abnormal physique long before this point.

**14:12–18. Samson's riddle.** It is not possible to solve the problem of the various references to time in this section. The feast lasted *seven days* (12); after *three days* the young men had not found the answer to the riddle (14); on *the seventh day* (15, AV, RV) they enlisted the aid of Samson's wife by threats; she wept for *the seven days* and Samson told her the solution on *the seventh day* (17). The LXX reads *on the fourth day* (15; *cf.* RSV, RV mg.), which eases the problem and makes sense of the reference in verse 14. But the first part of verse 17 remains inexplicable; obviously it *should* read 'And she wept before him until the seventh day' or something similar. This difficulty does not preclude an understanding of the general import of the passage, which centres on Samson's *riddle*. Riddles were highly esteemed in the ancient world, but those concerned with trivialities found little place in Hebrew life, according to the Old Testament evidence. The word is used of the 'hard questions' with which the Queen of Sheba plied Solomon (1 Ki. 10:1); it is also translated 'dark saying' in Psalms 49:4; 78:2; Proverbs 1:6.

In the generally festive atmosphere of the feast Samson's challenge was readily accepted, for the thirty men would consider the advantages of their combined wisdom and time to be on their side. In fact, the stakes were high. The *sheets*

(12,13, AV) were large rectangular pieces of fine linen which were worn next to the body by day or by night. The *change of garments* (AV; *cf.* RV) were properly *festal garments* (RSV) which were equivalent to the modern 'Sunday best'. These were garments of superior quality and decoration, which were not for everyday use but for special occasions such as weddings. The average person would possess only one such garment. Such attire was often the principal source of spoil in battle (*cf.* 5:30). Samson's riddle was in the form of a couplet, each line having three beats, the rhyme in our English rendering being accidental:

> '*Out of the eater came something to eat.*
> *Out of the strong came something sweet*' (RSV).

The answer to this riddle could hardly be found without the personal knowledge which only Samson possessed, and it is not surprising that, faced with considerable individual expense, the thirty guests were deeply concerned when they realized that a solution was beyond them. The atmosphere of the feast assumed an ugly, menacing aspect with their threat (15), in which they assumed that Samson's wife was implicated in a plot to strip them of their possessions. 15:6 shows that it was no idle threat. The woman, fearing for her life and her father's house, used the last resort of her sex, a flood of tears and the innuendo that Samson did not love her or he would keep no secrets from her – devices that have led to untold misery for both sexes! Samson was able to answer the innuendo by pointing out that his own parents, to whom he had the greater responsibility, were in ignorance of the answer (16); but he could not withstand the corrosive influence of three or four days of weeping. The suspense was maintained up to the last day. Samson, anticipating the consummation of the marriage, was anxious to stop the flow of tears. But the shared secret meant that the marriage was, in fact, never consummated, for, as the seventh day drew to its close, the riddle was answered. Samson never entered the bridal chamber and without this the marriage was considered invalid. His retort to the thirty companions is in the same form as the riddle, a three-beat couplet which, somewhat unusually in Hebrew poetry, has a rhyme formed by the repetition of the first person singular suffix to the nouns. C. F. Burney successfully renders this:

> 'If ye had not plowed with this heifer of mine,
> Ye would not have found out this riddle of mine.'[1]

**14:19, 20. Samson's exploit at Ashkelon.** Samson was obviously angered by his wife's disclosure of his secret, and as there was no reason for her to conceal from him the duress under which it was secured, he would be angry with the Philistines also. In this crisis he was again endued with supernatural strength, attributed as elsewhere to a sudden accession of *the Spirit of the Lord*. The payment of the wager and the desire for revenge put away all thoughts of his marriage and the Philistines themselves were made to pay. The choice of *Ashkelon*, on the coast about 23 miles from Timnah and one of the five principal cities of the Philistines, was probably to avoid any possibility of anyone connecting this exploit with the incident at the wedding feast. Had Samson slain thirty men in a nearby town or village, then the coincidence would point unmistakably to him and a rude vengeance would have been taken on his family at Zorah. The debt paid, Samson retired in high dudgeon to his own home, his feeling for his wife temporarily alienated. But it was a signal disgrace for a bride to be left in this embarrassing situation at the completion of the wedding festivities and she was given forthwith to Samson's *best man* (RSV), the 'friend of the bridegroom' (*cf.* Jn. 3:29). Problems remain for the modern student. For instance, it must have taken two days for the return journey to Ashkelon. Samson must have returned to Timnah with this considerable pile of raiment. Had his bride been given to the best man before he returned, or was it after his return to Zorah? It is important to observe that the narrator is concerned, not with

[1] Burney, p. 366.

the incidental details which perplex us, but with the fact of the slaughter of the Philistines.

**15:1, 2. Samson rejected.** Climatic conditions are slightly variable in the various regions of Palestine, so that the time of the *wheat harvest* is not uniform throughout the country. In Israel, of course, it was associated with the second of the three great harvest-festivals, Passover (barley), Weeks or Pentecost (wheat), and Tabernacles (figs, grapes, olives, *etc.*). In the region of Timnah the wheat harvest would come somewhere near the end of May or the beginning of June. Samson's anger had evaporated by this time and he made the journey to Timnah to cohabit with his wife. The gift of *a kid* was more than a device to remove her resentment; it was probably the prescribed offering for a husband visiting his wife in this kind of marriage, where the bride remained with her parents. The parents of the woman, however, had construed the abrupt action of Samson as a sign of complete alienation from their daughter and had sought to remove the stigma of disgrace by giving her to the best man. Their offer of the bride's *younger sister* (*cf.* 1 Sa. 18:19ff.) may reveal their consciousness that they themselves had acted hastily and improperly. Alternatively, it may have been caused by an acute personal fear of Samson and to placate his revengeful spirit. There could, in any case, be no question of an annulment of the marriage that had subsequently been contracted.

**15:3-6. Samson's revenge and its sequel.** Samson refused the offer of his intended bride's younger sister and, deeply offended, vowed vengeance upon the Philistines. His words indicate that he felt completely justified in such vindictive action. His action has frequently been compared to the ancient Roman custom in honour of Ceres, the corn goddess, when burning torches were secured to the brushes of foxes which were then hunted in the Circus, but the connection is only circumstantial. The large number of foxes, *three hundred*, has often been questioned. Some commentators explain it as due to hyperbole on the part of those responsible for the transmission of the story. In all probability the *foxes* were jackals. The same Hebrew word (*šū'āl*) describes both animals, which are closely related. But whereas the fox is solitary and avoids human beings the jackal hunts in packs and is more easily caught. Both animals are still found in Palestine.

The burning of *standing corn* was a common method of retaliation or revenge in the ancient world and its effect in an agricultural community was very serious. The prompt reaction of Joab to the ruse of Absalom to attract his attention may be instanced (2 Sa. 14:28–31). We can imagine the delight with which the Israelites would tell this story of revenge against the nation which was to oppress them so sorely. But such wanton cruelty to animals, whose sufferings must have been hideous, cannot be condoned.[1] The harvest was being gathered in at the time, for *shocks* (5) refers to the heaped sheaves. The hurt done to the Philistines was increased when the fire spread to the olive plantations. The reputation of Samson was such that the Philistines had no difficulty in discovering the identity of the incendiary, or his motive, and their words (6) confirm the suggestion made above, that the *Timnite* had acted hastily and inadvisably. In seeking to save his daughter's honour he had started a chain reaction that was to have disastrous consequences. It was easier for the Philistines to wreak vengeance on him and his daughter than to capture Samson himself, so the fate which Samson's intended wife endeavoured to escape by inveigling his secret from him befell her after all. Some Hebrew, Greek and Syriac manuscripts read 'burned her and her father's house', which would link with the threat of 14:15. It would have been wiser for her to have informed her husband as soon as it was made, for he was well able to take care of himself and of her and her father.

**15:7, 8. Further slaughter of the Philistines.** It is a truism that two wrongs never make a right. An act of revenge calls forth an answering act, and hurt pride can be so strong that there is no end to the process. Many a family, clan or tribe

[1] See Introduction, pp. 41ff.

has been wiped out, and its rivals decimated, in some of the feuds that have gone on for generations. At some point there has to be the absorption of wrong done, without retaliation, a fact illustrated supremely by Christ's death on the cross. But Samson was not this kind of man, and although he had brought a tragic end upon the family with which he once sought an alliance, he now vowed to make one final act of vengeance, as though it ever lies in the power of a man to decree when the blood-letting shall cease!

The number of Samson's victims is not specified, nor is the reference that *he smote them hip and thigh* (8) intelligible to us today. The suggestion that he hewed them in pieces with such violence that their limbs were piled up one on another is somewhat fanciful. More plausible is the suggestion that the expression was a proverbial one which originated in the art of wrestling, although something a little more potent than bare hands, brute strength and wrestling ability is called for to account for such slaughter of opponents who presumably were all armed. It is likely that the Philistines who died were the inhabitants of Timnah and its immediate vicinity. Realizing that reprisals would inevitably follow, Samson sought refuge *in the cleft of the rock of Etam* (RV, RSV). An Etam is mentioned in 2 Chronicles 11:6, but as this was probably between Bethlehem and Tekoa it would be too far away to connect with this incident. A site in the vicinity of Samson's home is much more likely and there is much to support the view that it was a cave in the cliffs above the Wady Isma'in, which was accessible only by descending through a fissure in the cliff-face, wide enough for one person to pass through at a time. This strongpoint, in an area well known to Samson, lay about two and a half miles south-east from Zorah. The context makes it clear that it was in Judaean territory, although Philistine pressure on the tribes of Dan and Judah had made their common border rather fluid.

**15:9–17. Samson's exploit at Lehi.** The massacre of their compatriots at Timnah led to the assembling of a force of at least a thousand Philistines (15, 16) to deal with this one-man menace. This is itself a tribute to Samson's strength. Their assembly-point, *Lehi*, meaning 'jawbone' is so called proleptically, in anticipation of Samson's exploit. The presence of such a considerable band of warriors caused understandable concern to the men of Judah resident in the vicinity. The story is illustrative of the conditions obtaining in the Shephelah at that time. It shows the Judaeans accepting the domination of the Philistines, and fearful of the consequences of Samson's exploits. No doubt they were secretly sympathetic with Samson, yet such was their fear of the Philistines that a band of three thousand thought only of binding him and handing him over to their common adversaries, rather than standing with this hero against them. It is clear also that the Philistines had no quarrel with the men of Judah.

If our identification of Samson's hiding-place be correct, then the order of events becomes clear. The Philistines were probably encamped in the valley when the men of Judah climbed to the top of the rock, descended through the fissure in the cliff-face as far as they dared and then called down to Samson. After securing their assurance that they would not slay him themselves, he permitted them to bind him and bring him up to the summit and then he accompanied them down to the Philistine camp. It was not fear that prompted his request to the Israelites (12), for it is obvious that he knew what he would do with the ropes that bound him, but had they made any attempt to harm him they themselves would have suffered, and his quarrel was with the Philistines, not his own countrymen. The shouts of triumph of the approaching Philistines was the stimulus that led to a sudden manifestation of power, attributed directly to *the Spirit of the Lord* (*cf.* 13:25; 14:6,19). The cords that bound him were snapped (*cf.* 16:9,12) and seizing a fresh jawbone of an ass he embarked on an orgy of destruction in which a thousand Philistines perished. It is clear that there was wholesale slaughter among the Philistines, but the reference to *a thousand* may be a round figure expressing a very large, but undefined, number. Probably the remainder of their demoralized army fled but, significantly, there is no mention of any intervention of the three thousand men of

Judah, who must have been the witnesses of the rout of their oppressors. Even this exploit failed to rouse them from their apathetic acceptance of the situation.

Samson's impromptu weapon, a *fresh* (lit. 'moist') *jawbone of an ass*, would be heavier and less brittle and therefore a more effective implement than a jawbone that was old and dry. His song of exultation was a four-beat couplet, with a play on the words *ass* and *heap* in the first line that is not easily reproduced in English. The words in Hebrew are identical (*ḥᵃmôr*). Moffatt's attempt is commendable, 'With the jawbone of an ass I have piled them in a mass!' C. F. Burney seizes upon the fact that *ḥᵃmôr* means literally 'the reddish-coloured animal' and notes the correspondence between this and the blood-stained pile of Philistine corpses. He renders the first line, 'With the red ass's jawbone I have reddened them right red.'[1] Such word-play is typically Hebrew and such a coarse illustration is typical of Samson.

A similarity of names links together three exploits: Shamgar slew six hundred Philistines (3:31); Samson slew one thousand Philistines at Lehi; Shammah, one of David's mighty men, slew an unspecified number of Philistines, and a slight emendation of the text, accepted by many scholars, sets this deed at Lehi (2 Sa. 23:11,12; *cf.* RSV). However, in view of the considerable differences in detail between these incidents, and the fact that the Philistine menace was continued for almost two centuries, the similarity of names may be viewed as purely coincidental. *Ramath-lehi*, the name bestowed by Samson upon the scene of his victory, means 'the height of the jawbone'.

**15:18-20. God's care for the overwrought Samson.** The battle over, a reaction set in and the prodigious energy expended in the slaughter of the Philistines left Samson with a raging thirst. The man who had not feared when he was delivered, bound, into the camp of the enemy now shrank in fear and distrust at the prospect of death through thirst, with the probability of the Philistines returning to mutilate his corpse. The scene is so typically human. It may be compared

[1] Burney, p. 372.

with Elijah's lone-handed triumph over the prophets and priests of Baal upon Carmel, after which he ran the whole distance from Carmel to Jezreel, and the aftermath, with the dejected, defeated and desperately weary prophet slumped under a juniper bush, asking the Lord to take away his life (1 Ki. 18;19). In each case God refrained from scolding His servants for their petulant outbursts and graciously provided for their acute physical needs. *The jaw* (19, AV) should be read as a place-name, *Lehi* (RV, RSV); *hollow place* is literally 'mortar', a word generally used for a hollowed stone or deep wooden bowl in which, for example, olives were crushed to produce the oil. Here it clearly indicates a circular depression from which the spring issued. There is no need to regard this incident as simply an aetiological legend explaining the name of *En-hakkore* ('the well of the one who called'). There is such a thing as a true aetiological story, *i.e.* a place-name is given because an incident actually took place there. The judgeship of Samson is noted as *twenty years*, and whilst any dates must be conjectural, the period *c.* 1080–1060 BC is most plausible. The nature of his office is clear from the records; it consisted of his lone exploits against the Philistines and appears completely devoid of judicial functions. His area of influence was confined to the small tract of country where the Philistines impinged upon the tribes of Dan and Judah. It is probable that Abimelech and Jephthah were contemporaries of Samson, but it is extremely unlikely that they had any mutual contact.

**16:1–3. Samson's exploit at Gaza.** *Gaza* was the southernmost of the five principal Philistine cities, although, with its strategic position on the trade-routes from Egypt to western Asia, it had a history going back to a period long before the Philistine occupation. It was captured by the Israelites at the time of the Conquest, but they were not able to retain it or any other of the coastal cities (see note on 1:18). It is not clear what brought Samson to Gaza, which was about 38 miles from Zorah; but on what appears to be a casual visit his wayward, sensual nature took him into the company of a Philistine prostitute. The man whose great strength made him a legend in his own lifetime was completely unable to bridle his own passions and this weakness was to lead to his eventual downfall. The editor makes no effort to cover up Samson's blemishes, and his exploits, which caused such delight to the contemporary generation, must have been somewhat embarrassing to a more enlightened age. Similarly the frailty and foibles of Abraham, Moses, David and other Old Testament characters are faithfully depicted. Although God greatly used these men and women in the working out of His purposes, none of them seems to have been a paragon of virtue.

The reputation of Samson had now extended far beyond the immediate vicinity of his exploits and his appearance in Gaza led to an attempt to apprehend him. The double reference to *all night* (2) has caused perplexity, since a guard at the gates of the city could not fail to be disturbed when Samson made his getaway in such an abrupt manner. There is no suggestion of any encounter with the guard; indeed, the whole point of the story is that the Philistines were taken by surprise. The difficulty is certainly eased by adopting the suggestion put forward by Kittel, that the first *all night* should read 'all day'. The sense would then be that the Philistines watched the gates all day, but trusting in the strength of the gates to contain their intended victim by night, they relaxed, thinking to fulfil their purpose the next morning. On the other hand, the guards at the gate may have relaxed their vigil with the passing of the hours and then been paralysed with fright and unable to act by the strange method of Samson's exit. He surprised them by breaking out of the city in the middle of the night, taking with him the doors and door-posts as well as the bar securing the doors, which was let into the posts. The incredible strength of Samson is shown in the fact that all this woodwork was transported 38 miles, mostly uphill, to Hebron! As the gates of ancient cities were often nail-studded and covered with metal to prevent them being burnt during an attack, the weight may have been greater than that of the timber itself. Many commentators have treated this feat of strength as wildly exaggerated tradition, but the fact that, in the Delilah episode, a band of armed Philistines dared make no attempt to fall upon a weaponless man until the source of his strength had been discovered points to completely abnormal power. However, as Hebron was in the vicinity of the highest point in southern Palestine, forming a prominent landmark over a wide area, the reference has been held to be figurative, *before Hebron* being viewed as equivalent to 'towards Hebron', which may suggest a hill near Gaza but in the general direction of Hebron.

**16:4, 5. Samson's love for Delilah.** It was written of King Solomon that he 'loved many strange women', and the editor duly notes that his wives 'turned away his heart' from following the Lord and contributed to the moral and religious decline of the people (1 Ki. 11:1–13). Samson had not the same opportunities as Solomon, but his unbridled passions were akin to those of the great king and brought about his downfall. The answer to his riddle had been wrested from him by the devices of a woman (14:12–17), now the greatest secret of his life was disclosed at the importunity of another lover. The name of *Delilah*, which means 'worshipper' or 'devotee', has become a synonym for the seductive woman. Delilah lived in *the valley of Sorek*, just below Zorah. Her name is Semitic, but as the Philistines intermarried freely with the peoples they dominated this is not significant, and the details of the narrative suggest that she was, in fact, a Philistine. It is strange that Samson's three loves should have been numbered amongst his inveterate enemies, the Philistines. We have already noted the wholesome respect with which the Philistines regarded Samson (see note on 15:9–17), now reflected in the fact that they dared not approach him until they had gained the secret of his strength. Two other factors attest to the seriousness of the situation and the effectiveness of Samson's single-handed campaign. Verse 5 notes the direct intervention of the five *lords of the Philistines* (*cf.* 3:3), the rulers of the pentapolis, suggesting that Samson was now regarded as a national menace. The second fact is the extent of the reward which they offered Delilah for information which would enable them to capture their enemy. The reference to *eleven hundred* *pieces of silver*, rather than the round thousand, is unusual, but it probably marks the generosity of their offer: 'We'll give you more than a thousand!' The weight of silver would be about 30 pounds from each of the five lords, making a combined total of 150 pounds, a very considerable reward (the value in AD 1967 would be over £1,100!). The risk was considerable, therefore the bribe had to outweigh the personal danger involved and the strength of the attachment with her lover.

**16:6–14. Samson's secret undisclosed.** Delilah went about her errand with a cold, heartless efficiency that causes the reader to wonder why Samson was so lacking in suspicion. In all probability he was so blinded by his passion and its gratification that no thought of insecurity entered his head. The liaison must have been a long-standing one for the Philistine lords to have heard of it and to have observed its potential usefulness to their aim. In the first three attempts made by Delilah Samson adopted a playful, teasing attitude. Six visits may have been made by Samson during this time, in three groups of two, on the first of which Delilah elicited the information and on the second of which, having secured the material from the Philistines, she carried it into effect. Alternatively, Delilah may have been given the new suggestion immediately following the failure of the previous one, which would reduce the minimum number of visits to four. The *seven green withs* (7, AV, RV) of the first attempt should be read as *seven fresh bowstrings* (RSV), which were made of twisted gut. The second attempt was made with *new ropes* (11, 12). Evidently the Philistines did not know, or else had overlooked, the fact that the men of Judah had already tried this method (15:13). It may have been the remembrance of this incident which prompted Samson to make this particular suggestion. The third attempt was perilously near the truth, for it concerned Samson's hair (13, 14) and this may reveal a stage in the breaking-down of his will.

The details of this particular method are not made clear in any of the versions. Indeed it is doubtful if this could be achieved without considerable amplification. The reference is to the weaving process. Primitive looms were either horizontal or upright; the former type would allow Delilah more freedom to deal with the hair of the sleeping Samson, assuming that his head was upon her lap, but the detail suggests the latter type. In the upright type of loom two vertical posts fixed in the ground were fastened at the top by a cross-beam from which the warp threads were suspended. The long hair of Samson was woven into the warp and then beaten up into the web with the pin (14), thus producing a firm piece of material.

To test the effectiveness of each method Delilah gave warning of the approach of the Philistines, with spectacular results. On the first occasion the bow-strings were snapped as easily as a thread of tow snaps when the flame licks (9; Heb. 'smells', *i.e.* having no direct contact) upon it; on the second occasion the new ropes were as effective as a fragile thread; on the third occasion it is possible that the whole loom was wrenched out and carried away. One wonders who was kind enough to disentangle Delilah's labours!

The temptress herself gently but persistently applied herself to her mission, increasing gradually the tone of hurt reproach as her endeavours were mocked. Whilst it is the principal actors that grip the attention of the readers, the suspense of the Philistine soldiers, armed but anxious, hiding in an inner chamber until the coast was quite clear, hopeful but frustrated on three occasions, can be imagined. The hypocrisy of Delilah, pretending to love but all the time plotting the death of her lover, can be left without comment.

**16:15-20. Samson's secret revealed.** It is evident that, after these three futile attempts, the Philistines had lost interest and retired from the scene, since Delilah had to make a special plea for their return (18). Verse 16 similarly indicates a considerable lapse of time. The fact that Samson continued to seek for her love did not soften the heart of Delilah or cause her to relent. Possibly the thought of immense wealth spurred her on; possibly there was an element of wounded pride in the realization that she had not been able to worm Samson's secret from him. The two sayings, 'Hell hath no fury like a woman scorned' and 'A continual dripping wears away the stone', may both be appropriate to this story. *Vexed to death* (16; our colloquial 'bored to death' is not an inaccurate rendering of the Hebrew) with her insistency, Samson at length capitulated and she knew that he had spoken the truth. The Nazirite vow was at last revealed. Mention has already been made that, of the three main provisions of such a vow, Samson had observed but one (see note on 13:5). He had often been in contact with the dead; he can hardly have kept himself from strong drink; but his hair still remained unshorn. In defence of Samson at this point, it may be that in the confused political situation and the generally low moral and spiritual tone of the age, some of the provisions of the Nazirite vow had been forgotten whilst this popular feature of the uncut hair was retained. The hair itself was not the source of Samson's unique strength. This lay in his separation to the Lord, of which the unshorn locks were the symbol. However, there remains the problem that this separation appears as a merely ceremonial concept, with little, if any, moral significance.

The Philistine lords came prepared to honour the promise they had given (18; *cf.* verse 5), and then the last act of treachery was enacted. Words are inadequate to describe the utter heartlessness of the woman who lulled her lover to sleep with his head in her lap, conscious of the fate into which she was delivering him. Was it nervousness that impelled her to call in a barber to clip Samson's seven locks? The precise meaning of *she began to afflict him* (19, AV, RV) is obscure, since Delilah herself would hardly dare attempt any hurt to Samson until she was quite sure that his strength was gone. Perhaps the verb should have Samson as its subject, 'and he began to be afflicted'. The warning call was given as on earlier occasions and Samson, awakened from his slumber, purposed to do as before, quite unaware of what had taken place. There is possibly no sadder verse in the Old Testament than the final sentence in verse 20. In Numbers 14:40–45 there is the sad picture of a nation temporarily forsaken by God; here there is the tragedy of a man unconscious of the fact that the Lord was no longer with him. In such a situation shame and defeat are inevitable (*cf.* Ex. 33:14,15).

**16:21, 22. Samson's humiliation.** The weakened Samson was now easily captured by the Philistines. His eyes were gouged out and he was brought down to Gaza, the scene of one of his earlier feats of strength (16:1-3), and put to work at the tedious task of grinding out corn, probably at a hand-mill, since there is no evidence of the larger, ass-powered mill until the fifth century BC. This occupation was not only menial, it was humiliating, since it was invariably women's work (see note on 9:53). *Fetters of brass* is a dual form, suggesting that his hands and his feet were both secured. It is surprising that his captors, having ascertained the secret of his great strength, did not take steps to see that he was shaved regularly; probably they thought that they had little to fear from this sightless, shambling wreck. Whilst it is not specifically stated, the inference is that his strength returned as his hair grew. It may be also that, during this confinement in prison, contemplating the shame and failure of his life, some spark of repentance was kindled, although there is little evidence of this in the text.

**16:23-30. Samson's final revenge.** At some unspecified point after Samson's capture the Philistines held a service of thanksgiving to *Dagon their god*. Dagon was commonly regarded as a fish-god until recently, but this identification rested solely upon a similarity with the Hebrew word for fish (*dāḡ*). Modern archaeological research has shown conclusively that he was a corn or vegetation-god, worshipped in Mesopotamia in the middle of the third millennium BC and brought to the eastern-Mediterranean countries by the Semitic migrations of the early second millennium. The common Hebrew word used for grain or corn (*dāḡān*) is possibly derived from the name of Dagon. There was a temple to Dagon in fourteenth-century Ugarit and he appears as the chief deity of the Philistines, who, as we have noted,[1] were a ruling class imposed upon a native population whose customs and religion they

[1] See p. 138.

adopted readily. Dagon was worshipped at Beth-shan in the reign of Saul (1 Sa. 31:10; *cf.* 1 Ch. 10:10) and at Ashdod until the Maccabean period (1 Sa. 5:2-7; 1 Macc. 10:83 -85). The wide diffusion of his worship is shown in the two settlements of Beth-dagon, one in Judah (Jos. 15:41) and the other in Asher (Jos. 19:27). There is a certain fluidity in the inter-relationships of the Canaanite deities, but in some texts Dagon appears as the father of Baal.

The influence of Samson's anti-Philistine activities is reflected in the national thanksgiving celebration and in their description of him as *the ravager of our country* (24, RSV). Such festivals, in which wine flowed freely, were often the occasion for debauchery, but on this occasion, when the strong drink had begun its influence, their inclinations took a more sadistic turn and they called for Samson, their prize-exhibit, that he might put on a performance for them and that they might bait him. The verb *make sport* comes from a root meaning 'to laugh' or 'deride'; possibly they wanted Samson to amuse them with the kind of performance we would associate with a strong man in a fair-booth. So the man whom armed Philistines had not dared to approach was led in by a single attendant.

A number of sites of ancient heathen temples have been recently discovered, and since they show certain common characteristics it is likely that the temple of Gaza was of a similar pattern. In all probability the officials and dignitaries were in a covered portion looking out upon a courtyard where Samson was made a spectacle, but separated from it by a series of wooden pillars set on stone bases, supporting the roof, on which the crowd gathered. It may be conjectured that the spectators on the roof, pressing forward to gain a good vantage-point, had made the whole structure unstable. Samson must have been aware of the form of construction and of the possibilities in such a situation. The performance over, or temporarily halted, Samson was brought *between the pillars* (25b), just under the shelter of the roof, so that the dignitaries within the portico could have a closer look at him.

Samson's last solemn prayer (28) in which he uses three

different titles of God, *Adonai*, *Yahweh* and *Elohim*, was for strength that vengeance might be taken on his persecutors for the loss of his two eyes. A possible alternative reading of verse 28, *that I may be avenged upon the Philistines for one of my two eyes* (RSV), would be a jest that appears out of place in this context. The fact that Samson *took hold* (AV, RV; lit. *grasped*, RSV) of the two central pillars indicates that, exerting his strength, he pushed forward either directly towards or directly away from the open courtyard. Had he pushed sideways he would not have 'grasped' the pillars. Aided by the weight of the crowd above, who would be pressing forward since Samson was now out of their sight, the main supporting pillars were displaced, causing them to slide off their stone bases. When the roof collapsed many would be killed instantly; others would be crushed in the ensuing panic. The exact number of casualties is not stated, but they are stated to have been more than the number killed by Samson in his lifetime, which at a conservative estimate would be in the vicinity of eleven hundred (14:19; 15:8,15).

**16:31. Samson's burial.** The Philistines' hatred of Samson must have been mitigated by respect for his achievements and they made no apparent effort to abuse his corpse or to refuse him burial in his family tomb (*cf.* the dishonouring of Saul's body, 1 Sa. 31:9,10). The treatment of a body after death was a matter of importance in the ancient world (*cf.* Am. 2:1; Je. 8:1,2). It is apparent that Manoah was dead at this time, and since Samson appears to have been an only child, the references to his *brethren* and his father's *house* must be understood generally as his fellow-countrymen and tribal group. He was buried in the hill-country overlooking the vale of Sorek, the scene of some of his greatest exploits and most abject failures. His life, which promised so much, was blighted and ultimately destroyed by his sensual passions and lack of true separation to the Lord. But it had not been in vain, since it had drawn attention to the peril of complete Philistine domination which had crept so insidiously upon the western fringes of Israel. The final sentence reiterates the statement of 15:20.

## III. APPENDICES (17:1 – 21:25)

The contents of this final section of the book of the Judges differ in character from the rest of the book. There is no suggestion of foreign domination apart from the inference that the Danite migration (18) is connected with the Philistine oppression, and no judge appears on the scene. The editorial comment, oft repeated in the earlier sections, that the Israelites did that which was evil in the sight of the Lord, is missing, to be replaced by the observation that 'in those days there was no king in Israel, but every man did that which was right in his own eyes' (17:6; 18:1; 19:1; 21:25). Thus the disorders of the time are attributed not so much to a falling-away from the Lord but to the absence of a strong central authority, and there is an absence of the religiously-motivated comment of the earlier section. This does not necessarily prove that these chapters were added by a different hand after the completion of the first draft of the book.[1] The incidents narrated in the appendices make their own vivid contribution to the whole. The original editor may well have included them without comment, allowing them to speak for themselves (*cf.* the Samson narratives, which have a minimum of editorial comment). But whatever the view of the composition of the book it is agreed that the material in these closing chapters, whilst it makes unedifying reading, is of the utmost importance. We are made vividly aware of the low moral standards, of the debased religious conceptions and of the disordered social structure. The picture must not be overdrawn, however, for the tribal structure itself survived and we see the intertribal organization, the amphictyonic league, at work, albeit imperfectly, dealing with the disorderly situation concerning Benjamin. Even in the horror of a civil war there is the evidence of a compassionate spirit for decimated Benjamin on the part of the other tribes which shows that the sense of solidarity still remained.

---

[1] See Introduction, p. 25.

## a. Micah's household and the Danite migration (17:1 – 18:31)

The first of the two appendices deals with domestic and religious affairs in the household of Micah and with his involvement with the migrating Danites. It is highly probable that these events came after those recorded in the second appendix (chapters 19–21), but being generally connected with chapters 13–16 (the Samson narratives), inasmuch as both are connected with the Philistine pressure on the tribe of Dan, they have been set first. Frequently in the Old Testament it may be observed that connection of subject-matter takes precedence over chronological sequence.

**17:1–6. Micah and his mother.** The tribal portion of Ephraim lay in mainly hilly country, but *the hill country of Ephraim* (RV, RSV) appears to refer to that wider tract of country between Bethel and Esdraelon which included a portion of western Manasseh. No more positive location of the home of Micah can be given, except for the fact that it lay on the general route between the tribal portion of Dan and the town of Laish in the extreme north. *Micah*, whose name is the shortened form of Micahyahu ('who is like Yahweh?'), which occurs in the Hebrew text in verses 1 and 4, is introduced in an unfavourable light as a thief who stole a large amount from his own mother. For a possible explanation of the *eleven hundred pieces of silver* see the note on 16:5. Micah's confession of his guilt and his restoration of this small fortune was undoubtedly conditioned by the curse which his mother had placed on the thief, and the fact that this was uttered in his hearing may suggest that she was not without her suspicions. The power of a curse was considered to be very real in the ancient world; 'not a mere sound on the lips but an agent sent forth . . . an active agent for hurt.'[1] The curse could, however, be countermanded by the blessing of the one who had pronounced it and this is the purpose of the blessing uttered by Micah's mother; the restoration of the money led to the revoking of the malediction. The sincerity of the woman is questionable; when the money was

[1] J. A. Motyer, 'Curse', in *NBD*, p. 283.

stolen she affirmed that she *had dedicated it* (AV, RV mg.) to the Lord, but when it was returned she gave only one-fifth of the total amount for this purpose (*cf.* Acts 5:1,2). It may be that her motive was to enhance the heinousness of the theft and thus to increase the possibility of restoration! Money dedicated to the deity was taboo and dared not be used for any other purpose.

A lamentable ignorance of the provisions of Israelite worship is also revealed, for the making of any *graven image* was expressly forbidden (Ex. 20:4,23; Dt. 4:16). Israel's faith was to be an imageless faith; Israel's God was not to be honoured by being cast into the likeness of any earthly creature. The *graven image* was probably carved out of wood or stones, possibly overlaid with silver, but the *molten image* (the word derived from the verb 'to pour out') was made of solid silver. However, there are indications in the text that there was only one image, for the pronoun *it* (as in RV, RSV) should stand in place of *they* (AV) at the end of verse 4 and only one image is mentioned in 18:20,30, 31. Possibly the older designation *graven image* was used generically and then qualified by *molten image* to define the method of construction. It has been suggested that the image may have been in the form of a bull, which is found throughout a wide area of the ancient world as the representation of the deity. The gods were often depicted as standing, or more rarely sitting, on the back of a bull, which by its strength and power of fertility well represented the essence of the nature cults. Aaron had made a bull or calf image while Moses was in the holy mountain (Ex. 32:4) and, at a later date, Jeroboam ben-Nebat made similar images to set up at the shrines at Dan and Bethel (1 Ki. 12:28-30). Most scholars accept that these were not intended to represent Yahweh but rather to serve as the visible throne upon which the invisible Yahweh was conceived to sit. But the great danger of associating the worship of Yahweh with the bull, the symbol of the Canaanite fertility cults, will be apparent. If this image of Micah's was indeed of this type, he must have been ignorant or forgetful of the fate which overtook the Israelites after Aaron's act (Ex. 32:19-35).

Other instances of irregularity appear in this narrative.

Exodus 20:24 provided for the setting up of a sanctuary at the place of a theophany, but Micah makes his shrine at the place of his own convenience, in his own home (5). Here he housed his molten image, an *ephod* (see note on 8:27) and a *teraphim*. The *teraphim* (the word is plural in form but singular in meaning) are frequently associated with the home throughout the Old Testament period and were almost certainly household gods. Like the ephod they were associated with divination. It may be that originally, *i.e.* before the patriarchal period, they were the mummified heads of the family forefathers, to be replaced at a later date by pottery figurines. Whenever they are mentioned in the Old Testament they are invariably condemned, either directly or indirectly.

The final aberration of Micah was the consecration of his own son as *priest*. Before the separation of the whole tribe of Levi to the priestly offices (Nu. 3:5ff.) it is likely that the priestly duties were fulfilled by the first-born (Jewish rabbinic scholarship regards Ex. 24:5 in this light). The by-passing of the Levitical priesthood by Micah may be due either to a breakdown in the distribution of the Levites amongst the community or to an overlooking, wilful or ignorant, of the provisions of the Law. It is striking that, when a Levite did appear on the scene, he was immediately preferred. The expression *consecrated* (5, AV, RV) is literally 'filled the hand of', which is the standard expression for induction into the priestly office. The background of this unusual figure of speech is the filling of the hand of the officiating priest with portions of a sacrifice, particularly the wave-offering (Ex. 29:24, *etc.*). The editor did not condemn these malpractices; he simply contented himself with the observation that there was no king in Israel, every man pleased himself. But since 'to do what was right in one's own eyes' is tantamount to saying that a state of anarchy existed, the inference is that this led inevitably to an undesirable and disorderly situation.

**17:7-13. Micah and the Levite.** Micah's private, well-equipped shrine, attended by his own son, sufficed him until the arrival of a genuine *Levite*. The Levites, according to the

Mosaic legislation, were allocated forty-eight cities for their personal use (Nu. 35:1ff.; Jos. 21:1ff.). These cities were evenly distributed throughout the land to ensure maximum effectiveness, but it is apparent that the political and social disorders of the judges' period had caused this organization to lapse. Micah does not seem to have had access to the services of a Levite up to this point. The clause *and he sojourned there* (7) appears out of place, since the Levite had left Beth-lehem-judah and had not yet been invited to settle in Micah's home at Mount Ephraim. Since the words *sojourned there* have exactly the same consonants as the name of Gershom, one of the two sons of Moses, and as the Levite is named in 18:30 as 'Jonathan, the son of Gershom, the son of Moses', it may be that this was the original reference here (see note on 18:30). The suggestion is strengthened by the incidental nature of the reference in 18:30. The latter part of verse 7 may therefore have been 'and he was the son of Gershom', or 'and he was Jonathan the son of Gershom', which probably signifies a descendant of Gershom, not his actual son.

Hitherto this young man had been resident in *Beth-lehem-judah of the family of Judah.* There is no cause for confusion here and no need to resort to a theory of duplicate narratives, one stating that the man was a true Levite and the other that he was a Judaean. Often associated with this view is the suggestion that the term *Levite* indicates one who exercises a particular function, not necessarily a member of the tribe of Levi. Support for this view is often claimed by reference to Samuel, who was an Ephraimite by birth (1 Sa. 1:1) and yet is listed with the tribe of Levi (1 Ch. 6:16–34). The fact that Samuel was 'given to the Lord' and brought up in the priestly sanctuary at Shiloh, where he was trained as a priest, made him an exceptional character; hence his inclusion in the Levitical list. A simpler explanation is that Beth-lehem-judah was virtually a composite name, distinguishing it from other places of the same name in other areas, so the repetition of the name Judah is not significant beyond indicating where the Levite was domiciled.

It is not clear why the Levite had been displaced from Bethlehem. Possibly it was because the support upon which the Levites depended was not forthcoming. Micah, hearing of his situation, gave an invitation to him to stay and minister to him. The terms of settlement, 'board and lodging', a new set of garments and ten pieces of silver (approximately £2) each year make very interesting reading in the light of the present high standard of living and working-conditions, as well as giving some indication of the relative value of the amounts in 16:5 and 17:2.

The relationship between Micah and Jonathan, his Levite, is also significant; Jonathan was to be a *father and a priest* to Micah, but he became like one of Micah's *sons* (10, 11). Many minister-congregation relationships would be improved if the former was a father in the things of God to his flock and the latter showed fatherly concern in providing material things for their minister. So Micah 'filled the hand of' the young man (see note on 17:5) and, with a certain superstition, faced the future with assurance now that he had a properly-qualified man to handle religious affairs.

**18:1–6. Micah's Levite and the Danite spies.** We have already noted the predicament of the tribe of Dan (1:34,35 and the Samson narratives). The Danites were quite unable to occupy the territory allocated to them (Jos. 19:41–46) due to the opposition of the Amorites and then the pressure of the Philistines. Pressed up into the hill-country, they were confined to a very small area in the region of Zorah and Eshtaol, where the activities of Samson centred (13:2,25), in territory which, according to Joshua 15:33, was also on the border of Judah. Probably the difficulties in settlement made for a lack of precision in the intertribal boundaries. The reference to the 'camp of Dan' (13:25; 18:12) also hints at an unsettled situation. At last, in desperation, a considerable group of them (see note on 18:11) decided to seek a more congenial and secure situation. Joshua 19:47 gives a summary of this northward migration and was added to the details of the Danite territory after the event. The sending of the five spies to reconnoitre the land recalls the incidents of Numbers 13. On their way they came to Mount Ephraim and recognized the voice of the Levite (3). Possibly he had passed through their territory on his journeyings or, due to the close connection between the tribes of Dan and Judah, they may conceivably have known him when he was at Beth-lehem. Alternatively, their recognition may not have been personal but of his southern accent or of one fulfilling the duties of a Levite. Their barrage of questions having been met with satisfactory replies, they requested guidance on their own mission (5). Since the sanctuary of Micah was designed to give such help it was readily forthcoming after the Levite had consulted the oracle. His favourable reply was to have an important bearing upon subsequent events.

**18:7–10. The report of the Danite spies.** The northward journey of the Danites took them about 100 miles from their starting-point before they found a satisfactory location for their proposed new settlement. They were now clear of the region occupied by the Israelites and in a small but very fertile area populated by people of Phoenician or Aramean stock (a very slight amendment to the word *man*, at the end of verse 7, gives the reading 'Aram'). *Laish* or Leshem (Jos. 19:47), which appears as *Lus(i)* in Egyptian texts of *c.* 1850–1825 BC, has been identified as the modern Tell el-Qâdi. The size of the mound, about half a mile in diameter, which was the site of the ancient city, witnesses to its importance. Its natural connections were with the area to the south, for it was cut off from Aram (Syria) by the bulk of Mount Hermon and from Phoenicia by the Lebanon range. There was an assured water-supply from the springs and streams which supplied the Jordan waters. Of great importance, in view of the relatively small fighting force of the Danites (11), was the fact that the inhabitants of the land, secure in their isolation, had taken no precautions against a surprise attack. The unanimous and enthusiastic report of the spies when they returned to their brethren and the urgency with which they advocated action are in marked contrast to the doleful account of the ten companions of Joshua and Caleb (Nu. 13:27–29, 31–33).

**18:11-20. The despoliation of Micah's sanctuary.** *Six hundred* Danite warriors responded to the challenge and moved northwards with their families and possessions (21), forming a party of about two or three thousand. The relatively small numbers may indicate the decimation of the tribe resulting from years of hostile pressure. Alternatively, it may be that when the moment of decision came a majority were unwilling to leave their familiar surroundings. If this incident be dated before the events described in the Samson narratives, then it is obvious that only a portion of the tribe left the region of Zorah and Eshtaol, but this is not clearly indicated in the text. The question of verse 19 suggests that the major part of the tribe migrated and so Jonathan was able to be *a priest unto a tribe and a family in Israel.*

The short journey of the first day took them in a north-easterly direction to the west (*behind*, AV, RV) of *Kiriath-jearim,* no more than 8 or 9 miles from their starting-point. Kiriath-jearim was one of the four towns of the Gibeonite confederacy which entered by guile into an alliance with Joshua (Jos. 9:17). *Mahaneh-dan* ('the camp of Dan') is not to be confused with the place of the same name in 13:25, since the latter was between Zorah and Eshtaol. The next day brought them to the vicinity of the house of Micah at Mount Ephraim. The repetition of certain expressions, such as *an ephod, and teraphim, and a graven image, and a molten image* (14, 17, 18, 20), and *the six hundred men appointed with their weapons of war* (16, 17) has suggested to some scholars a combination of narratives. A more plausible explanation is that an oral stage of the tradition is reflected, with a deliberate repetition on the part of the narrator, for the sake of effect. It is clear that he took a somewhat heartless delight in this brazen theft of the treasures of Micah's shrine, with 600 stalwarts standing by to intimidate the lawful owner.

The words at the end of the comment by the five spies (14) was a thinly-veiled suggestion, and a minor deviation brought the whole company to Micah's home. Here the five spies, no doubt influenced by the apparent success of their appeal to the oracle on their earlier visit, advanced and renewed their acquaintance with the Levite, while the 600 warriors took up a threatening station at the gate. *The gate* (16) is always used of the entrance to a village or city, never of the door of a house. But since no name is given to this particular place (Mount Ephraim gives only a vague idea of its whereabouts), and since only a few men were enlisted from the surrounding homes (22), it appears that it was little more than a cluster of dwellings around the home of Micah.

It is not clear whether the five spies, or a group from the main body, purloined the essential articles from the sanctuary. The feeble remonstrances of the Levite were soon silenced by the prospect of promotion, from being a spiritual counsellor for a small company to exercising the same function for a whole tribe. The complete lack of loyalty to Micah, overlooking the latter's kindness, and the mercenary attitude of the Levite reflect discreditably on him and on the standards of the age. The flock of God in all ages has been bedevilled by false shepherds who seek only their own self-interest and advancement. With gladness of heart the Levite connived at this act of armed robbery and went with his new masters, taking with him all the cultic trappings of the shrine of his original benefactor.

**18:21–26. Micah's abortive intervention.** The Danites, realizing that they could expect trouble, took the precaution of interposing their armed men between their dependants, cattle and baggage and any pursuing force, a device which would also indicate that they were not to be trifled with. Micah's more mobile force soon overtook them and from this point on the Danites blustered and threatened their way through, trampling over justice in the consciousness of their superior might. They knew full well why they were being pursued, but when this was made plain to them in tones of understandable indignation they threatened Micah and his men with force if he continued to disturb the peace. The expression *angry fellows* (25), lit. 'men bitter of soul', indicates men easily aroused and capable of fierce action (*cf.*2 Sa. 17:8 where the same phrase is translated 'chafed in their minds').

Enraged but helpless in the presence of such an aggressive attitude, Micah had no alternative but to return home empty-handed. The gods which he had made (24) were completely unable to avert this catastrophe (*cf.* Is. 44:9-20; 46:6,7). The incident is a sad commentary on the disturbed state of the land at this time, with no strong, centralized authority to ensure that justice was ultimately done. The revealing comment of 18:1 shows the editor's diagnosis of the situation.

**18:27-31. The capture of Laish.** The quiet security of the peaceable inhabitants of Laish was no protection against the weapons of the determined Danites and they were soon annihilated. Their isolation, in which they trusted, left them helpless, for there was no possibility of securing help from either Zidon or Aram (see note on verse 7). From the fire-stricken ruins there arose the city of Dan, named in honour of the tribal ancestor. Its location was *in the valley that lieth by Beth-rehob* (lit. 'house of the open place'), which may be the Rehob of Numbers 13:21, the most northerly city observed by the twelve spies. There the Danites set up a sanctuary and installed Jonathan as their priest. The AV follows an emendation introduced into the Hebrew text by reading *the son of Manasseh* (30). The consonants (*mšh*) are those of the name of *Moses* the father of Gershom (Ex. 2:21,22, *etc.*), but a supra-linear *n* has been introduced between the first two to give the consonants of Manasseh. It is universally agreed that the reference was originally to Moses. The reason for the amend-ment may have been to safeguard the reputation of this great leader by excluding him from the pedigree of this time-serving and idolatrous Levite. The alteration to Manasseh may have been designed to suggest a correspondence of character between the Levite and the most wicked of Judah's kings (2 Ki. 21), a device which would bring discredit upon the Danite priesthood instituted by Jonathan. Dan was one of the two sanctuaries set up by Jeroboam I at the time of the dis-ruption in order to counteract the centripetal influence of Jerusalem (1 Ki. 12:26-30). The golden calf or bull he set up may have been modelled after the molten image of Micah.

Dan and Bethel, the cult-centres of Jeroboam's debased priest-hood, were especially obnoxious to the priests of Judah.

**30.** *Until the day of the captivity of the land* is usually taken as a reference to the defeat of Israel and the deportation of many of its inhabitants by Tiglath-pileser III of Assyria in 733–732 BC, or to the final reduction of the land and the deportation under Sargon in 722–721 BC (2 Ki. 15:29; 17:6). In this case the historical reference could have been added by a later editor. But the reference to the house of God at *Shiloh* (31) suggests a link with an earlier period connected with the Philistines. This occasion could have been either after the twin defeat at Aphek (1 Sa. 4:1–11) or, more probably, after the death of Saul, when David reigned over Judah from Hebron, Ish-baal reigned over a truncated Israel from Mahanaim in Transjordania and the Philistines, presumably, controlled all the other areas including Dan (2 Sa. 2:8–11). It is inconceivable that David would have left untouched this idolatrous religious sanctuary at Dan, which suggests that it no longer functioned during his reign over the united kingdom. There is no record of the destruction of Shiloh in the historical books, but the event itself is noted in Jeremiah 7:12,14; 26:6; and Psalm 78:60. Archaeological evidence shows clearly that the temple there was destroyed about 1050 BC, which must have been immediately after the events of 1 Samuel 4.

It is frequently stated that these chapters were intended to justify the establishment of the northern sanctuary of Dan by pointing to its association with a descendant of Moses and its history going back as far as the shrine at Shiloh. The details of the narrative make this unlikely, however, for neither the Levite nor the Danites come out at all creditably. It is far easier to assume that the editor had no religious axe to grind, but incorporated these incidents to illustrate his main thesis, namely the disorder and irregularity of the political and religious life of Israel during the period.

## b. The outrage at Gibeah and the punishment of the Benjamites (19:1 – 21:25)

**19:1–9. The Levite and his concubine.** The reference to

time in the opening verse is quite indecisive and bears no necessary connection with the preceding chapters; indeed, it has already been observed that the incidents narrated in chapters 19–21 were earlier than those of chapters 17, 18.[1] Phinehas, the grandson of Aaron, is mentioned (20:28) and the amphictyonic league is still functioning and able to take combined action, as in the incident described in Joshua 22:9–34. There is no mention of Philistine domination which would have made impossible such concerted action on the part of all the tribes during the latter part of the judges' period. Bethel appears as the major sanctuary, not Shiloh, as in the Philistine period. The reference *from Dan to Beer-sheba* (20:1), which became a proverbial expression for the whole land, was probably added by a later narrator or editor and does not demand a date after the establishment of Dan (18:29).

The Levite of the story, like Micah (17:1), had his home in *the remote parts of the hill country of Ephraim* (RSV). As the main line of communication ran north and south along the centre of the hill-country it is probable that the eastern or western flank of the hill-country is indicated, but the references to place-names, Jerusalem, Gibeah and Ramah, do not point conclusively to either. A further connection existing between the two appendices is shown in the reference to *Beth-lehem-judah* (*cf.* 17:7), where the Levite's concubine returned to her family. The reason for her return given in many ancient versions, 'because she was angry with him' (followed by RSV), is more plausible than that supplied in the AV and RV that she *played the whore against him*. The penalty against the adulteress was death (Lv. 20:10), but a heated argument would allow the Levite to seek a reconciliation when the passions of temper had subsided. The expression *to speak kindly to her* (3, RV, RSV) is in Hebrew 'to speak to her heart', a frequently used and most suggestive idiom. One of the asses would be for her use on the return journey. The attitude of the concubine's father suggests that nothing serious was involved, and since the disgrace of his daughter's separation from her husband would fall upon him, his joy at seeing the Levite, and the

[1] See p. 183.

festivities that followed, is understandable. The leisureliness of the East, particularly in connection with festive occasions (*cf.* Gn 24:55) showed itself in the hospitality pressed upon the Levite, whose attempt to return on the fourth day was completely thwarted. Similar endeavours, reflecting the social etiquette of the period, were almost successful in retaining the party for another complete day. The language of this hospitable man of Beth-lehem (9) is most picturesque and contains several allusions to the years spent in the semi-nomadic wanderings of the wilderness period. *The day draws to its close* (RSV) is lit. 'the encamping of the day', *i.e.* the time to pitch camp for the night, and the word translated *home* is actually 'tent'. Such expressions survive long after changing circumstances have made them out of date. On this occasion, however, the will of the Levite was asserted and he made his departure somewhere about the middle of the afternoon (see note on verse 14). As events turned out, he would have done better to have asserted himself earlier in the day, or else to have yielded to his host's importunities to stay yet another night.

**19:10–15. From Beth-lehem-judah to Gibeah.** It can be imagined that the Levite would make good speed in an endeavour to make up for the late start. *Jerusalem* (see note on 1:8) lay about 6 miles north of Beth-lehem, a journey which would take under two hours. It was occupied by the Jebusites (hence the alternative name of the city, *Jebus*), who were probably of Amorite stock, until it was captured by David and his men (2 Sa. 5:6–9). The Levite's attendant, apprehensive of the approach of night and the peril of attack by wild beasts or armed bands, urged his master to sojourn there, but his suggestion was refused. The basis of this refusal, that it was preferable to seek shelter in a city of Israel rather than among strangers, shows the subsequent conduct of the men of Gibeah in a more reprehensible light. *Gibeah*, the modern Tell el-Fûl, was about 4 miles north of Jerusalem, *i.e.* no more than 10 miles from Beth-lehem, and as the sun set when they were there their time of departure cannot have been much earlier than 3 p.m. *Ramah*, mentioned as an alternative resting-place, was 2 miles further north than Gibeah. The setting of the sun would leave no alternative but to seek accommodation in the nearest city, and this happened to be Gibeah, a city which was founded about the time of the Israelite invasion. This first city was destroyed by fire in the middle part of the twelfth century BC, an event which almost certainly connects with the events of 20:37ff. A break in occupation of almost a century followed this destruction, and the second city became famous as the birth-place and subsequent capital of Saul (1 Sa. 10:26; 11:4; *cf.* the numerous references in 1 Sa. 13–15). The Levite and his party sat down in the open place of the city, probably just inside the gate, which served as the meeting-place for social, business and judicial purposes, waiting for the expected hospitality which was not forthcoming. This failure to offer hospitality, a sacred duty in the East, was downright boorish on the part of the Benjamites, for the two laden asses gave the assurance that no great liability would be incurred (*cf.* verse 19). Such a breach of etiquette was an indictment of the men of Gibeah and an ominous warning of what was to come. Once more we must admire the consummate skill of the narrator, whose delicate hints build up the atmosphere and add point to the crime of the inhabitants of this Benjamite city.

**19:16–21. The gracious hospitality of a stranger in Gibeah.** The inference is that the Levite and his party would have waited in vain but for the arrival of an old man, who was himself a native of Mount Ephraim and a stranger in the city. His question elicited the facts which are already known to the reader, with one puzzling exception, the reference to the journey *to the house of the Lord* (18, AV, RV). It may be that this was a part of the Levite's purpose, perhaps to offer a sacrifice of thanksgiving for the reconciliation with his concubine, although this had not been suggested up to this point. Or it may have been a stratagem on his part, since if it were known that his journey was for a religious purpose hospitality might be the more readily forthcoming. A third alternative, based on the LXX, which is accepted by most scholars, is that 'my house' (*cf.* RSV, *my home*) should be read, the first person singular pronominal suffix indicating possession (the letter *yôdh*) having been wrongly regarded as an abbreviation of Yahweh. The Levite was careful to point out that no obligation need be incurred in offering hospitality to a party of three, with two laden asses, since they were self-sufficient, an innuendo which was graciously and hospitably set aside by the old man, now become their host. His first and greatest concern was that shelter should be extended to them, as was demanded by the canons of eastern etiquette. No item was overlooked: the beasts were attended to, the travel stains of his guests were washed away and there was an ample provision for their physical needs. The fears which attended their journey must have been quite relieved by this hospitality and the storm which followed comes as a greater shock, precisely as the narrator intended.

**19:22–28. The bestiality of the men of Gibeah.** The festivity inside was abruptly disturbed when the house was surrounded by the men of Gibeah, described as *sons of Belial* (AV, RV). The word is a compound form (*bᵉlîyaʿal*) of obscure derivation, although the general meaning is plain. The usual interpretation links it with the Hebrew *yāʿal* (meaning 'to profit' or 'help'), so giving the meaning 'worthlessness'. Alternatively some have connected it with the Babylonian goddess of vegetation, who was possibly also the goddess of the underworld, which makes it synonymous with the Abyss or Sheol, the place of no return. This view is strengthened by a consideration of Psalm 18: 4,5 where Belial ('ungodly men', AV; 'ungodliness', RV) corresponds to death and Sheol in the parallelism of the verses. A third and less likely view links it with the verb *ʿālâ* ('to come up'), giving a sense of 'ne'er-do-well' or, in modern parlance, 'layabout'. Not only their words but their actions also must have been frightening, for the word *beat* (22) is a *hithpaʿel* form having intensive force. G. R. Driver observes, 'The ruffians were dashing themselves against, hurling themselves on the door in an attempt to break it down and gain an entrance'.[1] As no attempt was made subsequently by the rulers of Gibeah to punish the offenders, or to repudiate

[1] Driver, p. 19.

their vicious actions, it appears that the men of the city generally were involved, and not just a lewd minority. It may be that their motive was, in part, a sense of offended pride that a sojourner in their city should put them to shame by proffering the hospitality which they had withheld. Their request to the old man (22) revealed the extent of their sexual perversion, whilst his answer to them (23, 24) showed his immediate and horrified recoil at such conduct which would shatter all the conventions of hospitality (*cf.* the treacherous action of Jael, 4:17–21). In one of the Ugaritic texts reference is made to the ideal son 'who may drive away any who would molest his (*i.e.* the father's) night-guest.'[1] The word *folly* (AV, RV) is inadequate to convey the meaning of *nᵉbālâh*, which indicates an insensibility to the claims of God or man, and is best rendered 'impiety', 'churlishness' (*cf.* Nabal, 1 Sa. 25:25) or 'wantonness'. There are many parallels between this grisly incident and the one recorded in Genesis 19:1ff.,[2] but at Gibeah there were no angels to thwart the evil intentions of the men of the city.

In his concern for the accepted conventions of hospitality the old man was willing to shatter a code which, to the modern reader, appears of infinitely more importance, namely, the care and protection of the weak and helpless. Womanhood was but lightly esteemed in the ancient world; indeed it is largely due to the precepts of the Jewish faith, and particularly the enlightenment which has come through the Christian faith, that women enjoy their present position. The old man was willing to sacrifice his own virgin daughter and the Levite's concubine to the distorted lusts of the besiegers, rather than allow any harm to befall his principal guest. His suggestion, however, fell on deaf ears, so the Levite himself, with a callous disregard for the one he professed to love, or, perhaps more pertinently, with a greater concern for his own skin, took his concubine by force and thrust her out to the men. The narrator does not dwell on the harrowing details, but if ever a human being endured a night of utter horror it was the

[1] *DOTT*, p. 124.
[2] See F. D. Kidner, *Genesis* (Tyndale Press, 1967), pp. 133–137.

Levite's concubine on that night, which must have seemed as interminable as eternity and as dark as the pit itself. It is not only the action of the men of Gibeah which reveals the abysmally low moral standards of the age; the indifference of the Levite, who prepared to depart in the morning without any apparent concern to ascertain the fate of his concubine, and his curt, unfeeling command when he saw her lying on the threshhold (27, 28), these show that, in spite of his religion, he was devoid of the finer emotions. The sense of outrage does not appear to have influenced him until he realized that she was dead, when he lifted her body on to one of his asses and continued his journey. The whole shocking incident made an indelible impression upon Israel, and was referred to by the prophet Hosea as one of the greatest examples of corruption (Ho. 9:9; 10:9).

**19:29, 30. The summons to the nation.** The action of the Levite had an almost sacramental significance, perhaps suggesting the unity of those who responded with the sacrificial significance of the life that had been taken. Originally it may have had magical associations, involving the curse of blood on those who failed to respond. The action is paralleled and illuminated by Saul's method of rallying the nation to his side in support of the men of Jabesh-gilead; only in this case a yoke of oxen were dismembered (1 Sa. 11:1–8). The verb 'to divide' is used of ritual dissection (Ex. 29:17; Lv. 1:6,12; 8:20) and the number of the pieces corresponds to the twelve tribes, which suggests a period before the isolation of Judah and Simeon in the south.

It is assumed that the tribe of Benjamin was included in the summons but they withheld their support, thus automatically identifying themselves with the men of Gibeah; hence the parenthetical reference in 20:3. The messengers who bore these grisly tokens to the various tribes were no doubt commissioned to tell the story of the outrage of the men of Gibeah and verse 30, especially the latter part, comes more naturally from their lips, although their words would be echoed in shocked tones by those addressed. This foul deed was considered to be the outstanding atrocity since the time of the Exodus, the decisive event which was the foundation of the nation.

**20:1-7. The Levite reports to the assembly.** The summons met an immediate response from the tribes, which points, with other factors, to a very early point in the period of the judges, when the intertribal organization was still functioning normally, before the onset of the periods of foreign domination. The reference *from Dan to Beer-sheba* does not exclude a date before the capture of Laish by the Danites (18:29); it was probably included by the editor, by which time it had become a proverbial expression for the whole land. At this early period Bethel was the central sanctuary (20:18, 26,27) but the assembly point of the tribes was *Mizpah*, which was itself an ancient shrine (1 Sa. 7:5,6,16; 10:17). Two main identifications have been made for this city: the first, Tell en-Nasbeh which is about 8 miles north of Jerusalem and a few miles south of Bethel; the second, Nebi Samwil, about 5 miles north-west of Jerusalem. The former has the stronger support. The conjunction of Bethel and Mizpah does not indicate a composite account: Mizpah, being nearer to Gibeah, was chosen as the centre of the confederate army, and the ark may conceivably have been moved there in this emergency, but the main sanctuary at Bethel was within easy reach.

The very large number of the Israelite force, *four hundred thousand* (2), has caused difficulty, for in the full-scale assault on Jericho only forty thousand were involved and the same figure is given as the fighting force of Israel in the time of Deborah (5:8). The word which is translated *thousand* (*'eleþ*) is also used to refer to clan or family units (as in Jdg. 6:15; 1 Sa. 10:19; Mi. 5:2) and possibly to denote the officers over the military divisions.[1] It is not a question of gross inflation of the numbers for reasons of prestige, nor of inaccuracy in the figures themselves; it is a question of interpretation, and most scholars would admit that no really satisfactory key to the understanding of the large numbers of the Old Testament has yet been

[1] *Cf.* R. E. D. Clark, 'The Large Numbers of the Old Testament', in *Journal of the Transactions of the Victoria Institute*, LXXXVII, 1955, pp. 82–92.

found.[1] The Levite's report to the assembled tribes (4–7) corresponds with the actual event with the single addition that the men of Gibeah purposed his death (5). However, in the light of the fate of his concubine, it was a reasonable inference that the men of the city intended more than their foul suggestion of 19:22.

**20:8–11. The resolution of the assembly.** The minds of the Israelites were doubtless made up before they assembled together, but, none the less, this formal affirmation of their unity and strength of purpose is striking. The parallelism of *tent* and *house* (8) is reminiscent of the wilderness period, and an indication that Israel was not far removed from the stage of transition in its settlement in the land. The absence of the men of Benjamin from the assembly was an obvious indication that they could expect no easy or speedy success and they wisely laid their plans to allow for a protracted campaign, with an adequate supply-organization. The expression of unity here is in marked contrast to the disintegration and lack of co-operation which was manifested later in the period of the judges. *Folly* (10, AV, RV; *cf.* verse 6, and see note on 19:23) is altogether inadequate to convey the strength of the Hebrew; 'wantonness' (*cf.* RSV, *wanton crime*) or 'impiety' is to be preferred. Martin Noth regards the phrase 'folly wrought in Israel' as a technical term signifying a violation of the divine law then in force in the tribal society, which was especially strict in sexual matters, in direct and intentional contrast to Canaanite practices (*cf.* Gn. 34:7; Dt. 22:21; Jos. 7:15; 2 Sa. 13:12).[2]

**20:12–17. The approach to the tribe of Benjamin.** Before the commencement of the punitive expedition the delegates of the amphictyony made a formal request to the tribe of Benjamin that the offenders be delivered up for

---

[1] R. A. H. Gunner, in his article 'Number', in *NBD*, pp. 895–898, discusses fully the issues involved. See also J. W. Wenham, 'The Large Numbers of the Old Testament', in *Tyndale Bulletin*, 18, 1967, pp. 24ff.

[2] Noth, p. 105.

execution. The expression *put away evil from Israel* (13) is
reminiscent of Deuteronomy 17:12. Unless sin was dealt with
thoroughly, evil consequences could be anticipated (*cf.* Jos. 7;
2 Sa. 21:1–14). The appeal was unheeded; instead, the men of
Benjamin mobilized their own forces to fight on behalf of
these evil men against their own *brethren the children of Israel* (13).
The precise number of the Benjamites is not clear: verse 15
mentions 26,700; verse 35 records 25,100 casualties; verses
44–47 note 25,000 casualties and 600 survivors. The differences
may be accounted for by the unrecorded casualties of the first
two days, although the divergency in the numbers given for
verse 15 in different recensions of the LXX (Vaticanus reads
23,000; Alexandrinus 25,000) warns against an easy solution
of the problem. However, laying aside the difficulty which is
found in interpreting the numbers of the Old Testament, the
general picture is clear. We have the combined resources of
eleven tribes massed against the total available manpower of
Benjamin. It has been suggested that *seven hundred chosen men*
(15) has been repeated in verse 16 by dittography, in which
case this élite group can be identified with the men of Gibeah,
who, like Ehud (see note on 3:15), were *left-handed*. The prowess
of the men of Benjamin is hinted at in the Blessing of Jacob
(Gn. 49:27) and attested in the cases of Ehud and Saul, as
well as in the more general references in 1 Chronicles 8:40;
12:2. The *sling*, which was employed with a left-handed motion,
must not be confused with a modern schoolboy's catapult; it
was a formidable weapon of war used in the Assyrian, Egyptian
and Babylonian armies as well as in Israel. David's encounter
with the Philistine, Goliath, is a telling example of the power
and accuracy of this weapon (1 Sa. 17:49). It has been estimated that stones weighing up to one pound could be projected with uncanny accuracy at speeds up to 90 m.p.h.!

**20:18–23. The first encounter.** The hilly terrain in the
vicinity of Gibeah favoured a defensive force rather than an
attacking force, especially if the former was in a strong position,
as was likely in this case, since the Benjamites were familiar
with their own tribal portion. In such a situation superior

numbers were of limited value, since they could not be effectively deployed, and a determined group of men armed with slings could inflict heavy casualties on an attacking force. A realization of the danger confronting the vanguard of the army probably lay behind the request which was made to the divine oracle, and the choice of the tribe of *Judah* for this invidious task rested on the fact that Judah was a tribe renowned for its fighting qualities, whose territory was similar to that of Benjamin. *Beth-el* (RV, RSV) should be read in place of *the house of God* (AV), for where the latter is indicated the word *Elohim* is invariably used, not the shorter *El*. Beth-el was within 5 miles of Mizpah and while the ark of the covenant may have accompanied the army the oracle possibly remained in the sanctuary. In the battle which ensued the psychological advantage lay with the Benjamites. They would fight desperately because they were fighting for their lives, whereas the opposing force, while convinced of the rightness of their cause, may have had little heart to engage in a civil war. The Benjamites inflicted heavy casualties upon the confederate army, who were forced to withdraw. The logical place of verse 23 is before verse 22, as the context makes clear. Since the Israelites had time to wait on the Lord for further guidance, and still assemble themselves and give battle on the second day, the inference is that their first attack and shattering defeat took place in a relatively short period early in the first day.

**20:24-28. The second encounter.** Having confirmed their purpose by a second consultation of the oracle, it must have been a devastating experience for the Israelites to suffer a second, humiliating defeat at the hands of the Benjamites. The success of the latter issued in a self-confidence which preceded defeat, but the failure of the former sent them back to the Lord in deep humility. To the tears of the day before (23) were now added the discipline of fasting and the offering of sacrifices (26), all of which suggest the sense of urgency with which they now sought the Lord. It may be that their vastly superior numbers had made their earlier approaches to Him somewhat perfunctory, with fatal results. The two classes of sacrifice, *burnt* *offerings* and *peace offerings*, showed both their repentance and their desire for reconciliation which would restore their communion with God (*cf.* Lv. 1:4; 7:16). Only after these tokens of their evident sincerity was the oracle consulted, and on this third occasion the command to go up was accompanied by an assurance of victory.

Some scholars have suggested that the reference to the pedigree of *Phinehas* (28) may be a gloss added in error by a scribe who was unaware that there was another officiating priest of the same name at a later date. However, such an excision is not really necessary. We have observed at many points that the evidence consistently points to an early date for these narratives and this view is strengthened by the fact that Beth-el was the central sanctuary at this time. In the post-Mosaic period the central shrine was first of all, and probably for a very limited period, at Shechem (Jos. 8:30–35; 24), then at Shiloh itself for an equally short period (Jos. 18:1; 22:12; see note on Jdg. 21:10–12), next at Beth-el and finally at Shiloh again, where a more permanent structure was established (1 Sa. 1:9; 3:15). Judges 21:12 appears conclusive evidence that Shiloh was not the amphictyonic shrine at this time, for the focal point of the tribal association would hardly be described as 'Shiloh, which is in the land of Canaan'. Phinehas was one of Israel's truly great and devoted men. As a young man his resolute action had saved the situation at Shittim, an action which won him a unique commendation from the Lord (Nu. 25:1–15). He had taken a prominent part in the campaign against Midian (Nu. 31:6) and an equally prominent part when the tribes east of Jordan were suspected of disunity and apostasy in the erection of their memorial altar (Jos. 22:9–34). The name itself is, like that of Moses, of Egyptian origin and means 'the Nubian' or 'the child of dark complexion'. Such names would hardly be invented by Israelites of a later age, which verifies the actual existence of these two central characters. The *ark of the covenant* (27) is not mentioned elsewhere in the book of Judges.

**20: 29–36. The third encounter.** Although they were

assured of success, the Israelites were not careless in their method of deployment. On earlier occasions a direct frontal assault had been decisively repulsed; now their strategy was to lure the over-confident Benjamites out of their secure position, destroy the city by a force left in ambush and then trap their enemy, demoralized by the severing of their escape route, in a pincers movement. A similar ruse, adopted with conspicuous success by Joshua at Ai (Jos. 8:3-28), may have provided the inspiration on this occasion. The historian has not set out the facts of the campaign as orderly as the modern reader, conditioned by his concept of history, would desire, but the main facts are clear. The slight, initial success of the Benjamites aroused expectations of a victory as decisive as on the previous days, a state of mind which the Israelite force fostered by its feigned retreat. The movement of the battle along the roads between Beth-el and Gibeah and in the surrounding countryside is clearly indicated, although the mention of two *highways*, as distinct from one inter-connecting road, may show that Gibeon, north-west of Gibeah, should be read instead of *Gibeah* (31).

Meanwhile the Israelite force in ambush seized its opportunity to attack the virtually defenceless city of Gibeah. They numbered *ten thousand* men (34), a fraction of the entire army, for the suspicions of the Benjamites would be aroused if they were confronted with a greatly depleted main force. The location of *Baal-tamar* (33) is uncertain and the reference to *the meadows of Gibeah* (AV) is not clear, since open meadows would hardly conceal such a large force. A change of one consonant gives the reading preserved in the LXX, *west of Gebah* (*cf.* RSV), which seems preferable. Geba was a few miles north-east of Gibeah. The fury with which the men in ambush made their onslaught is concealed in the AV, *came forth* (33). The verb means 'to break forth' and is used of water gushing forth, or of a child bursting out of the womb. The direction of the attack was probably from the east. (The Hebrew *neḡeḏ* corresponds to *lip̄nê*, 'before', with the sense of 'eastward of'.) The historian could not resist interrupting his account of the ambush by glancing at the fortunes of the main contestants

Diagrammatic sketch of the third encounter between the Benjamite and Israelite forces
(Judges 20:29-48)

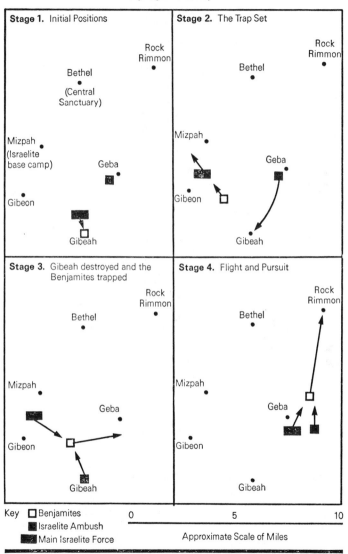

(34b): the battle was fierce, but the Benjamites were unaware of the events already in motion which were to seal their doom. His thought was then drawn to note the extent of the impending disaster and the fearful casualties inflicted on the Benjamites (35) and then, somewhat illogically, he noted their reaction, at a point before the final slaughter, when they saw that they had been duped.

**20:37-44. The defeat of Benjamin.** The account now focuses on the part played by the small force of valiant warriors entrusted with the task of destroying Gibeah. Entrance into the city appears to have been easily effected, since the main Benjamite army had been drawn away in the opposite direction, on which side the attention of the remaining defenders would also be centred. The pre-arranged *signal* (38, RSV) for the springing of the trap was also the sign that the force in ambush had completed its task, the firing of the city itself. The word for *sign* (AV, RV) is found in Jeremiah 6:1 with the meaning of fire-beacon, and the same graphic signal is also mentioned in the Lachish ostraca (iv. 10) at the time of the Babylonian devastation of Judah.[1] When the smoke of the doomed city was seen by the main Israelite force they turned back (AV *retired* gives quite the wrong sense) and the Benjamite force, flushed with the thought of their initial success, also observed the sign that caused their self-confidence to evaporate in a moment, to be replaced by abject fear and precipitate flight.

There are certain topographical references which are not clear, but those which are identifiable enable us to make a reasonable reconstruction of the whole campaign from the beginning. The main Israelite force had approached and then withdrawn towards the north-west, *i.e.* towards Gibeon, drawing the defenders away in this direction. The smaller Israelite force had been in ambush in the vicinity of Geba, north-east of Gibeah, and they attacked the condemned city from the east. The fleeing Benjamites headed in an easterly direction, *unto the way of the wilderness* (42) away from the main

[1] *DOTT*, p. 216.

Israelite force which was westward of them. The fact that the Israelites *inclosed the Benjamites round about* (43, AV, RV) suggests that *cities* (42) should be singular, as in many Greek manuscripts. In this case the reference is to the Israelites, who, having destroyed Gibeah, now emerged from the burning city to cut off the escape route of the Benjamites. In this pincers movement 18,000 Benjamites perished, but the survivors broke out of the trap and continued their flight. The reference to *Gibeah toward the sunrising* (*i.e.* eastwards, 43, AV, RV) is not impossible, but as it is unlikely that the Benjamites would flee directly towards the doomed city, and as their ultimate destination was *the rock of Rimmon*, which was 6 miles north-north-east of Geba, it is likely that Geba should be read instead of Gibeah. Thus the general line of retreat was in a north-easterly direction.

Two references in this section are quite obscure. In verse 43 *with ease over against* (AV) is, in Hebrew, '(at their) resting-place' (*cf.* RV, RSV mg.). It may be that the Benjamites, imagining that they had eluded their pursuers, had made a temporary halt eastward of Geba, only to be caught up by the Israelites. Alternatively, 'resting-place' could be read as a proper name, *Nohah* (*cf.* RSV), which appears in 1 Chronicles 8:2 as the name of the fourth son of Benjamin, and thus may have been the name of a city. But such a site has not been identified. A further possibility is that it should be translated 'without respite', which fits admirably into the context.[1] The second problem relates to *Gidom* (45), which is quite unknown apart from this reference. Possibly it was in the vicinity of the rock of Rimmon, but it has been conjectured that it should be read as Geba, and that this city marked the area where the pursuit was terminated. In the final stages of the pursuit 5,000 Benjamites were cut off in the highways and a further 2,000, accepting the conjectural explanation offered above, perished when the Israelites again surprised the Benjamites at their temporary bivouac east of Geba. The Israelites apparently made no attempt to pursue the surviving 600 Benjamites, who made good their escape to *the rock of Rimmon*, which is identified

[1] Driver, p. 20.

with the modern Rummūn, a village on the summit of a conical chalky hill about 4 miles east of Beth-el. Instead, the Israelites turned in judgment upon the other Benjamite cities, which by their intervention on behalf of the men of Gibeah had become associated in its guilt. As all the able-bodied men of Benjamin were doubtless involved in the earlier battles, this would be no difficult task, but rather a slaughter of the helpless, if not, by Israelite standards, the innocent. The justification for this action may be found in Deuteronomy 13:12-18, where the crime specified is that of idolatry, but the evidence of Judges 21 shows that either the Israelites bitterly regretted their revengeful action, or that they performed their punitive duties with little heart.

**21:1-9. The grief of the Israelites.** When the heat of the battle was over and the memory of the shameful events of the first two days had been set in a healthier perspective by the ultimate victory, the Israelites had occasion to reflect and to repent. Their action had been necessitated by the outrage of the men of Gibeah, and the war was, in a sense, a holy war. But it had brought in its wake a sense of shattered brotherhood and a realization that, in the heat of the crisis, some of their vows had been extreme. It is obvious that, at this stage, a keen sense of unity prevailed, which was not always in evidence in later generations. In particular they regretted their solemn vow not to allow any intermarriage between their daughters and the men of Benjamin, since this meant that a tribe of Israel must inevitably perish. It was a tragedy when a family in Israel was in danger of extinction, hence the device of levirate marriage. But the tragedy was greater when a whole tribe was involved. However, a vow once made, even if it was rash and ill-considered, could not be revoked; so the people mourned before God at His sanctuary in Bethel (*cf.* 20:18,26). Their action in building an altar on which to offer sacrifices appears strange, since there was an altar at Bethel where sacrifices had already been offered (20:26). The most likely explanation is that the location of the altar was at *Mizpah*, which was, as we have noted (20:1), the base-camp of the assembled tribes (*cf.* the reference to *the camp*, 8). There is strong evidence that altars were not erected indiscriminately in Israel. They were normally erected in places where a theophany had occurred but they were built at other places in a time of national peril or rejoicing, often before or after a battle (*cf.* 1 Sa. 7:9; 13:8ff.; 14:35). This occasion, being in the nature of an emergency, merited such an exceptional procedure.

At about this time the remembrance of another great vow suggested a possible way out of their dilemma, for the summons to the tribes to assemble and deal with the situation in Gibeah was of such a solemn nature that any group not responding came under the curse of destruction. A quick survey showed that there were no participants from the city of *Jabesh-gilead*, 9 miles south-east of Beth-shean and about 2 miles east of the Jordan. The Gileadites were descended from Manasseh, the grandson of Rachel, and thus there was a blood-tie with the descendants of Benjamin, Rachel's son. In the subsequent history there was a very close link between the tribe of Benjamin and the men of Jabesh-gilead. When the latter were threatened by the Ammonites they turned for succour to Saul the *Benjamite* (1 Sa. 11:1ff.); and it was the men of Jabesh-gilead who recovered the bodies of Saul and his sons from their ignominious position on the wall of Beth-shan (1 Sa. 31:11-13; *cf.* 2 Sa. 2:4-7). But this close link may have been the result of this incident, *i.e.* the extensive intermarriage between the Benjamites and the maidens of Jabesh-gilead, rather than the cause of the non-intervention of the men of Jabesh-gilead against the inhabitants of Gibeah.

**21:10-12. Wives for the surviving Benjamites.** A considerable force was then despatched to Jabesh-gilead in a plan to fulfil one vow and to circumvent another. The inhabitants of the city were to be destroyed for failing to honour their obligations within the covenant community, but the *virgins* were to be spared and brought back as wives for the surviving 600 Benjamites. The suggestion that this act of destruction was not carried out, but that the inhabitants of Jabesh-gilead delivered over their virgin daughters, finds no support in the text, although subsequent history shows that there were survivors. The action appears cruel in the extreme to the modern reader, but the virtual sacredness of the bond linking the several tribes into the amphictyony must be appreciated, and the sin of Jabesh-gilead seen in its light.

The victorious Israelites, and their terrified prisoners, returned to *the camp* at *Shiloh*. The reference to Shiloh has caused great and unnecessary perplexity to commentators, the main reason for this being that Shiloh afterwards became the greatest central sanctuary of the period of the judges. It seems obvious that it was not thus honoured at the time of this incident, for the detailed geographical descriptions of verses 12 and 19 would be most inappropriate if Shiloh was the major sanctuary. Shiloh was, of course, the central sanctuary for what appears to have been a brief period in the lifetime of Joshua (Jos. 18:1) and it was the assembly point for the tribes when action was contemplated against the two and a half tribes eastward of Jordan (Jos. 22:12). But the evidence points to the fact that Shiloh, like Shechem and possibly Gilgal, did not long remain the central sanctuary in this early period, when the ark of the covenant appears to have moved from one place to another.[1] The 'feast of the Lord' referred to (verses 19ff.) was evidently of a rustic and local character, and hardly to be equated with the cultus at Israel's chief shrine. A glance at a map shows the simplest and most plausible explanation. There was no need for the main Israelite force to remain at Mizpah or Bethel, since the Benjamite crisis had been conclusively dealt with. The scene of operations had now been transferred to Jabesh-gilead, about 45 miles to the north-east, and it is in this general direction that the Israelites moved, to deal with any emergency which might arise and to effect a more convenient link-up at Shiloh, about 13 miles north-north-east of Mizpah. A supplementary reason which

[1] M. Noth comments, 'But possibly at this early period an occasional change of the central place of worship was provided for because the Ark was formerly a travelling shrine which it was not intended should become the object of a local cult after the manner of the Canaanites' (Noth, p. 94).

made a move desirable was that the 600 Benjamites were at the rock Rimmon, so that the transfer to Shiloh grouped both Israelite forces to their northward, thus making for greater security. The site of Shiloh was excavated by Danish archaeologists in 1926–9 and 1932 and it has been established that the settlement there was destroyed *c.* 1050 BC, almost certainly after the events of 1 Samuel 4.

**21:13–15. The embassy to the Benjamites.** The fact that 400 prospective wives had been procured for them must have convinced the Benjamites of the sincerity of the endeavours of their brethren to effect a reconciliation. There was still a deficiency of 200 maidens, however, and it is clear that the contrite Israelites felt themselves responsible for making up this lack, although their vow made it impossible for them to give their own daughters in marriage. The sparing of the 600, who were as guilty as their fellow-Benjamites who had perished, seems to have been prompted by the consideration that, in any case, sufficient punishment had been meted out, and that the breach must not be made absolute by the complete annihilation of one tribe.

**21:16–24. More wives for the Benjamites.** The elders of Israel continued their efforts to procure wives for the surviving Benjamites. The reference to *an inheritance* (17) is not clear, since it is the provision of wives, not a tribal portion (the usual meaning of 'inheritance'), which is required. Possibly there is compression of thought; the remnant of Benjamin were to be allowed to return in peace to their own territory, but unless wives were provided then the line of Benjamin would cease, and a tribe would be blotted out in Israel. In this predicament their fertile imagination suggested another alternative, possibly prompted by the fact that the camp was now at Shiloh. The words of verse 19 are addressed to the 200 Benjamites without wives, and the precision of the description suggests that Shiloh was a small settlement off the main highway. The geographic allusions make it clear that Shiloh was the modern Seilūn, between 9 and 10 miles north-north-east of Bethel, about 3 miles south of Lebonah (the modern el-Lubbān), and approximately 2 miles east of the main road connecting Bethel and Shechem.

It has been conjectured that the annual *feast* (19) or pilgrimage (so the meaning of the Heb. *ḥāḡ*) was the Passover, and that the dancing commemorated the rejoicing of Miriam and the women of Israel after the crossing of the Red Sea (Ex. 15:20,21). More plausible, in the light of the mention of *vineyards* (20), is that it was the Feast of Tabernacles, in the time of the vintage-harvest. Since Shiloh is described as *in the land of Canaan* (12) it is at least plausible that this particular area, like the area of Shechem (see introductory note on 9:1–57), was a Canaanite enclave within Israel. This particular pilgrimage, therefore, may have been of a local character, having its origins in the pre-Israelite worship of the locality. Such an explanation could ease the problem of accounting for the absence of any representative from Shiloh in the council of the eleven tribes which hatched this scheme to deprive them of two hundred of their maidens! The council anticipated that this Israelite 'rape of the Sabines' (Livy, *Hist.* i.9) would provoke a very strong complaint to the tribal assembly and they had prepared for this. Their appeal was to the forbearance of the men of Shiloh, a forbearance which would enable them to steer a middle course between two perilous extremes: the 200 Benjamites would not be guilty of seizing the maidens by an act of war; nor would the men of Shiloh give their daughters to the Benjamites, and thus be guilty of violating the vow of 21:1. Whether this appeal to the men of Shiloh was met with willing acquiescence is conjectural. Most probably, like Micah and his neighbours, they were powerless to do anything to undo this *fait accompli* (18:22–26). The scheme worked out according to plan, the Benjamites were able to set about restoring their shattered cities, and the rest of the Israelites were able to disperse to their tribal portions.

**21:25. Finale.** The book closes with the reflection of the editor that the absence of the strong hand of a king was largely responsible for the disorders of the land in this earlier age.

The editor thereby shows his own background to be one of stability and security, conditions which obtained in the major part of David's reign and in the earlier part of Solomon's reign, when, most likely, this portion of Israel's history was completed. However, the historical perspective of the editor was not to be the final assessment, for the monarchy itself was to deteriorate and proved to be no lasting remedy for the evils of the land. Moreover, it is to a judge, not a king, to whom we must look for the initial improvement, for it was Samuel who led his people out of the period of the judges into the period of the monarchy; out of the turbulence and apostasy of the period of the judges and into the relative stability which confronts us when we consider Saul and his successors. But the reader must take up this story in another book.

*Nevertheless they were disobedient, and rebelled against thee, and cast thy law behind their back . . . and they wrought great provocations.*
*Nevertheless in thy manifold mercies thou didst not make a full end of them, nor forsake them; for thou art a gracious and merciful God* (Ne. 9:26,31, RV).

Israel in the Time of the Judges

The Twelve Tribes and Israel's Neighbours

0    10    20
Scale of Miles

PHOENICIANS

Asher

Naphtali

Zebulun

Issachar

BASHAN

Manasseh

Manasseh

Ephraim

Gad

Dan    Benjamin

AMMON

PHILISTINES

Judah

Reuben

Simeon

MOAB

EDOM

215

# RUTH

*AN INTRODUCTION AND COMMENTARY*
by
LEON MORRIS, B.SC., M.TH., PH.D.
*Principal, Ridley College, Melbourne*

# CONTENTS

## AUTHOR'S PREFACE

THERE are not many commentaries in English on the book of Ruth, so no apology is needed for producing this one. It is meant primarily for the general reader. For this reason it is not a technical work, and the translation most often referred to is the Authorized Version, since this is most generally available. But I hope that the general reader will not mind the fact that, since there are so few commentaries on this book, I have sometimes ventured on a rather technical piece of information for the benefit of the student who reads Hebrew. These notes are all brief and can be passed over by those who have no use for them.

It may help, too, if I explain for the non-Hebraist that Hebrew was originally (and often still is) written without vowels. When we speak of 'the consonantal text' we mean the text written without vowels. Usually this presents no problem, for the Hebraist becomes quite used to reading the vowelless text. Now and then it results in ambiguity, for it is sometimes possible to think of more than one set of vowels which might be supplied to the consonants. Because of this there are some passages where the possibilities must be looked at very carefully.

In the early centuries of our era certain Jewish scholars, whom we call 'the Massoretes', did a great deal of work on the text of the Hebrew Bible. They compared the manuscripts known to them and copied only those which seemed superior. In this way they standardized the text, which is thus called 'the Massoretic text'. And, as a help to those who followed them, they developed a system for indicating the vowels which the consonantal text lacked. They had a great reverence for the sacred text, so they did not disturb it. Their vowel-signs, or 'points', were little marks for the most part placed above or below the consonants. This process is called 'pointing', and the old text they worked on may be called 'the unpointed text' as well as 'the consonantal text'.

Before the Massoretes did their work, the Old Testament was translated into Greek, the translation being called 'the Septuagint'. This translation sometimes appears to have been made from a text slightly different from the Massoretic, and it thus repays careful study. Almost all the Hebrew manuscripts of the biblical books known to us contain the Massoretic text. Thus lacking anything with which to compare it, we cannot tell whether the Massoretes decided wisely or not. But when the Septuagint enables us to say, 'Such and such a Hebrew text must have been before the translators who produced this translation', we can compare this reading with that in the Massoretic text. The Septuagint is thus valuable as giving us information about textual variants which otherwise would be lost to us. A similar comment may be made about other ancient translations, notably those into Latin and Syriac.

The book of Ruth is sometimes regarded as very simple, so simple indeed that no commentary on it is required. Obviously I do not share that opinion! It is true that much in the book is straightforward. But it is also true that there are quite a few difficulties, including some which seem insoluble in the light of our present knowledge. But there is much that can be learned from a close study of the text, and by taking into consideration recent archaeological discoveries, notably those at Mari, Nuzi, Alalakh and Ugarit. I trust that this commentary will be useful in helping to bring before the general reader some of this new knowledge.

In conclusion, may I express my indebtedness to Professor Donald Wiseman for his careful reading of the typescript and his helpful comments. I have benefited greatly from his advice. I have also profited from suggestions made by the Rev. Professor F. I. Andersen. His expertise in Moabite studies,[1] allied as it is to a wide knowledge of Hebrew, made his comments particularly valuable for a book with a Moabitess as a principal character. I am also grateful to my colleague the Rev. Gordon Garner, and to my former colleague the Rev. James Fraser, for their help on a number of points on which I

---

[1] See, for example, his authoritative study entitled 'Moabite Syntax' in *Orientalia*, 35, 1966, pp. 81–120.

consulted them. These good friends are not, of course, responsible for the imperfections that remain. But this book would have been a good deal poorer without their help.

LEON MORRIS

# CHIEF ABBREVIATIONS

| | |
|---|---|
| AV | English Authorized Version (King James) |
| BDB | *Hebrew-English Lexicon of the Old Testament* by F. Brown, S. R. Driver and C. A. Briggs (Oxford University Press, 1907). |
| Berkeley | *The Holy Bible, The Berkeley Version in Modern English* (Zondervan, 1959). |
| Cassel | *Joshua, Judges and Ruth* by P. Cassel (Vol. IV of *A Commentary on the Holy Scriptures* edited by J. P. Lange) (T. & T. Clark, n.d.). |
| Cooke | *The Book of Ruth* by G. A. Cooke (*Cambridge Bible for Schools and Colleges*) (Cambridge University Press, 1913). |
| FF | *The Holy Bible in Modern English* by F. Fenton (Partridge, 1922). |
| Gerleman | *Ruth* by G. Gerleman (*Biblischer Kommentar Altes Testament*) (Kreis Moers, 1960). |
| Herbert | A. S. Herbert in *Peake's Commentary on the Bible* edited by M. Black and H. H. Rowley (Nelson, 1962). |
| Hertzberg | *Die Bücher Josua, Richter, Ruth* by H. W. Hertzberg (*Das Alte Testament Deutsch*) (Vandenhoeck & Ruprecht, 1959). |
| *HS* | *Hebrew Syntax* by A. B. Davidson (T. & T. Clark, 1924). |
| *IB* | *Interpreter's Bible*, Vol. 2 (Leviticus–Samuel) (Nelson, 1953). *Ruth*: introduction and exegesis by L. P. Smith; exposition by J. T. Cleland. |
| Joüon | *Ruth Commentaire Philologique et Exégétique* by P. Joüon (Institut Biblique Pontifical, 1953). |
| KB | *Lexicon in Veteris Testamenti Libros* by L. Koehler and W. Baumgartner (Brill, 1953). |
| KD | *Joshua, Judges, Ruth* by C. F. Keil and F. Delitzsch (*Biblical Commentary on the Old Testament*, Vol. IV) (T. & T. Clark, 1887). |

| | |
|---|---|
| Knight | *Ruth and Jonah* by G. A. F. Knight (*The Torch Bible Commentaries*) (S.C.M. Press, 1950). |
| Knox | *The Holy Bible, A Translation from the Latin Vulgate in the Light of the Hebrew and Greek Originals* by R. Knox (Burns & Oates, 1955). |
| Lattey | *The Book of Ruth* by C. Lattey (*The Westminster Version of the Sacred Scriptures*) (Longmans, 1935). |
| Learoyd | W. H. A. Learoyd in *A New Commentary on Holy Scripture* edited by C. Gore, H. L. Goudge and A. Guillaume (S.P.C.K., 1937). |
| LXX | The Septuagint (pre-Christian Greek version of the Old Testament). |
| Macdonald | A. Macdonald in *The New Bible Commentary*[2] edited by F. Davidson, A. M. Stibbs and E. F. Kevan (I.V.F., 1954). |
| mg. | margin. |
| Moffatt | *A New Translation of the Old Testament* by J. Moffatt (Hodder and Stoughton, 1924). |
| MT | Massoretic Text. |
| Myers | *The Linguistic and Literary Form of the Book of Ruth* by J. M. Myers (Brill, 1955). |
| *NBD* | *The New Bible Dictionary* edited by J. D. Douglas, F. F. Bruce, J. I. Packer, R. V. G. Tasker and D. J. Wiseman (I.V.F., 1962). |
| RSV | American Revised Standard Version, 1952. |
| Rudolph | *Das Buch Ruth – Das Hohe Lied – Die Klagelieder* by W. Rudolph (*Kommentar zum Alten Testament*) (Gerd Mohn, 1962). |
| Rust | *Judges, Ruth, I & II Samuel* by E. C. Rust (*Layman's Bible Commentaries*) (S.C.M. Press, 1961). |
| Simeon | *Horae Homileticae*, III by Charles Simeon (H. G. Bohn, 1847). |
| Slotki | J. J. Slotki in *The Five Megilloth* edited by A. Cohen (Soncino, 1946). |
| *TWNT* | *Theologisches Wörterbuch zum Neuen Testament* (W. Kohlhammer, 1949– ). |

Vulg.            The Vulgate (translation of the Bible into Latin, by Jerome).

Wright          *The Book of Ruth in Hebrew* by C. H. H. Wright (Williams & Norgate, 1864).

# INTRODUCTION

THE little book of Ruth has drawn tributes from very many, and it has even been described as 'the perfect story'.[1] It is indeed a splendid example of the storyteller's art and it is more than a little interesting to find in this book which comes down from a remote antiquity a tale which conforms so exactly to the standards looked for in a good story in modern times.

It is told simply and directly. It deals with the period of the judges, but it forms a contrast with the book of that name. The book of Judges tells of war and strife, but this is a quiet story of ordinary people going about their quiet lives. In one way it is a tale of two women. It relates how one of them, Naomi, underwent much hardship, but eventually won through to peace and security. It tells how the other, Ruth, attached herself firmly to her mother-in-law and to her mother-in-law's God and how she received the blessing of that God. But most of all the book is a book about God. It deals with unimportant people and unimportant matters. But it deals with them in such a way as to show that God is active in the affairs of men. He works His purpose out and blesses them that trust Him.

## I. DATE

There are few indications of the date of this book. The author, of course, is quite unknown. There is a Rabbinic tradition that Samuel composed the book (Talmud, Baba Bathra, 14b), but the tradition is late and does not appear to be soundly based.

Most scholars date the book late. They point out that it is found in the Hebrew Bible in the *Ketûbîm*, the third division of the Canon, among the five *Megillôt*, or 'rolls' (the others

---

[1] A. Weiser cites Goethe's view that Ruth is 'the loveliest complete work on a small scale', and that of Rud. Alexander Schröder: 'No poet in the world has written a more beautiful short story' (*Introduction to the Old Testament* (Darton, Longman and Todd, 1961), p. 305).

being Esther, Song of Solomon, Ecclesiastes and Lamentations), which is taken to indicate that the book was written later than the prophetic writings. This, however, obviously does not follow. It simply raises the question, 'When was Ruth first put among the *Keṯûḇîm*?' There is nothing to indicate that this arrangement was primitive and a good deal to show that it was not.

It is difficult to be sure of the date of order of the books in the LXX, but it is certainly old. Most agree that it is our oldest evidence. In this order Ruth is placed among the historical books, immediately after Judges. Gerleman notes that this is the case with other ancient versions also, and he sees in it evidence for an old Jewish tradition that Ruth has a close connection with the historical books.[1] This is apparently supported by Josephus, who says there are twenty-two books in the Canon.[2] Though Josephus does not say in so many words that Judges and Ruth were numbered together as one book, it is generally agreed that this must have been the case (no hypothesis which rejects this seems to have any plausibility). The idea that there are twenty-two books in the Old Testament is very common in early discussions. P. Katz speaks of it as the earliest arrangement we can trace.[3] He cites and approves T. Zahn's statement 'that from 90 to 400 AD we have an almost unbroken chain of witnesses for the fact that the Palestinian Jews not only had a theory about the 22 books of the Canon, but also as a rule used a Bible consisting of 22 scrolls'.[4] Another way of counting up the books made the total twenty-four (as in 4 Ezra 14:44f.; G. H. Box commenting on this verse says, 'In the Talmud and Midrash the O.T. is regularly termed "the twenty-four holy Scriptures" '[5]). This appears to mean that Ruth was separated from Judges (and Lamentations from Jeremiah). Whether the order was

[1] Gerleman, p. 1.
[2] *Contra Apion*, i. 8.
[3] *Zeitschrift für die Neutestamentliche Wissenschaft*, XLVII, 1956, p. 201.
[4] *Op. cit.*, p. 199.
[5] *The Apocrypha and Pseudepigrapha of the Old Testament*, ed. R. H. Charles, II (Oxford, 1963), p. 624. The point is made clear by H. B. Swete, *An Introduction to the Old Testament in Greek* (Cambridge, 1902), pp. 220f.

the same as in the twenty-two book classification we do not know. Yet another piece of information comes from Melito of Sardis (second century AD). Eusebius cites a letter written by Melito in which he says that he visited Palestine and there took pains to ascertain for his correspondent 'the accurate facts about the ancient writings, how many they are in number, and what is their order'. In the resultant list he places Ruth immediately after Judges.[1]

A further piece of evidence, not generally noticed, is the very old Hebrew–Aramaic list of the books of the Old Testament given in MS. 54 of the library of the Greek patriarchate in Jerusalem.[2] This list, which Paul E. Kahle thinks 'is possibly the oldest list available to us',[3] arranges the books of the Old Testament in a curious order. It begins: Genesis, Exodus, Leviticus, Joshua, Deuteronomy, Numbers, Ruth, Job, Judges. For our purpose, the important thing is this further piece of early evidence that Ruth was not put among the Writings, but among the books reckoned as historical.

Lattey maintains that the first evidence for regarding Ruth as part of the *Ketûbîm* is not found until the time of Jerome, who mentions it, but who also speaks of the twenty-two book arrangement.[4] This may not be taking seriously the point made, for example, by Rudolph,[5] that the Targum of Jonathan (first century AD), which deals with the prophets, does not include Ruth and Lamentations, from which the conclusion is drawn that it must be reckoning them among the *Ketûbîm*. But this conclusion is obviously far from certain. And Jerome's view is not lightly to be dismissed. He was not a casual visitor to Palestine, but lived there. And he was a learned Hebraist. He did not depend for his information on the LXX.

It is sometimes urged in favour of the view that the book is

[1] *Historia Ecclesiastica*, iv. 26. 13f., cited from the Loeb edn., ed. K. Lake (Heinemann, 1926).
[2] See the Note entitled 'A Hebrew-Aramaic List of Books of the Old Testament in Greek Transcription', by J.-P. Audet, *Journal of Theological Studies*, New Series, I, 1950, pp. 135–154.
[3] *The Cairo Geniza* (Blackwell, 1959), p. 218.
[4] Lattey, p. xxxviii.
[5] Rudolph, p. 24.

late that no good reason can be given for moving it from the historical books to the *Keṯûḇîm*, whereas the reverse process is easily understood. P. Katz, however, denies this. He points out that the arrangement in the earliest Hebrew selections of books varies, and that in any case it is bound up with ideas which are late. His argument that the order in the LXX is earlier than that in the Hebrew lists so far known to us is convincing. It should further be pointed out that those who maintain that no reason can be given for transferring the book from the historical books to the *Keṯûḇîm* overlook the fact that Ruth, in common with the other *Megillôṯ*, came to be used liturgically. The five were read at major festivals, so there was every reason for grouping them together. When this was done they had to be placed among the *Keṯûḇîm*, for three of them could by no stretch of imagination be classed among the historical books.[1]

There is a statement in the Talmud that the book of Ruth precedes Psalms (Baba Bathra, 14b). This may indicate a tradition that Ruth was of an earlier date than the Psalms. But on the other hand, it may be due to nothing more profound than a recognition that the subject-matter of the book is early.

It is suggested by some that the writer of Ruth knew the Deuteronomic edition of Judges, and that he made use of a genealogy in a form used by the Priestly Code and by the author of Chronicles. But the former contention seems pure assertion. It is far from being proven. And the latter simply raises the question of who borrowed from whom. Lattey regards the argument from the genealogy as 'a further example of the perverse treatment from which the book has suffered, that whereas the concluding genealogy ends with David, this has been seized upon as a proof, not that it was written in that reign, but that it came into being long afterwards . . . there is no valid reason for assuming that a genealogy cannot be early'.[2]

An argument from language is that the book is said to contain Aramaisms and words characteristic of late Hebrew. Examples cited are: *nāśā nāšîm* (1:4), *lāhēn* (1:13), the verb

---

[1] *Cf.* W. W. Cannon, *Theology*, XVI, 1928, p. 318.
[2] Lattey, p. xxxix.

'*āgan* (1:13), *mārā*' for *mārâh* (1:20), '*ānâh b*ᵉ (1:21), *miqreh* (2:3), *ta*ᶜᵃ*ḫûrî* (2:8), *yiqṣōrûn* (2:9), *tidbāqîn* (2:21), *yāradty* (3:3), *šākaḇty* (3:4), *ta*ᶜᵃ*śîn* (3:4), *marg*ᵉ*lōṯ* (3:7,8,14), *tēḏ*ᵉᶜ*în* (3:18), *p*ᵉ*lōnî* '*almōnî* (4:1), *qayyēm* (4:7), *šālap na*ᶜᵃ*lô* (4:7). Some find *ṭrwm* (3:14) an Aramaism, but Cassel thinks this unlikely, as the form is not found in Aramaic.[1]

Yet it should be noted that there are legitimate doubts about all this. In the first instance, not all scholars are sure that these forms are Aramaisms. F. I. Andersen says firmly, 'Several of these words are pure old Canaanite'. If this is so, the words are evidence for an early rather than a late date. Then in the second place, it is not clear that, even if genuine Aramaisms are present, they are late.[2] Thus H. Gunkel says, 'we cannot always deduce a late origin from an Aramaic expression, for, as Hans Bauer and Leander maintain, Hebrew was from the beginning a mixed language, and possessed Aramaic words from the first. The task of distinguishing Aramaic words which are to be found in the most ancient texts from those which were not introduced till later times, is a problem for the future. In the meantime it is only with the greatest reservation that we should draw the conclusion of a late origin from Aramaisms.'[3] KD make the point that the alleged Aramaisms are found only in speeches, not in the author's own narrative. The conclusion is that these forms were not the author's own, but those of the time of the Judges.[4] Wright points out that they 'occur in all the books, and if such are sufficient to prove lateness of date, then we have no ancient

---

[1] Cassel, *in loc.*

[2] D. J. Wiseman informs me that 'Aramaic' words are now known from the Middle Babylonian and Middle Assyrian period, *c.* 1400 BC! He points out that the evidence for early Aramaisms is abundant. *Cf.* the article, 'Studies in Aramaic Lexicography', *Journal of the American Oriental Society*, 82, 1962, pp. 290–299.

[3] *Old Testament Essays*, papers read before the Society for Old Testament Study (Charles Griffin, 1927), p. 119.

[4] KD, p. 469. *Cf.* Cassel: 'The narrative exhibits life in its popular aspect, and probably makes use of popular forms of speech which to us seem Chaldaizing' (Cassel, p. 6). 'He makes his rustics talk in rustic fashion, while yet, when Boaz speaks on elevated subjects, the language rises to the level of the theme'(*ibid.*, p. 8).

Hebrew at all'.[1] A remark of Myers also has relevance. On *qayyēm* in 4:7, he says, 'several middle weak forms are found in the *Piel* in early documents. ... Since it is an explanatory insertion, an Aramaic borrowing would not affect the question of date of the original, but only that of its final prose edition.'[2] An occasional late word may well be evidence of scribal activity rather than of a late date for the book as a whole. And in any case we must bear in mind that 'the number of relatively late words is at best very small'.[3] Rudolph points out that the number of 'late' words noted by earlier scholars has been drastically reduced in recent writing. Thus Joüon[4] finds only four expressions typical of late speech, and Rudolph[5] proceeds to show that none of these is necessarily late. The conclusion is inescapable that the language of the book as a whole does not prove a late date. Indeed, as far as the language is concerned, the indications are that the book is early. Only a very small number of words is cited for a late date, and, as we have seen, they do not prove it. By contrast, the overwhelming majority of words and constructions points to an early date, to a time when classical Hebrew was the norm. An early date is perhaps not proven beyond all doubt, but it is supported by the bulk of the evidence.

Some allege that the shoe custom described in Ruth 4 was obsolete when this chapter was written and that this indicates a late date. This argument is very weak. It depends on one verse (4:7), which could have been a gloss inserted at a later time.

---

[1] Wright, p. XLII.

[2] Myers, p. 19.

[3] Myers, p. 28. *Cf.* also A. Bentzen, 'The *Aramaisms* in the book are not numerous enough to account for a late date' (*Introduction to the Old Testament*, ii (Copenhagen, 1949), p. 185). Similarly S. R. Driver decides that the language does not point to a late date. It is classical, and 'stands on a level with the best parts of Samuel' (*An Introduction to the Literature of the Old Testament* (T. & T. Clark, 1909), p. 454). He gives it as his opinion that 'the general beauty and purity of the style of Ruth point more decidedly to the pre-exilic period than do the isolated expressions quoted to the period after the exile' (*op. cit.*, p. 455). W. W. Cannon finds that the language, so far from indicating a post-exilic date, is 'almost incompatible' with it (*op. cit.*, p. 317), while W. F. Albright says roundly, 'a post-exilic date is impossible' (*Journal of Biblical Literature*, LXI, 1942, p. 124).

[4] Joüon, p. 11.

[5] Rudolph, p. 28.

In any case, while the words point to a date later than that of the events described, they do not necessarily indicate a very late date. The writer knows the old custom, which may indicate that he lived near enough to the change-over to remember what the previous custom was. Again, almost exactly the same expression is found in 1 Samuel 9:9 in the passage explaining that formerly in Israel a prophet was called a 'seer'. Yet no-one argues that this is convincing evidence for a very late date. A somewhat similar suggestion is that the author misunderstood the custom, which is given in its true form in Deuteronomy. But this is pure assumption. There is no contradiction with Deuteronomy, which describes what happens when a relation refuses to do his duty. Ruth 4 is concerned rather with how he transfers it with the consent of all concerned. See further my note on the passage (pp. 305ff., below). The Nuzi parallels there mentioned, and which date from *c.* 1500 BC, make it very difficult to hold to a late date.

Though the evidence for this late date is thus far from conclusive, most scholars hold that a date between 450 and 250 BC should be accepted. The earlier part of this period is favoured by those who think that the book was written to oppose the prohibition of mixed marriages in Nehemiah 13:23ff. On this Lattey comments, 'The fresh and simple story is above suspicion of such sophisticated composition'.[1] Those who think the book was written to oppose objections to the making of proselytes tend to date the work in the Greek period.

On the other hand, there are arguments for a much earlier date. Thus it is pointed out that the style and language are classic Hebrew and so point to early times. Learoyd thinks that 'The literary and linguistic style of Ruth is far more like that of Samuel than that of late books like Chronicles'.[2] Myers classes it with the JE narratives of the Pentateuch, Joshua, Judges, Samuel and Kings and says, 'The simplicity of the story itself, the short but telling phrases and sentences employed as its vehicle, and the general impression created in the mind of the reader compel its classification with the early literature of

[1] Lattey, p. xxxiv.
[2] Learoyd, p. 214.

Israel.'[1] 'In general, there are few constructions which cannot be paralleled in the earlier writings of the Hebrew Bible.'[2]

The language of this book contains some unusual forms, some of which appear to be early. Myers lists a number of archaic forms. He cites as especially noteworthy archaic forms *tiḏbāqîn* (2:8,21), *yiqṣōrûn* (2:9), *yiš"ᵃḇûn* (2:9), *wᵉyāraḏty* (3:3), *wᵉšāḵāḇty* (3:4), *taᶜᵃśîn* (3:4), *tēḏᵉᶜîn* (3:18), *qānîṯāy* (4:5).[3] He also lists *śdy* (1:1), *tēᶜāgēnâh* (1:13; Myers sees development from a primitive form[4]), *taᶜᵃḇûrî* (2:8)[5], *qnyty* (4:5; confusion of genders and thus archaic 2f.s.).[6] He cites *'ānōḵî* as occurring seven times with *'ᵃnî* twice, a mark of early date.[7]

These forms are hard to explain in a late document. Cooke suggests that the author deliberately adopted certain older phrases to accord with the setting of his narrative.[8] But this is to apply modern standards of verisimilitude. Writers in antiquity do not seem to have thought like this. But if the early forms are hard to account for in a late document, late forms in an early document are not so difficult, provided they are not the characteristic language of the book. For, as Myers points out, 'all of the Hebrew Bible passed through the hands of Judean editors . . . This fact would at once indicate that the materials which they handled were made to conform at least in part to current Jerusalemite spelling standards.'[9]

On gender Myers points out that the confusion of gender found in Ruth is not characteristic of Hebrew, early or late. 'It follows, probably, that it was a relatively early dialectical peculiarity, submerged by the later spread of standard grammatical forms.'[1]

---

[1] Myers, p. 4.
[2] *Ibid.*, p. 27. See also p. 234, n. 3 above.
[3] *Ibid.*, p. 20.
[4] *Ibid.*, p. 16.
[5] *Ibid.*, p. 10.
[6] *Ibid.*, p. 19.
[7] *Ibid.*, pp. 19f. We should add that the archaic character of these forms largely concerns morphology, the grammatical forms, rather than orthography, the spelling.
[8] Cooke, p. xv.
[9] Myers, p. 12.
[1] *Ibid.*, p. 20. F. I. Andersen speaks of 'the alleged confusions of gender' as

On idiomatic expressions, Myers says, 'The book of Ruth partakes of the regular idioms prevalent in the classical litera-ture of Israel. While some of these idioms are current also in the later period of Hebrew literary development, a glance at the references cited above or a perusal of the concordance will demonstrate that they belong overwhelmingly to the early period.'[1] 'There is not a single linguistic feature of the book that cannot be explained satisfactorily on the basis of a later reduction to writing of a story perpetuated orally for centuries.'[2]

The narrative itself gives indications of early elements so that even those who think of a late date often suggest that parts of the book at any rate go back to a remote antiquity. Upholders of an early date suggest that the undoubtedly early elements carry the rest of the book (which after all is quite short) with them. Lattey, for example, says, 'There is much in this story that points to an early date both for the facts and for the writing of them, and very little makes for a late date. The modern perspective in ancient history, and that not least in Palestine, makes the craze for later dating appear somewhat antiquated ... we may reasonably ask that the evidence for the date should be weighed impartially, and that the work should not be assigned the latest date possible that is not positively ridiculous – if indeed even that limit is always observed.'[3]

There is also the fact that according to the Deuteronomic legislation Moabites were not permitted to enter the con-gregation. That the heroine was a Moabite points to a time like that of Judges when foreign wives were not so likely to be objected to. A post-exilic date has to be supported by making the book a counterblast to Ezra-Nehemiah.

Cassel argues from the tenderness shown to foreigners in David's reign that the book must date from then. In addition

'among the most authentic archaisms in the book'. Some he thinks of as 'duals, used correctly, which have survived later normalization'.
[1] *Ibid.*, pp. 31f.
[2] *Ibid.* p. 32.
[3] Lattey, p. xxxiii.

to commending his parents to the care of the King of Moab in a time of crisis (1 Sa. 22:3) David remembered that the King of Ammon had shown him kindness (2 Sa. 10:2). His bodyguard included foreigners like Cherethites and Pelethites (2 Sa. 8:18). He lived for some time in Philistine Gath (1 Sa. 27). He attached to himself men like Uriah the Hittite (2 Sa. 11:3), and Zelek the Ammonite (2 Sa. 23:37). He deposited the Ark in the house of a Gittite (2 Sa. 6:10). At the time of Absalom's rebellion he was given provisions by an Ammonite (2 Sa. 17:27), counsel by Hushai the Archite (2 Sa. 15:32ff.), and military support by Ittai the Gittite (2 Sa. 15:19ff.). 'Never again, in the history of the ancient Israel, do such relations come to view.'

While this falls short of proof it should at least be considered. There is more to be said for a date in David's reign than is commonly allowed.

The office of 'kinsman' (*gō'ēl*) is evidently early. Lattey sees it not yet 'limited in actual practice to the law of the levirate' and feels there is no evidence that the latter expanded in later times.[1]

The book is certainly later than the events it describes. Ruth 4 contains a clear indication that the custom of loosening the shoe had fallen out of use by the time the book was written and of course the book ends with a genealogy which takes us on to the time of David at least, though it is possible that this was added later than the rest of the book. But it is difficult to think of this as being penned at a very late date. David became the ideal king, the man after God's own heart. It is not easy to think that when such ideas were held strongly a statement which ascribes to David a Moabite grandmother (and serves no other purpose) should be appended to a book which originally had nothing to do with him. This indicates that 4:17 at any rate was from the first a part of the book, and that it rests on a very old tradition.

A further argument is drawn from the general tone of the book. The narrative is serene and pleasant, not at all the sort of thing one would expect to find issuing from the life of the

[1] *Op. cit.*, p. xxxiv.

poverty-stricken and struggling post-exilic community. With this we might take the freshness of the narrative. It does not seem as though the main facts recorded have to do with a remote past. Indeed, the fact that the shoe custom is explained in Ruth 4, but nothing else is, shows that the rest of the narrative would have been quite familiar, *i.e.*, the date must not be set too far from the facts recorded.

The inconclusiveness of the evidence, and the difficulty of dating the book, is shown by the wide variety of dates to which scholars have assigned it. Thus C. F. Keil and, more recently, J. E. Steinmueller see it as coming from the time of the early monarchy; S. R. Driver from the period between David and the exile; S. Davidson from the time of Hezekiah; H. Ewald, F. E. König and others from the exilic period; J. Wellhausen and others, including, more recently, P. Joüon, W. O. E. Oesterley and T. H. Robinson, and R. H. Pfeiffer, from the post-exilic period.[1] W. Rudolph favours the period of the later monarchy[2] and W. F. Albright 'about the eighth century BC'.[3]

In view of the lack of firm evidence, it is impossible to be dogmatic. But the language, the acquaintance with early customs, and the general atmosphere of the book seem to show that a date during the early monarchy probably best satisfies the conditions. It is difficult to be more precise.

II. PURPOSE

Various suggestions are made as to the purpose of the book.

*a. Universalism*

Some suggest that it was written to counter exclusivist tendencies. There were Jews who thought so highly of the privileged position of their nation that they regarded all other men as outside the sphere of God's care and interest. To

---

[1] The references are given by H. H. Rowley, *Harvard Theological Review*, XL, 1947, p. 78, n. 4.
[2] Rudolph, pp. 26–29.
[3] *Journal of Biblical Literature*, LXI, 1942, p. 124.

counter such tendencies this book was written with its heroine a Moabitess, and a Moabitess who became an ancestress of the great King David. This view is usually made specific by suggesting that the book is a protest against the legislation of Ezra and Nehemiah prohibiting foreign marriages. No evidence is cited for this, it being regarded as self-evident.

But it is far from self-evident. As polemic the book is a curious piece of work. The controversial point is made so gently that one fears most readers would have missed it.[1] Moreover, it is not easy to see how the story effects the postulated polemic. After all, Ruth was not simply a foreigner. She was devotedly attached to an Israelite mother-in-law and she was a convert to the Jewish religion.

Hertzberg[2] makes the point that, had the book really been a polemic against Ezra and Nehemiah, the unnamed kinsman's refusal to marry Ruth would surely have been on the grounds that she was a Moabitess (Boaz expressly informs him of this, 4:5). Boaz would have replied repudiating such prejudices. As polemic the book is curiously reticent. Indeed, H. H. Rowley thinks it would be as easy to read it as a defence of the policy of Ezra-Nehemiah as to think of it as attacking this policy.[3]

The view, moreover, demands a late date, not only for the final writing of the book, but also for the whole story. This ignores the evidence we have noted for the main story as being very old. And Joüon reasonably asks whether a book written late, and which opposes Ezra and Nehemiah, would ever have been admitted to the Canon.[4]

A variant is the view of Herbert. He rejects the idea that the book is a polemic against Ezra and Nehemiah, but thinks of it rather as a parable to teach the Israelites an important

---

[1] Cooke maintains that 'it argues a singular lack of imagination and literary insight to treat the Book of Ruth as a counter-blast or manifesto ... We may question whether Jewish readers in the time of Nehemiah would have detected a protest against his policy any more readily than we do in such a guileless piece of literature' (Cooke, p. xiii).

[2] Hertzberg, p. 258.

[3] *Harvard Theological Review*, XL, 1947, p. 78.

[4] Joüon, p. 6.

lesson. 'They have received the great revelation of God which must be kept free from the contaminations and dilutions of paganism, yet must be available for all, even a Moabite woman.'[1] This is a little better, but again it is difficult to see how the book does this. Ruth is not simply 'a Moabite woman'. She is a proselyte.

### b. Friendship

The book is a book about friendship. The devotion that Ruth shows to Naomi and the care that Naomi exercises towards Ruth run through the book. Some suggest that there is no grandiose purpose in the book. It is simply a tale of friendship.

But it is worth noticing that all three of the principal characters of the book are depicted as being mindful of their obligations to the family. Ruth does not forget her duty to Naomi, and consequently to Elimelech; Naomi seeks out a marriage that will preserve the name of her deceased husband, while Boaz marries the Moabitess to raise up the name of the dead. It is more plausible to argue that this is a book setting out the obligations of piety within the family, than to speak of it as a tale of friendship.

### c. The genealogy of David

It is an interesting fact that though David is the greatest king spoken of in the historical books, and though he is looked on by subsequent generations as the ideal king, there is no genealogy of him in 1 Samuel. There he is simply 'the son of Jesse'. The book of Ruth closes with a genealogy running back to Pharez, the son of Judah. It is suggested that the book was written to supply the missing genealogy. 'In this simple fact (*i.e.* the inclusion of the genealogy) the author very plainly shows that his intention was not to give a picture of the family life of pious Israelites in the time of the judges from a civil and a religious point of view, but rather to give a biographical sketch of the pious ancestors of David the king.'[2] Some ask

[1] Herbert, p. 316.
[2] KD, p. 469.

whether anyone would have taken the trouble to write or to preserve the book had the great king's name not been attached to it. Against this is the fact that nothing in the book, right up to the preceding verse, gives us the impression that it is leading up to anything like this. The genealogy appears rather as an appendix than as a climax.

### d. Levirate marriage
The story deals with the plight of the childless widow. According to the levirate law, the brother of a man who had died childless was required to marry the widow. The first child of the marriage was reckoned as the child of the deceased, whose name was thus perpetuated (Dt. 25:5f.). It is suggested that this book was written to inculcate the importance of carrying out this duty. The suggestion is difficult to accept, if for no other reason than that, though we have three widows, in no case does a brother of the deceased marry one of them. There is no example of levirate marriage in the proper sense.

### e. The sovereignty of God
It is better to see it as a tale told because it is true and because it shows something of the relationship between God and man. There is a good deal to be said for the view that the key verse is 2:12, 'The Lord recompense thy work, and a full reward be given thee of the Lord God of Israel, under whose wings thou art come to trust' (AV). That is what the book is about. It is not without its interest that the initiative is with Ruth in chapter 2, with Naomi in chapter 3 and with Boaz in chapter 4. None of them can be said to be the person about whom the book is written. But the implication throughout is that God is watching over His people, and that He brings to pass what is good. The book is a book about God. He rules over all and brings blessing to those who trust Him.

### III. POETICAL FORMS
Myers thinks that, while the book of Ruth as it stands is undoubtedly prose, there underlies it a poetic original. He

draws attention to many occurrences of parallelism, to the occurrence of poetic words and phrases, to the way various scenes in the book lend themselves to poetic treatment, and to many passages which scholars have regarded as poetry. It is possible that parts, at any rate, of the book were at one time poetry. If so, the core of the book in origin is older than the date at which it was reduced to writing in its present form. But there is a good deal that is speculative here, and perhaps we should not rest too much on it.

### IV. DIALECT

It is beyond doubt that there is something strange about the language of this book. While on the whole it is good classical Hebrew, there are some very unusual forms, as noted above. Myers refers to 'archaisms' and one wonders why such forms should be preserved in a book of this sort and why they should be located as precisely as they are in speeches. D. B. Macdonald thinks of Ruth as 'the first "dialect story" ', and he points out that 'Boaz, the wealthy and elderly farmer of Bethlehem, talks countrified dialect as contrasted with the more literary Hebrew of Ruth'.[1] There seems little doubt but that the book faithfully records certain dialectical peculiarities. It thus provides us with a valuable addition to our knowledge of the richness and variety of the Hebrew language.

[1] *The Hebrew Literary Genius* (Princeton, 1933), pp. 121, 122.

# ANALYSIS

# COMMENTARY

## I. AN ISRAELITE FAMILY IN MOAB

### (1:1–5)

The introduction is a brief account of the scene and the *dramatis personae*. Without going into detail, it tells of an Israelite family which went to neighbouring Moab in a time of famine, and there fell on evil days.

**1.** The opening words[1] date the action of the book, namely, during the time of the judges. The form of expression shows that the days of the judges were past and that this book was written at a later period. Joüon points out that the expression rendered *days* (*yᵉmê* from *yāmîm*) usually expresses duration of time (as against *'ēth* which gives us the point of time). In other words, no attempt is made to date the story closely. It is loosely assigned to the time of the judges. *Ruled* (AV, RSV) is literally

---

[1] A problem is posed by the very first word of this book, namely, whether the book of Ruth was originally an appendage to some other writing or whether it existed from the first as a separate entity. The *now* of AV represents a Hebrew *waw* consecutive. In Hebrew narrative of past events the first verb is usually in the perfect tense, and succeeding verbs go into the imperfect with *waw* prefixed, but are understood as though they were perfects. (I am here, of course, using commonly accepted terms. I am not unmindful of G. R. Driver's suggestion that the *waw* consecutive construction is the survival of an ancient preterite; *cf. Problems of the Hebrew Verbal System* (Edinburgh, 1936), pp. 85–97. If this is correct there is no reason why a book should not begin with the construction.) Here, however, we have *waw*+imperfect as the opening of the book and it is not surprising, accordingly, that some have suggested that originally something preceded. However, this phenomenon is not confined to Ruth. We find it also at the beginning of Leviticus, Numbers, Joshua, Judges, 1 Samuel, 2 Kings, Ezekiel, Esther, Nehemiah and 2 Chronicles. While it may well be that some of these books originally followed others and were not in origin complete wholes, it is difficult to think that this was so in every case. Davidson suggests that Hebrew showed a dislike for beginning a sentence without 'and' (*HS*, 136 R1). This is a possible explanation, though in point of fact there are many sentences which do just that. It is probably better to think that the *waw* consecutive construction so dominated the language that speakers and writers used it instinctively without stopping to inquire whether they were at the beginning of a narrative or not. This construction then is no reason for doubting that Ruth was always a unit.

245

*judged* (RV) and, while we need not quarrel with the AV and
RSV, we should not overlook the fact that verb and noun are
cognate. 'Judging' in ancient Israel was a complex affair.[1]
It included an element of discrimination between right and
wrong, and the taking of action as a result. This often yields
the meaning 'rule', for the sovereign was the supreme judge
in the land. But we should not overlook the connection with
justice. *The judges*, of course, are the leaders mentioned in the
book of Judges. They are not to be understood primarily as
legal functionaries, but as men raised up by God to be the
nation's deliverers in time of trouble. We need not doubt that
they did exercise legal functions, but their primary importance
was in their delivering of the people. Moffatt translates *heroes*,
and while this is not exact it brings out the fact that they were
not legal men.

At this time, then, there was a famine in the land. *The land*
is not further defined, but for a Hebrew only one country was
*the land*. This was the land God had given to His people, the
land of Canaan. Palestine has a rather uncertain rainfall, hence
times of drought and, consequently, of *famine* are not uncommon. The Old Testament refers to such famines quite a
number of times (*e.g.*, Gn. 12:10; 26:1; 41:56; 2 Sa. 21:1;
1 Ki. 18:2; 2 Ki. 6:25). But droughts are strange affairs and
sometimes conditions vary widely over comparatively small
areas (Gerleman overlooks this when he finds it 'scarcely conceivable' that there should be a fleeing to Moab on account of a
famine in Judah; on the contrary, it is quite conceivable given
the right conditions). So on this occasion there was famine in
the land of Israel, but not in nearby Moab. (On another occasion of famine in Israel a certain woman obtained relief by
going in another direction, namely, to the country of the
Philistines, 2 Ki. 8:1f.) Knight thinks that the famine was
caused in part at least by the devastation brought about during
the chaotic time of the judges when 'every man did that which
was right in his own eyes' (Jdg. 21:25, AV, RV; the kind of thing
that happened is seen in Jdg. 6:3f.). There was evidently no

[1] See on this my *The Biblical Doctrine of Judgment* (Tyndale Press, 1960),
chs. I, II.

intention of a permanent migration. The use of the verb *gûr*, 'to sojourn', shows that the man planned to return in due course (Berkeley renders, *to live for a while*). It is the regular word for a resident alien. Such had certain rights in Israel, but we do not know whether this was so in Moab or not. *The country of Moab* employs an expression which appears to mean literally 'the fields of Moab'. This may be no more than a very natural way of describing a predominantly rural country. With the use of the singular instead of the plural, the expression is not at all unusual. We read, for example, of 'the field of the Philistines' (1 Sa. 6:1) and of 'the field of Ephraim and the field of Samaria' (Ob. 19, RV). It is the plural form used here that is unusual. It occurs only in this book and always in the expression 'the fields of Moab' (1:1f., 6, 22; 2:6). In each of the passages where it is found there is some textual support for the more usual singular, both in Hebrew manuscripts and in such versions as the LXX, Syriac, and Vulg. Most scholars, however, agree that the plural form is correct. Its significance is not so clear. To begin with, it is not certain that it is a genuine plural. Myers accepts the reading of MT, but takes the form to be the construct singular of an archaic poetic form *śāḏay*.[1] If this can be accepted, the meaning will be 'the territory of Moab'. Those who take it as a genuine plural are divided on the meaning. FF translates 'plain' or 'plains' of Moab according as the singular or plural is found. This can scarcely be justified, since the word does not mean 'plain'. It means 'field', as its use in 2:2f. plainly shows. FF might possibly, however, be on the right lines in regarding the expression as pointing to a part only of the country. In view of the established idiom, the singular undoubtedly simply means 'the territory of Moab'. But where the form under discussion occurs, if it is really plural, it may well designate a particular area. Joüon thinks it refers to the high, cultivated plateaux. Plausibility is lent to this by the fact that much of Moab is mountainous and rugged and would be impossible for cultivation. Macdonald is a little more

---

[1] Myers, p. 9. So also Rudolph. F. I. Andersen has no doubt about its being a singular. He points out that in this book an individual 'field' is *ḥelqaṯ-haśśāḏeh*.

specific, with his suggestion that it probably means 'the rolling plateau south of the Arnon, still a rich pastureland'. Some such area seems to me to be the likely meaning if the term is plural, though it is impossible to be certain at this distance in time exactly which. But the suggestion that it is an archaic singular seems full of merit and may well be right. In that case, as we have noted, the meaning will be 'the territory of Moab'. Perhaps we should also notice Slotki's view that the expression signifies 'that Elimelech did not settle in one city permanently, but moved from place to place'. This is difficult to derive from the text, and is inherently unlikely. It is better to see a reference to the land of Moab.

It is possible that instead of *a certain man of Bethlehem-judah* we should take the passage to mean 'a certain man went from Bethlehem-judah . . .' (taking *mibbeth leḥem* with the verb). The man's movements would in that case be given here, and his place of origin in the next verse. The addition *Judah* is to distinguish this Bethlehem from other places of the same name. There was one, for example, in the north, in the territory allotted to Zebulun (Jos. 19:15). Bethlehem in Judah was by far the most famous and it is mentioned often. The name *Bethlehem* probably signifies 'house of bread', *i.e.*, 'granary'. Such a word might well, of course, be used of various places. Incidentally, it draws attention to the fertility of the region. Some scholars see in the name a reference to the name of a god rather than to a granary. This is supported by citing a place-name mentioned in the Amarna letters.[1] But there is little evidence for such a god, and the reference to a granary seems much more likely. An earlier name of the city was Ephrath (Gn. 35:19; 48:7).

**2.** Now come the names[2] of the various members of the

---

[1] In letter No. 290 there is a reference to 'a town of the land of Jerusalem, Bit-*Lahmi* by name' (cited from *Ancient Near Eastern Texts*, ed. J. B. Pritchard (Princeton, 1955), p. 489). This almost certainly refers to our Bethlehem, and in a form favouring a meaning 'house of Lahmi'. But this is scarcely sufficient to establish the point.

[2] W. E. Staples brings the names into an argument to show that the book is to be explained in terms of the fertility cults (*American Journal of Semitic Languages and Literatures*, LIII, 1937, pp. 145–157). This whole thesis is most unconvincing and few have been persuaded.

migrating family. The head of the household was called *Elimelech*, a name which means 'God is King', or perhaps 'My God is King'. Names in ancient times often reflected profound religious convictions, and this is one such. To name the name of God upon a child was to associate him in some way with God, and thus many Old Testament personal names include the name of the deity. Elimelech's consort was called *Naomi* (which would be more accurately transliterated as $N^{o'}omi$), a name which signifies 'pleasant', 'lovely', 'delightful'. Some have suggested that the name is not good Hebrew, but Aramaic. The point is not important, but Hebrew seems more probable. In the first place, it is somewhat unlikely that one member only of this family group should have an Aramaic name while all the rest have Hebrew names. And in the second place, the words of Naomi to the women of Bethlehem (who would probably not know Aramaic) about the meaning of her name (verse 20) show it was understood as Hebrew. The names of the two sons follow. *Mahlon* is possibly from a root *ḥlh*, 'to be weak' or 'sick', in which case he had evidently been a sickly child. *Chilion* is likewise a name with an unpleasant ring, for it signifies something like 'failing', 'pining', or even 'annihilation'. It is worth noticing that all these names are found at Ugarit, so that they are good old Canaanite names.

These people are then called *Ephrathites of Bethlehem-judah* (AV, RV). Ephrath was an earlier name for Bethlehem, as we have already noted (Gn. 35:19; 48:7; Ru. 4:11; Mi. 5:2, Hebrew verse 1), and sometimes Ephrath is mentioned without Bethlehem (Gn. 35:16). It is not certain whether the name was Ephrath or Ephrathah (in some passages which contain the longer form the final *-ah* could simply express motion, 'to Ephrath', but Ru. 4:11 seems decisive for the longer form). The use of the older name in such a connection may point us to the old-established families, the local aristocracy (the Midrash records an interpretation of the word as meaning 'aristocrats', ii. 5). At any rate, the indications we have are in favour of this family as being somewhat distinguished. At the end of the chapter, when Naomi returned, 'all the city' was interested, which argues for the return of someone well known and not a mere nobody. This may also be behind the question 'Is this Naomi?' (verse 19). Naomi could say, 'I went out full' (verse 21), which seems to indicate prosperity. The term *Ephrathite* sometimes means 'Ephraimite' (Jdg. 12:5; 1 Sa. 1:1; 1 Ki. 11:26). But it also refers to inhabitants of Bethlehem (1 Sa. 17:12) and this is clearly the meaning here. These people, then, went to 'the fields of Moab' and remained there.

**3.** We do not know how long they were there. Nothing is recounted of their doings until the death of the head of the household. Interestingly he is called *Naomi's husband* (AV, RV), though it is rare for a man to be characterized with reference to a woman. But in this story he plays no part, whereas Naomi is a central figure. Naomi *was left*, *i.e.*, 'left in life', 'remained alive'.

**4.** Now the sons contracted marriages. Nothing is said of any activity of Naomi's in this connection, and perhaps the young men took the initiative. Due to the circumstances it was probably inevitable that their wives should be Moabitesses, but this fact is stated in so many terms. It may be that the author does not want the point to be missed. He is no rigorist, and he draws attention to the intermingling with Moab. There was a prohibition against admitting Moabites into the congregation and the offspring of marriage with a Moabite were not to be admitted to the congregation to the tenth generation (Dt. 23:3). But, as KD point out, there was no prohibition of marriage with a Moabite. Deuteronomy 7:3 is sometimes cited in this connection, but this refers only to Canaanites and other dwellers in the land. The law did not prohibit marriage with a Moabite, whatever restrictions it laid on the issue. Slotki cites the Midrash to show that this verse is a silent protest against intermarriage and he says this is the unanimous view of Jewish commentators. At the same time, he affirms that marriage with a Moabite woman was not forbidden, and that the prohibition is concerned exclusively with males (Dt. 23:3). The names of the wives are given, but it is not certain how far we should attach meaning to them. We have little knowledge of the Moabite language, but the name *Orpah* is apparently from the same root as the Hebrew word for 'neck' ('*ōrep*). If the Moabite was similar it may signify something like 'firmness' (*cf*. 'stiff-necked'). Or, with ideas of feminine beauty rather different from ours, it may signify something like that which is said in the Song of Solomon, 'Thy neck is like the tower of David builded for an armoury, whereon there hang a thousand bucklers, all shields of mighty men' (Ct. 4:4, AV, RV, though in this passage the word for 'neck' is different). It is also possible that the name is a Hebrew designation given after her return to Moab. Then 'stiff-necked' will have derogatory associations (*cf*. Ex. 32:9; Pr. 29:1, *etc*.). *Ruth* may signify 'friendship' (a name singularly apt in view of the events narrated in this book), if we can connect it with the root we see in *r^eʿût* ('(woman) friend'). But this is not certain since, in the first place, we do not know whether the Moabite language had this root or not, and in the second, it is unlikely that the middle consonant would be lost. On the fact that Elimelech, Naomi, Mahlon are all good Hebrew names, whereas Orpah and Ruth, the names of foreigners, are not, Knight comments, 'Our author is careful to be accurate with his historical facts.'

After marriage, the young men settled down with their wives. The statement that *they dwelled there about ten years* probably covers the whole of their time there, and not simply the time of their married life. We have no way of knowing how old the sons were when they went to Moab, nor at what time they contracted their marriages. But probably these took place toward the end rather than the beginning of the ten years. Otherwise it is difficult to see why there should be no mention of children or of childlessness. But if the marriages were of fairly short duration the point would not arise.

**5.** At the end of the ten years both Mahlon and Chilion died. It is perhaps unusual that the three males of the household should perish. The Talmud regards it as a punishment for leaving Judah (Baba Bathra, 91a). No cause of death is given, but for the purposes of the story this is not important. It is the reactions of the women that matter. Naomi had now been bereaved of husband and all children. She was completely alone. For *left* see comment on verse 3. Literally translated, the Hebrew says 'left from'. The meaning will be 'she was left in separation from, far from, her two sons and her husband' (so Joüon, who says this use of *min* is not noticed by BDB, but *cf.* 2:18). Sons (AV, RSV) renders a word which may be used of small children (*cf.* 4:16) or of adults, but this is apparently the only place where it is used of married men.

## II. THE RETURN TO JUDAH (1:6–22)

### a. Ruth's steadfastness (1:6–18)

Naomi had no further stake in Moab. The news that the famine that had brought the family there in the first place was over was sufficient to cause her to decide to return home. This led to a problem for her daughters-in-law which they faced in different ways. It brought from Ruth a magnificent declaration of loyalty.

**6.** Naomi began to return home. The verb translated *arose* (*qûm*), though often used of a literal rising from a prone position, is also frequently used to indicate the commencement of an action, especially of a journey (*e.g.*, 1 Sa. 9:3,'And Kish said to Saul his son, Take now one of the servants with thee, and arise, go seek the asses', AV, RV). It is used in such a sense here, *cf.* RSV, *Then she started.* . . . The part the daughters-in-law played here is not certain. The verbs are all in the singular, so they describe Naomi's actions. It seems likely that she took the initiative in setting about her return home, and at first the younger widows associated themselves with her. The reason assigned for her return was that a report reached her in Moab that God had *visited* His people. This verb is rarely, if at all, used in our sense of going to see someone briefly. It is often used of the divine activity in the Old Testament. It sometimes carries overtones of punishment (*e.g.*, Je. 25:12, where it is translated 'punish'); sometimes, as here, of blessing. When God visits, everything depends on the state of affairs He finds. The verb is a warning against presuming on the holiness of God and a reminder that God delights to bless. On this occasion His visit means the end of the famine. The bread now available is regarded as God's gift. Incidentally, in this verse there is a slight difference in the Hebrew in the two expressions rendered *the country of Moab*: the first time it is the apparent plural, 'the fields of Moab', and in the second the form is singular, 'the field of Moab' (see note on verse 1). The fact that there seems no difference in meaning supports the view that in the former we have an archaic singular.

**7.** The initiative is clearly with Naomi. The verb is singular. She went out. Then it is added that her two daughters-in-law were with her and the next verb, *went*, is plural. The three of them took the road to Judah. A minor point is that whereas Moab is referred to as 'the fields of Moab', Judah is called *the land of Judah*. The territory of Judah (or Israel) is characteristically referred to in this way with the use of the term *'ereṣ* (as for that matter is the territory of most nations).

The impression one gets is of a very poor household, so that Naomi's preparations for the journey were soon made. The three women could thus walk together in the road to Judah before a final decision was reached as to whether they were all actually going there.

**8, 9.** These verses introduce us to the author's characteristic use of dialogue. Over fifty out of his total of eighty-five verses are taken up with dialogue, so it is obvious that he prefers to tell his story through conversations. Naomi now invites the younger widows to leave her and return to their homes. It is no part of her plan to involve them in a change of country. So she tells them to return, each to her mother's house. It is interesting that she refers to the mother rather than the father. This is a book written from a woman's point of view. Ruth, at least, had a father alive (2:11) and possibly Orpah did, too. But in a polygamous society the place for such as Ruth and Orpah would be the women's quarters presided over by the mother (*cf.* Ct. 3:4; 8:2). Yet the expression remains curious, all the more so since the 'father's house' is the general Old Testament way of referring to the place of a woman, even a widow returning home as here (*cf.* Gn. 38:11; Lv. 22:13; Nu. 30:16; Dt. 22:21). Naomi prays that Yahweh may *deal kindly* with them as they have done with the dead and with Naomi herself. We should not overlook the fact that she uses the

name 'Yahweh', the personal name of the God of Israel. It
might have been expected that in speaking of Moabite women
in Moabite territory she would use either the general word
'God' (*'elōhîm*) or else 'Chemosh' the name of one of the principal gods of the Moabites (Nu. 21:29; 1 Ki. 11:7). It is very
revealing that in the circumstances Naomi uses the name
'Yahweh'. For her, Chemosh need not be taken into consideration. She knew but one God and quite naturally she spoke of
Him. Such a use of the divine name springs from a deep-
seated monotheism. *Deal kindly with* represents a Hebrew
expression difficult to translate. The key word is *ḥesed*, often
rendered 'loving-kindness'. It is a word which on occasion
means something very like loyalty, and on occasion something
very like love. In the Old Testament it is often related to the
covenant, and it indicates the kind of warm and loyal attitude
that the parties ought to have for one another. The translation
of the AV brings out the thought of kindness that the word
includes, but not that of reliability. Naomi recognizes that
Yahweh is a God who is faithful and loving and prays that He
will deal with the daughters-in-law accordingly. She sees a
fitness in this because the young widows have been loyal
and loving to their deceased husbands and also to Naomi
herself. Thus her prayer is that their constancy may receive
an appropriate reward. Knox translates *you have shewn kindness
to the memory of the dead*. . . . This is not quite it. Naomi is thinking of their kindness to the dead men themselves, not to their
memory. Slotki takes the words as a statement, 'the Lord will
deal kindly', but a prayer seems more appropriate.

Naomi adds a prayer for the future prosperity of Ruth and
Orpah. Again she uses the personal name 'Yahweh', and again
she looks for Him to be active in the land of Moab. She prays
specifically that each of them may settle down with a new
husband. RSV reads, *The Lord grant that you may find a home*, but
AV's *that ye may find rest* is nearer to the Hebrew *m'nûḥâh* (*cf.* 3:1).
It is true that *rest* with a husband implies a home, but it is the
former and not the latter that is meant. It is also to be borne
in mind that for the Hebrew 'rest' could mean more than a
cessation from toil or trouble. To read such a passage as Joshua

21:43 – 22:8 is to see that 'rest' signifies more than the end of war: it means security and the blessing of the Lord, 'There failed not ought of any good thing which the Lord had spoken unto the house of Israel' (Jos. 21:45, AV, RV). In antiquity there were, of course, few jobs for women, especially in rural areas, so that marriage was almost the only career open to a woman. It was the one thing which promised stability. Naomi saw no future for the young women in her own country. Being Moabites they would be less likely to remarry in Israel. And what else could they do there other than share her poverty? So she kissed them in farewell and the trio joined in the loud weeping which was the Eastern expression of grief.[1]

**10.** Orpah and Ruth agree in rejecting the suggestion. They assure Naomi that they will certainly go back with her to her people. There is a difficulty about *kî* rendered *Surely* in AV, and *No* in RSV (also KB, Gerleman, *etc.*). The conjunction is common in the senses, 'that, for, when' (BDB). BDB think that it introduces the exact words of a speaker like the Greek *hoti*, but Joüon is doubtful whether this usage ever occurs. He thinks the *kî* of affirmation very rare, and prefers the meaning 'but' (as often after a negation). He supposes an original *lō* to have become corrupted to *lāh* or else to have dropped out of the text (so also Rudolph). This is perhaps over-elaborate, but an adversative meaning does seem to be required. Perhaps 'No' is as good a translation as we can find.

**11.** But Naomi will not commit them to her uncertain life.

---

[1] In these verses there are some grammatical points of interest. Although the reference is to women, there are masculine forms both for the suffixes denoting the personal pronouns and also for the verb. Similar forms are found in verses 11, 13, 19, 22; 4:11 and *cf. ḥayyîm* in 2:20. Some hold that this indicates a late date for the book when there was a weakening of grammatical gender. But this is not proved and as, in any case, grammarians seem agreed that the masculine was the prior gender, the point does not prove much. F. I. Andersen gives his opinion that these forms 'are perfectly good Old Hebrew duals (common gender and so distinguishable from plurals in consonantal writing only for feminines)'. They may be colloquial forms (except for 1:19,22 all are in conversation). All that can be said with certainty is that the forms are not used with the precision required in later times. The verb rendered *that ye may find* is unusual. It is a feminine imperative but, very exceptionally, lacks the final *he*. We might have expected a jussive in this place, but the imperative is somewhat more vigorous.

They are young and may well remarry in their own land and thus find security. She is too old for marriage. She has no prospect of providing them with a comfortable home. With her there is likely to be nothing but poverty and uncertainty. So she addresses them tenderly as *my daughters* (they are called 'daughters-in-law' three verses back) and tells them to turn back. She points to the hopelessness of their staying with her by reminding them that she will bear no more sons to be their husbands. The reference is to the custom of levirate marriage, whereby the brother of a man who died childless married the widow to raise up an heir for the deceased. The custom is regulated in Deuteronomy 25:5ff. (*cf.* Mt. 22:24ff.). Evidently the first child was accounted as though the son of the dead man.[1] Naomi is saying that there is no prospect of such a marriage in this case. This view is denied by some who affirm that the levirate marriage would be performed by Naomi to raise up the name of Elimelech. This would indeed be so were she not so old. But in any case what of Mahlon and Chilion? They had died childless and their widows might normally have looked to levirate marriage to preserve the names of the deceased. In this verse Naomi speaks of having no sons in her womb. She is not pregnant. In the next she proceeds to the thought that she is too old to remarry.

[1] This appears to be the distinctive Old Testament idea. Levirate marriage was widespread in the Ancient Near East and there is an extensive literature. See particularly H. H. Rowley, 'The Marriage of Ruth', *Harvard Theological Review*, XL, 1947, pp. 77–99, and the literature there cited; M. Burrows, *The Basis of Israelite Marriage* (American Oriental Society, 1938), 'The Ancient Oriental Background of Hebrew Levirate Marriage', *Bulletin of the American Schools of Oriental Research*, 77, Feb. 1940, pp. 2–15; E. Neufeld, *Ancient Hebrew Marriage Laws* (Longmans, 1944), pp. 23–55; H. Granqvist, 'Marriage Conditions in a Palestinian Village', ii (*Commentationes Humanarum Litterarum*, Helsingfors, 1935), pp. 303–310. H. H. Rowley cites Morgenstern on levirate marriage as a means of raising up a son to the deceased. 'This is an altogether new motif, not without occasional, though not frequent, parallels in the marriage practice of other, non-Semitic peoples, but entirely without parallel in Semitic practice, at least so far as present evidence goes. It is this motif which is characteristically Israelite, and which indicates that the institution of levirate marriage must have had an independent development in Israel' (*Harvard Theological Review*, XL, 1947, p. 82, n. 21). In Rabbinic times levirate marriage does not appear to be required with a Gentile woman (Yeb. 2:5), but there is no reason for thinking that this attitude is as old as the book of Ruth.

**12, 13.** She draws attention to her age. She is too old for marriage. Then she embarks on a somewhat different argument, but calculated, like the preceding, to show the impossibility of the young women's coming with her. Even should she become a wife again and bear sons, they could not wait for the boys to grow up. Naomi is clear that there is no point in their continuing with her. They should seek marriage elsewhere. Her *go your way* employs the same curious feminine imperative without the final *he* that we saw in verse 9 (p. 255 footnote [1]). It is also worth noting that she does not employ the usual construction for a conditional in the expression *If I should say*. Normally one would expect to find the imperfect, a tense which can denote very various degrees of contingency. Naomi, however, uses the perfect tense, which conceives the condition as actual, 'If I have said. . . . 'She obtains the maximum effect in bringing out the absurdity of the position by presenting the supposition realistically. There is a further peculiarity in the twice-repeated *hᵃlāhēn* rendered *for them* in AV and *therefore* in RSV. The latter understanding of it views it as an Aramaic word, not Hebrew. But it is not at all certain that the word *lāhēn* meaning 'therefore' exists in Aramaic. Lattey's examination of the problem concludes, 'The case for a *lahen* meaning "therefore" in biblical Aramaic is thus so weak that it appears safer to treat it as a mistake here, no less than in Hebrew.'[1] G. R. Driver also has grave doubts whether this form ever occurs in Aramaic meaning 'therefore' and takes the meaning here to be 'for those things'.[2] Joüon amends the text to *lāhem*, the usual masculine 'for them' (he also recognizes the possibility that the feminine *lāhen* was used in the sense of the masculine, but the end result is the same). There is also the possibility, as Gerleman thinks, of taking the form as a feminine plural used in a neuter sense referring to the conditions Naomi has just laid down, 'Could you in these cir-

[1] Lattey, p. xxxvii.

[2] *Miscellanea Orientalia, dedicata Antonio Deimel annos LXX complenti* (Pontificio Istituto Biblico, 1935), pp. 64–66. Myers also doubts whether this is Aramaic. He notes the possibility and proceeds, 'but in view of LXX reading and the constant confusion of gender in Ruth that cannot be proved' (Myers, p. 27)

cumstances wait?' (*i.e.*, on the basis of the fulfilment of these uncertain and improbable events). It is possibly best taken as an inexact piece of Hebrew, equivalent to *hᵃlāhem*. This yields the meaning *for them* as AV. 'For them' seems also to be the meaning understood by the LXX, Vulg. and Syriac versions, and it should be accepted. From its position it is emphatic, 'for *them*'. BDB think the verb rendered *tarry* (AV, RV) is an Aramaism, but it is found in Hebrew (*cf.* Ps. 119:166).

So Naomi rejects with decision the thought that Orpah and Ruth should continue with her. Her *nay* (AV, RV) has a ring of finality about it. This is not an easy decision for her and she goes on to express regret. *It grieveth me much* (AV, RV) is literally, 'It is very bitter to me' (an impersonal use of the verb; in verse 20, God is the subject of the same verb). *Your* is another example of the use of a masculine form of the pronoun though applied to the women (unless it is a dual; see note on verses 8,9).

*It grieveth me much for your sakes that the hand of the Lord* (AV) does not give the sense of the Hebrew (which is comparative in form) as well as does the RV margin, 'it is far more bitter for me than for you'. Nor does it accord so well with the context. They had each lost a husband. Naomi had lost a husband and two sons as well. Moreover, the young widows could remarry and thus find security and happiness. For Naomi there was no prospect other than a lonely old age, embittered by the thought that *the hand of the Lord is gone out against me* (AV). These concluding words arise from a conviction that underlies the whole of this book, namely, that things do not happen by chance. God is a sovereign God and He brings to pass what He will. Thus Naomi can ascribe responsibility for what has befallen her to no-one but Him. *The hand of the Lord* is an anthropomorphism in fairly common use. The Old Testament uses parts of the body freely to express inward states and the like, and does this even when speaking of God. God's *hand* is a way, then, of speaking of God's activity. The verb *gone out* is sometimes used of an army going out with hostile intent, and this may be behind the usage here (*cf.* BDB). Naomi cannot encourage the girls to stay with her. Yahweh is her enemy.

**14.** Naomi's words provoked more tears. Again the women raised their voice in lamentation. But this time there was also action. The meaning of Naomi's words sank in and each of the two younger widows reacted. Orpah *kissed her mother in law*. In verse 9, Naomi had kissed Orpah, but on that occasion Orpah had not realized what was involved and did not take it as final. Now she understood and she took the initiative by kissing Naomi. This was farewell and they both knew it (for the kiss of farewell, *cf.* Gn. 31:28; 1 Ki. 19:20). Orpah is usually blamed, but J. T. Cleland in *IB* reminds us of her 'submissive obedience'. He points out that 'she was dissuaded by the sensible counsel of the older woman; she returned to Moab. There is no good cause to disparage her. Obedience is not a virtue either to be overlooked or censured.' We may feel that Ruth showed more imagination and deeper love. But let us not be too quick to blame Orpah. At the same time we must notice that Ruth was not so easily persuaded. She had given her loyalty to Naomi and she would not lightly withdraw it. So when Orpah kissed Naomi goodbye Ruth *clung to her* (RSV). Cassel points out that 'the same cause induced Orpah to go and Ruth to remain, the fact, namely, that Naomi had no longer either son or husband. The one wished to become a wife again, the other to remain a daughter.'

**15.** The subject of *said* is not expressed, but the context shows plainly that it is Naomi. She uses the example of Orpah as a lever to induce Ruth to follow suit. She does not speak of Orpah as having returned home, or to her own country, but to *her people* and *her gods* (AV, RSV) (or perhaps *her god* (RV); it is possible to take *'elohîm* as either singular or plural, and Chemosh was the god of the Moabites, Nu. 21:29; 1 Ki. 11:7). *Her people* means 'her nation', not her family as the English expression might perhaps indicate. The reference to the gods is sometimes held to point to a belief that a god and a certain piece of territory were closely connected, so that the god can be worshipped only on the soil of his own country. The classic example of this is said to be Naaman, who, having become a worshipper of Yahweh, took back to Syria with him 'two mules' burden of earth' so that he could worship Him (2 Ki.

5:17). But the idea was far from being universally held. There are, for example, instances cited of kings and others in vassal-states worshipping the deities of their foreign overlords. For that matter Solomon worshipped Chemosh on the soil of Judah without the pressure of a foreign overlord (1 Ki. 11:7). We have already noticed that Naomi thought of Yahweh as active in Moab (verses 8,9,13), so it is plain that she held no such idea. She may possibly have thought that Ruth would have been attracted by the idea and so referred to it. But her words need mean no more than that the Moabites were the community of Chemosh-worshippers. If Ruth were to continue to worship Chemosh she would be well advised to go where he was venerated. It is perhaps worth adding that, while the Bible never takes seriously the existence of other gods than Yahweh as real gods, it always assumes their reality as objects of worship. Chemosh was certainly worshipped in Moab, and Orpah must be assumed to be worshipping him.

**16.** Ruth's answer is a classic expression of faithfulness. She declares her undying devotion to Naomi and refuses to leave her now or at any time. She first tells Naomi to cease to entreat her to leave her. Then she affirms her determination to go where Naomi goes, and to stay where Naomi stays. The verb in the expression *where thou lodgest, I will lodge* (AV) is not usually used of a long stay (other than in poetry), but this appears to be Ruth's meaning. She realizes what this means as the following expression indicates. She will be cut off from her own people Moab, but she will make Naomi's people her own. And her decision has religious implications of which she is not unaware. Naomi's God will be her God. This does not mean that she has no religious principles or that she rates friendship above faith. In the very next verse she invokes Yahweh, which indicates that already she has come to trust in Him (*cf.* 2:12). Her trust may not have been well informed, but it was real. Simeon remarks, 'Her views of religion might not be clear: but it is evident that a principle of vital godliness was rooted in her heart, and powerfully operative in her life. In fact, she acted in perfect conformity with that injunction that was afterwards given by our Lord, "Whosoever he be of you that forsaketh not all that he hath, he cannot be my disciple".'[1]

**17.** Ruth's determination to be with Naomi is not meant to be short-lived. She will stay with Naomi until death, and die where Naomi dies. As Ruth was much younger than Naomi and would presumably live longer this implies that she will so identify herself with Naomi's community that she will stay on there after Naomi's death. The reference to burial seems scarcely to be needed, but we must bear in mind that for the ancient world proper burial was of great importance. Even after death Ruth plans to be with Naomi. She concludes by calling down divine punishment upon herself should she fail to keep her word. The formula she uses is found in this full form only in the books of Samuel and Kings besides Ruth (though a shorter form occurs elsewhere).[2] It suggests but does not define the punishment that should follow the breaking of the oath. *So* was perhaps accompanied by some expressive gesture (touching the throat?). Otherwise it is incomprehensible. The addition *and more also* to the undefined *do so to me* indicates the direst possible consequences. There can be no doubt that Ruth is in earnest. We should not overlook her use of the divine name 'Yahweh'. She does not invoke Chemosh or the gods generally. She has taken Yahweh to be her God and it is upon Him accordingly that she calls. AV and RV perhaps misrepresent her point by saying *if ought but death part thee and me.* KD deny that *kî* here means 'if', and think it introduces the terms of the oath, thus signifying, 'I swear that death, and nothing else than death, shall separate us.' But more probably Ruth is saying, 'if death itself part thee and me', or as RSV expresses it, *if even death parts me from you.* This is supported by the emphatic position of the word *death* in the Hebrew. It accords with this that she goes on to speak of being buried with Naomi. Ruth is determined that nothing, not even death, shall separate them.

**18.** This little speech greatly impressed Naomi. She saw that Ruth was determined. The verb *was stedfastly minded* (AV, RV)

[1] Simeon, p. 91.
[2] D. J. Wiseman informs me that the same formula is found at Mari and Alalakh in the eighteenth century BC.

is used in a great variety of senses, for example, of giving the clouds their place, or repairing the Temple, of physical vigour, *etc.* It indicates an unshakable firmness. So Naomi accepted the situation and stopped arguing. Indeed after Ruth had concluded with a solemn oath there would have been something impious or very close to it in seeking to dissuade her.

### b. The arrival in Bethlehem (1:19–22)
The journey back to Israel is not described, but the reception of the two widows by the women of Bethlehem is. They received a welcome, but Naomi could not but contrast her present difficult state with her condition when she had left the village.

**19.** The pair journeyed till they came to Bethlehem. As they approached the city there was a buzz of excitement. The whole place was involved. But as soon as we come to a place where the sex can be determined, namely, the verb *they said* (AV), the feminine form shows that it is *the women* (RV, RSV) with whom the story is concerned (*cf.* Knox, *all the gossips were saying*). This is almost inevitably the case since the men were at work on the harvest (verse 22). The women of Bethlehem saw the pair approaching, and came excitedly out to greet them. They asked *Is this Naomi?* Years had passed since she lived there, and those years had dealt harshly with her. It would not be surprising, accordingly, if she was sufficiently altered in appearance to make such a question appropriate.

**20.** Naomi puts stress on the meaning of her name (see on verse 2). Her experiences have been anything but pleasant, and she disclaims the name 'Pleasant' accordingly. She suggests that the women (the forms of pronoun and verb are feminine) should call her *Mara'*, a word which means 'bitter' (the form of this word with final *aleph* instead of *he* is Aramaic or perhaps Moabitic rather than Hebrew). Her reason is that God has dealt very bitterly with her (*cf.* Jb. 13:26). Moffatt brings out something of the word-play in the Hebrew with, *call me Mara, for the Almighty has cruelly marred me.* Naomi does not think of chance or of the work of the gods of the heathen. She is sure that her God is over all, so that the explanation of the bitter things she has experienced must be with Him. The name she uses for God is *šadday*, not the commonest of names, and one which appears to mean 'Almighty' (see Additional Note, pp. 264ff.). Naomi thinks of the irresistible power of God. When He determined that bitterness should enter her life there was no other possibility. It is worth noticing that, while the name *šadday* is sometimes used in contexts of blessing, it is also found when it is the severity as well as the power of the Lord that is in mind (*e.g.*, Is. 13:6; Joel 1:15). This is one of very few places where it stands alone in prose (this is not unusual in poetry, but in prose 'God Almighty' is more common). F. I. Andersen points out that Naomi's speech may well be poetry. In verse 22 *šadday* is found in good, poetic parallelism.

**21.** Naomi contrasts her departure from Bethlehem with her return. *Full* and *empty* occupy emphatic positions in their respective clauses. The latter term is actually the adverb 'emptily' and not the adjective which we would have expected (*cf.* also 3:17, though there the adverb is more in place). Naomi uses the personal pronoun in the first clause, though this is not strictly necessary as the verb would give the meaning by its form. This emphatic pronoun sets Naomi over against the Lord. She for her part went out prosperous, but He brought her back indigent. She uses the covenant name 'Yahweh'. Yet again there is the thought that this God is supreme in Moab as elsewhere. Naomi asks accordingly why they use her name 'Pleasant', since Yahweh has 'made answer against' her or perhaps better 'afflicted' her. It is a question of the correct vocalization of the text. That behind AV, *testified*, demands *'ānâh* (favoured by Rudolph), but LXX, Syriac and Vulg. presuppose *'innâh*, 'afflicted', and this fits the context better (though a difficulty is the following *bᵉ* which is not natural after this verb). *Cf.* RSV, *the Lord has afflicted me and the Almighty has brought calamity upon me*. Naomi uses the name *šadday* once more. She is helpless in the face of God's almighty power.

**22.** For *the Moabitess* see on 2:2. This verse simply rounds off the narrative of the return. It locates it at the beginning of barley harvest (*i.e.*, towards the end of April), but otherwise simply says that it took place. As Ruth had not, as far as we know, ever been in Judah the verb *returned* seems a curious one to use of her. It is perhaps worth noting that this verb (*šûḇ*) occurs twelve times in this chapter (of return to Moab, verses 8, 11, 12, 15 (twice), 16; of return to Bethlehem, 6, 7, 10, 21, 22 (twice)) and that it is a verb which for the Hebrew was full of associations. It meant a return to the land of God's people. Used thus of Ruth at the end of the chapter it may be meant to signify something of this.[1] The expression *barley harvest* is found in the Gezer Calendar which speaks of 'Month of pulling flax. Month of barley harvest. Month when everything (else) is harvested.'[2]

## Additional Note on *šadday*

The divine name rendered *the Almighty* in Ruth 1:21 is the Hebrew *šadday*. This term is used in this way forty-eight times. It is especially common in the book of Job where it is found thirty-one times. In prose it is often linked with *'el* in the expression translated 'God almighty', but in poetry it commonly stands alone, though *'el* may be used in parallelism (*e.g.*, Jb. 8:3). The significance to be attached to *šadday* is not immediately obvious, and very varied suggestions have been made. Mostly they centre round the thoughts of power or compassion.

An obvious approach is the etymological one. Many have felt that by starting with the root meaning of the word we will

[1] There are some minor grammatical peculiarities. Thus the pronoun *they* is masculine in form, though referring to two woman (or it may be dual; see note on 1:8, 9). The form rendered *which returned* in the consonantal text appears to be the participle preceded by the article. The Massoretes, however, inserted the vowels of the perfect, a tense which could not have the article. The reason for this is far from clear, unless it is that they wanted to bring out the past tense. Joüon thinks that they have given the article the value of a relative pronoun.

[2] J. Mauchline in *Documents from Old Testament Times*, ed. D. Winton Thomas (Nelson, 1958), p. 201. Mauchline speaks of the Calendar as 'the most ancient inscription in Early Hebrew writing, as old as the age of Saul or David' (*ibid.*). J. B. Segal dates it in 'the tenth to ninth century, the period to which it is already assigned by most scholars' (*Journal of Semitic Studies*, VII, 1962, p. 218).

be led to its significance as a divine name. Unfortunately, however, there is little agreement among scholars as to what the root meaning is. Thus Norman Walker, in an important article, lists and rejects eleven suggested derivations and proceeds to add another of his own.[1] He notes three from the Hebrew, namely 'My destroyer' (*sh-d-d*, 'destroy') favoured by Franz Delitzsch, A. Dillmann and B. Stade, 'My Rain-giver' (*sh-d-h*, 'give rain') favoured by W. Robertson Smith, and 'My Demon' (*shēd*, 'demon') suggested by T. Nöldeke. Eight he sees as based on the view that ultimately the term comes from the Assyrian *shadû*, 'mountain'. He lists 'My Mountain' (Friedrich Delitzsch), 'of the Mountains' (C. J. Ball), 'Mountain' (through the Aramaic; F. Baethgen, S. A. Cook), 'Mountain-Moon' (*shadû+ai*, 'moon'; F. Hommel), 'of the Two Mountains' (dual form; H. Radau), 'of the Hill-Country' (G. A. Barton), 'of the Mountains' (W. F. Albright), and 'of the Mountains' (through the Amorite *shadê*; Garrow Duncan). To this impressive list Norman Walker adds his own derivation of the term. He thinks it comes from the Sumerian *šazu*, the eighteenth of the god Marduk's fifty names. This he sees as meaning 'All-knowing', which 'seems more in keeping with the thoughts of the devoutly religious, like Abraham, Naomi and Job, than the Greek rendering "All-ruling, Almighty" of the Septuagint'.[2]

Even this dozen suggestions does not exhaust the possibilities. H. F. Stevenson holds to 'the traditional view that *Shaddai* is derived from the word "invariably used in Scripture for a woman's breast" (Schofield)'.[3] He thinks that the term denotes 'the Breasted One' and maintains that it points to the compassion of God. He cites G. Campbell Morgan and Canon R. B. Girdlestone in support of this view, the former rendering it by 'God All-bountiful' or 'God All-sufficient'.

John Skinner mentions yet other suggestions. He reminds us of the traditional Jewish derivation from *š*=*ᵃšer* and *day*, 'the

---

[1] 'A New Interpretation of the Divine Name "Shaddai" ', *Zeitschrift für die Alttestamentliche Wissenschaft*, 72, 1960, pp. 64–66.
[2] *Op. cit.*, p. 66.
[3] *Titles of the Triune God* (Marshall, Morgan & Scott, 1955), p. 38.

all-sufficient' or 'self-sufficient'. He refers to others we have listed, and to some, like that from the Syriac meaning 'to hurl', that we have not.[1]

But it is clear that we have gone far enough along this road. Etymology yields such varied results that there can be no doubt but that it is a dubious guide to the meaning of the word. There is nothing at all that gives us conclusive information about its derivation.[2] All conclusions based on etymology must be regarded as hazardous in our present state of knowledge.

We turn to the way the word is used. *šadday* is an ancient name, for God said to Moses, 'I appeared unto Abraham, unto Isaac, and unto Jacob, by the name of '*el šadday*' (Ex. 6:3, AV). This is borne out by a study of Genesis. The first occurrence of the name is in the Lord's appearance to Abraham when that patriarch was ninety-nine years old. God said, 'I am '*el šadday*' (Gn. 17:1), after which He commanded him to walk before Him and be perfect, and promised to make a covenant with him. Isaac called on '*el šadday* to bless Jacob on the occasion when he was about to set out for Padan-aram (Gn. 28:3). When God appeared to Jacob and changed his name to Israel He told him, 'I am '*el šadday*: be fruitful and multiply . . . the land which I gave Abraham and Isaac, to thee I will give it' (Gn. 35:11f., AV). In each of these passages there is the thought of the power of God. He disposes as He sees fit, and no obstacle need be taken into account. But equally every one of the passages we have cited could be understood of a compassionate God, who had mercy on Abraham and on Isaac and on Jacob and blessed them all. It would also not be difficult to make out a case for omniscience, with the 'All-Knowing' declaring in each case exactly what will come to

---

[1] *Genesis, International Critical Commentary* (T. & T. Clark, 1951), pp. 290f.

[2] S. R. Driver could say, 'The real meaning of *Shaddai* is extremely uncertain, neither tradition nor philology throwing any certain light upon it'; 'as regards the real meaning of *Shaddai*, we are entirely in the dark: neither Hebrew nor any of the cognate Semitic languages offers any convincing explanation of it' (*The Book of Genesis* (Methuen, 1904), pp. 404, 406). The choice of this word he sees as due sometimes at any rate to the thought of God's power either in the way of blessing and protection, or of punishment.

pass. This is a difficulty which often meets us. In many passages more than one suggested meaning yields a satisfactory sense.

There are some places, however, where the thought of power seems more appropriate than any other meaning, as when we read in Psalm 68:14 of the time 'When *šadday* scattered kings', or when *šadday* is the abiding place of him 'that dwelleth in the secret place of the most High'. This man 'shall abide under the shadow of *šadday*. I will say of the Lord, He is my refuge and my fortress' (Ps. 91:1f., AV; *cf.* Jb. 22:25). The thought here is surely that of strength. So is it when Isaiah calls on men to howl, 'for the day of the Lord is at hand; it shall come as a destruction from *šadday*' (Is. 13:6, AV). Joel also speaks of the day of the Lord as at hand, and he tells us that 'as a destruction from *šadday* shall it come' (Joel 1:15, AV). Ezekiel twice refers to the voice of *šadday*, likening it to the sound of many waters and to the noise of the wings of the cherubim (Ezk. 1:24; 10:5). There are also some passages in Job where the thought of power seems appropriate, as when the patriarch is exhorted, 'despise not thou the chastening of *šadday*: for he maketh sore, and bindeth up: he woundeth, and his hands make whole' (Jb. 5:17f., AV). So Job can say, 'the arrows of *šadday* are within me, the poison whereof drinketh up my spirit: the terrors of God do set themselves in array against me' (Jb. 6:4, AV; *cf.* 23:16; 27:2). Similarly, Zophar's series of questions indicates the greatness of God: 'Canst thou by searching find out God? canst thou find out *šadday* unto perfection?' (Jb. 11:7, AV). Again, Elihu could say, 'Touching *šadday*, we cannot find him out' (Jb. 37:23, AV).

From all this it seems that the thought of power does attach to the name. There are many passages wherein this is the most appropriate meaning, and very few, if any, where it is not acceptable. We should accordingly take this to be the basic force of *šadday* as a name of God.

When Naomi then says '*šadday* hath dealt very bitterly with me' and '*šadday* hath afflicted me' (Ru. 1:20f., AV) the emphasis will be on God's great power. He cannot be resisted. If He sends disaster on anyone, that disaster cannot be averted. The book, of course, goes on to bring out the complementary thought that God in His grace has mercy on His people. But our author does not choose to use this name of God when he brings out the point.

## III. RUTH THE GLEANER (2:1-23)

This chapter gives us a glimpse of the life of the poor in ancient Palestine. There were not many ways of making a living open to widows but one such was provided by the custom of gleaning. It was laid down in the law that at harvest-time a man must not reap his land to the very border, nor should he pick up what was left after the reapers went through (Lv. 19:9; 23:22). Indeed, if he forgot a sheaf and left it in the field he was forbidden to go back for it (Dt. 24:19). In such ways as these a certain provision was made for the poor. They could go through the fields after the reapers and glean what they could. Similar provision was made concerning grape harvest (Lv. 19:10; Dt. 24:21) and olive harvest (Dt. 24:20), but these do not concern us here. Ruth and Naomi were obviously very poor, and it was well for them that they arrived in their new home at the beginning of harvest. It enabled them to get some food immediately.

### a. The field of Boaz (2:1-3)

Ruth, the younger and more able-bodied, sets out to glean and finds herself in the field of a kinsman.

**1.** Boaz is now brought on the scene. He is described as a *kinsman* of Elimelech's, though the exact relationship is not defined. In rendering *kinsman*, AV, *etc.* follow the Massoretic pointing. The consonantal text designates Boaz as an acquaintance only, but this is not in accordance with later statements (2:20; 3:2, 12; 4:3). Most commentators agree with AV. Joüon is of opinion that we should not translate *of her husband's*, but 'by her husband'. Boaz was not a relation of Naomi. He was connected with her only 'by' Elimelech. This is important. It was because of the connection with Elimelech that Boaz could be the *gōʼēl*. Relationship to Naomi would not have sufficed. *Family* here denotes a larger group than does a family with us, though a close community is certainly implied. It is rather like a Scottish 'clan'. The exact expression rendered *a mighty man of wealth* (AV, RV) is elsewhere translated 'a mighty man of valour' (*e.g.*, Jdg. 11:1). We perhaps get the force of it by thinking of our word 'knight'. This applied originally to a man distinguished for military prowess, but it is now used widely of those whose excellence lies in other fields. In the Old Testament it most often has to do with fighting capacity. Boaz may have been a warrior, for these were troubled times and any man might have to fight. But in this book he appears rather as a solid citizen, a man of influence and integrity in the community and it is likely that this is what the term denotes here. Some suggest 'a powerful landowner'. The word rendered 'valour' is used of general moral worth in 3:11 (where see note), and something of this may be implied here. The name *Boaz* is found again as the name of one of the pillars in Solomon's Temple (1 Ki. 7:21; 2 Ch. 3:17; D. J. Wiseman thinks that there it may be the first word of an oracle ascribing strength to the Davidic dynasty; see *NBD*, p. 593). Its meaning is not certain, but it may connect with the idea of quickness or of strength (Cassel derives it from *ben 'āz*, 'son of strength').

**2.** Ruth now takes the initiative by suggesting that she should go to the field and glean. Notice that our author is not losing sight of his heroine's origin, for he speaks of her as *the Moabitess*, a designation which is found five times (1:22; 2:2,21; 4:5,10) out of twelve occurrences of the name of Ruth. The Moabite nationality of his heroine is an important part of his story. *Field* is singular. We are not to think of many farms about the village with each man owning his own fields. There appears to be a common field where all grow their crops, with ownership vested in parts of the one great field. Ruth suggested that she *glean ears*[1] after one with whom she should find favour

[1] As is often the case the verb *lqt* is followed by *bᵉ* (*cf.* RSV, *glean among the ears*). This is classed by BDB (*sub lqt*) as *b* loc. or partitive, *i.e.*, it designates the place where the gleaning is carried on, or that one gleans some of the ears. The former is unsatisfactory for one gleans ears, not among ears, so we accept the latter. Joüon, however, rejects this in favour of what he calls '*bᵉ participatif*', *i.e.*, 'I will work at the gleaning of the ears'. W. L. Moran points out that Ugaritic use has clarified our understanding of certain Hebrew prepositions, and specifically that it shows that the preposition *bᵉ* is often

(Berkeley, *someone who is kind to me*). The reference to *him in whose sight I shall find grace* is interesting for the law laid it down uncompromisingly that the land was not to be reaped in its entirety, but something was to be left for the poor to glean (Lv. 19:9f.; 23:22; Dt. 24:19). Gleaning was not dependent on the whims of landowners. It was a right and, moreover, a right specifically granted in the law to the widow (Dt. 24:19). But in the first place, Ruth may not have been fully conversant with the laws of her adopted country, and in the second, we need not doubt that a hostile landowner would have ways of making gleaning difficult for the friendless. It was better for Ruth to look for someone who would regard her with favour.

**3.** So Ruth went to the field and gleaned after the reapers. Slotki understands *she went, and came* (AV, RV) to mean, 'She repeated the act of going out and coming back home again so as to familiarize herself with the bewildering network of country lanes, while at the same time making the acquaintance of decent folk to whom she could safely attach herself.' But this seems to be reading a lot into the expression. *Her hap was* (AV, RV) is the translation of an expression which makes it clear that Ruth did not understand the full significance of what she was doing. She did not know the people, nor did she know the owners of the land. She came to the field and, apparently by chance, worked in a particular section of the field, the section which belonged to Boaz. Almost exactly the same expression is found in Ecclesiastes 2:14f. ('one event happeneth' to all men) and nowhere else in the Old Testament. It points to the truth that men do not control events, but that the hand of God is behind them as He works His purpose out. It was the fact that she came to this field and no other that was to lead to her acquaintance with Boaz and subsequent marriage with all that that involved (including, for example, the fact that it led up to the birth of David). Our author thinks of God as being in all this. The Hebrew refers to 'the piece of the field belonging to Boaz' and not 'a part of the field of Boaz'. This probably

used where we would say 'from' (*The Bible and the Ancient Near East*, ed. G. E. Wright (New York, 1961), p. 61).

means 'that part of the common field which belonged to Boaz'. It is said that grain fields were not divided from one another by a fence or hedge, but that the boundary was simply indicated by stones (*cf*. Hackett, cited in Cassel). Alternatively, 'the field-portion of Boaz' might mean 'the fields belonging to Boaz'. Our author repeats the information that Boaz was from Elimelech's clan. The hand of God is over Ruth's action, and he does not want us to miss this.

### b. Boaz' provision for Ruth (2:4-17)
Boaz had heard of Ruth's kindness to Naomi, and when he found her gleaning in his part of the field he took steps to see that she should work unmolested.

**4.** *Behold* brings a touch of vividness to the narrative. The author sees the events happening (*cf*. Berkeley, *Then, look . . .*). The verb rendered *came* could be either the participle, in which case the writer sees Boaz 'coming' from the town, or the perfect, when he would be thinking of him as having arrived. Perhaps the latter is a little more likely so that AV gives the sense of it. Boaz evidently lived in Bethlehem, and came out to the scene of labour after the reapers had started their work. He seems to have been one of those who believe that their religious faith should enter their daily work, for his greeting to his employees was *The Lord be with you* (the Syriac reads 'Peace be with you'). This elicited the kindred response, *The Lord bless thee* (AV, RV). There is nothing to show that this form of greeting was considered unusual, but it does not appear to be attested elsewhere. If it was a conventional greeting we should not read too much into it (*cf*. our 'Goodbye', which retains little of its original religious flavour).

**5.** Boaz' attention was immediately attracted by Ruth. He addressed a question about her to his 'boy' set over the reapers. The word rendered *servant* has quite a wide range of meaning. It can denote a baby (Ex. 2:6) or a lad seventeen years old (Gn. 37:2). But it can also mean a servant (as in other languages). Indeed this is a very frequent use of the term. It is not without its interest that *damsel* (AV, RV) is the feminine form of the same word, a word play impossible to reproduce in

English. The feminine usually refers to an unmarried woman. An exception occurs in 4:12, where it is used of Ruth by the elders, though they know her to have been married. We should take it here as general, *i.e.*, 'young woman'. Boaz assumes that Ruth is a servant girl, but he does not recognize her. So he inquires as to her owner.

**6.** His boy answers that she is *the* (so LXX; the Hebrew has no article) Moabite girl who returned with Naomi from 'the field of Moab'. For this expression see note on 1:1. The expression *that came back* (AV, RV) is the same as that rendered 'which returned' in 1:22 (see note on this). We should probably take it as a participle with the article, to give the meaning, 'a Moabite young woman, the one who came back with Naomi'. She is first described as 'a' Moabite, then as 'the' one which came with Naomi.

**7.** The boy's report continues. Ruth had asked him, he said, to let her glean and gather among the sheaves (this latter is lacking in the Syriac and Vulg.). This implies more than simply going over the field after the reapers. It indicates that anything that fell from the sheaves (though originally gathered by the reapers) was regarded as belonging to the gleaners. There is a difficulty in that gleaning among the sheaves is regarded as a special favour (verse 15) and Ruth would scarcely have sought more than the common lot of gleaners. Joüon thinks of a *bᵉ participatif* as in verse 2, and he vocalizes the consonants '*mrym* to read "*mīrîm*, 'stalks', instead of MT, "*mārîm*, 'sheaves'. This makes the verse rather like verse 2, and may be the sense of it. The boy comments on Ruth's persistence. She came (this verb may indicate that the conversation took place some distance from where the reaping was being done) in the morning and continued right up till the time of speaking (though, of course, we do not know what time of day that was). Evidently he had taken good notice of Ruth, for he had observed that she spent a short time *in the house* (AV, RV). There are difficulties about the last part of this verse. One concerns the meaning of *the house*. Knox and FF take it to mean Ruth's own home, but one would have thought that that would be too far off for a short rest, which is what is

envisaged. If the word be read, it is better to think of a
house, perhaps a temporary shelter, adjacent to the field being
reaped. It is unlikely to mean a regular house in such a situation, for houses tended to be grouped for protection, with the
fields outside the villages. An isolated house would be unusual.
But then there are textual difficulties. Literally the Hebrew
reads 'this her sitting the house a little'. AV and RV make as
good sense of this as seems possible. But the versions presuppose a different text. LXX reads, 'from morning to evening she
did not rest in the field a little', and Vulg., 'and she did not
return home', while the Syriac omits some of the words. The
commentators adopt various conjectures. Thus Gerleman omits
*the house* (thinking the word has been inserted by dittography)
and removes *zeh* ('this') by taking it closely with the preceding
'*attâh* ('just now'). The result is 'from morning until just now
she has rested only a little'. Joüon replaces *zeh* with *lō* (as LXX),
points the next word *šāḇʿṭâh* instead of MT, *šiḇtāh*, and alters
*habbayiṯ* to *šabbāṯ* to give the sense 'she has not allowed herself
(even) a little rest'. A different meaning is assigned to the
Hebrew text by Lattey, who renders, 'Her dwelling in her
present home hath been but short.' This has the advantage of
sticking to the Hebrew text, but the disadvantage of appearing
to be irrelevant. Wright takes *zeh* to mean the present state of
affairs: 'This her sitting in the house has been but for a little',
which he paraphrases as, 'she has been sitting in the house, as
you see her now, only for a short time.' *House* on this view
denotes a tent or other temporary shelter provided for the
convenience of the workers. L. P. Smith in *IB* takes a similar
view, but if there were such a shelter one would perhaps have
expected it to be mentioned in verse 14. The resolution of the
difficulty is not easy. Though the Hebrew text is difficult it
seems better to rely on it than on the versions (which introduce
difficulties of their own). Thus, whatever be the decision on
minor points, the meaning of the words will be as AV. Ruth
has worked hard all the morning, but she did take one short
rest.

**8.** Boaz now addresses Ruth. His *Hearest thou not, my daughter?*
(AV, RV) secures her attention for what follows. The verb

*šāmaʿ* sometimes means 'understand' and not simply 'hear' (as in Gn. 11:7; 42:23) and this may well be the case here. The form of the question looks for an affirmative answer. The form of address, *my daughter*, points to a disparity of ages. He instructs her not to glean elsewhere. *Neither go* (AV) represents an emphatic prohibition in the Hebrew (*lōʾ* rather than *ʿal*). This seems to imply that there might be advantages for the gleaner in moving about from one farmer's crop to that of another. Boaz, however, takes steps to ensure that Ruth will be better off by remaining in this part of the field. He now gives her a direction to remain with his maidservants. This apparently indicates some form of status in Boaz' household. The verb rendered *abide* (AV, RV) is here followed by an unusual preposition (*dāḇaq ʿim*), a construction found only here and in verse 21, both times ascribed to Boaz. Joüon thinks this a provincialism or solecism which the author himself does not employ, for he uses the correct *bᵉ* (1:14; 2:23). It is a piece of local colour as being the way Boaz would speak. The word rendered *here* in the AV, RV (*kōh*) is unexpected in view of the preceding *from hence* (RV), but it is arbitrary with Joüon to alter to *kî*, 'but', and drop the *wᵉ*.

**9.** Boaz tells Ruth to keep her eyes on the field which they are reaping and to go after them. *Them* is feminine in form and it indicates that Boaz' maidens had some function to perform in the reaping. Perhaps the men cut the crop and the girls tied the bundles. Alternatively, the maidens did some reaping, the masculine verb *reap* being used of the feminine (as in 1:8). Men and women normally worked together at harvest. There was an urgency about the task that demanded the fullest effort from everybody. Joüon thinks the feminine form a textual error. He argues that had there been maidens Ruth should have drunk with them and not the men (but this verse does not speak of drinking with the men, only of drinking what the men have drawn), that she should have sat with the maidens rather than the men (verse 14), and that when Ruth is reporting these same words of Boaz she uses the masculine (verse 21). But the feminine form occurs a number of times (8, 9, 22, 23; 3:2) and accidental error seems an impossible explanation in every case. It is better to take the natural meaning and see a reference to young women. Boaz further encourages Ruth by letting her know that he has given orders to the young men not to molest her. One can imagine that the enthusiasm of the gleaners would cause them to encroach on the legitimate property of the owners of the crops unless they were checked, and that accordingly the reapers might repulse, by force, if necessary, any who came too near before the owners were through. Ruth would know this and keep her distance. Boaz' instruction to Ruth enabled her to work close to the reapers in a position specially favourable for gleaning. But this very position exposed her to the possibility of rude jests and even mishandling from the workmen. He now tells her that he has guarded against this by giving instructions to the reapers that they were to leave her alone. His order would allow her to approach before other gleaners and thus ensure that she obtained a good reward for her labours, and this without being treated disrespectfully. But Boaz' kindness does not stop there. Ruth is bidden help herself when she is thirsty from what the young men have drawn. The liquid is not specified, but probably water is meant (though Joüon thinks of wine, or a mixture of water and wine). This would be a valuable provision, for gleaning in the heat of harvest-time would be thirsty work, and no doubt the water so laboriously drawn and carried to the place of reaping would be jealously guarded from all but those entitled to make use of it. Valuable time would be lost if a gleaner had to draw her own water. Boaz was going out of his way to be kind to Ruth.

**10.** Ruth prostrated herself before Boaz in token of humility and gratitude. She recognized that Boaz was doing more than was in strictness required and she was grateful accordingly. But she did not presume on his kindness, being content to take a lowly place. Still, she was not without her curiosity and she inquired why Boaz should show her such signal favour though she was but a foreigner.

**11.** Boaz replied that it had certainly been told him (the infinitive absolute strengthens the idea of the verb: *fully*) all that she had done for Naomi. In strictness his word is 'with' not *for* your mother-in-law, so that Boaz may mean that Ruth had been helping Naomi as the two worked together. Boaz is also impressed with Ruth's sacrifice in leaving parents and native land (this expression means 'land of your kindred'; the strong family sense should be noted: the emphasis is on the relations rather than one's birth or the like). Was he reminded of the faith of the great ancestor of his race, Abraham, who left his country and his kindred in obedience to the divine command (Gn. 12:1)? Whether Boaz had this in mind or not it seems likely that the author of the book did . He makes no express mention of Abraham, but Ruth, like the patriarch, went out not knowing whither she went. And like Abraham she trusted Yahweh. Again, Abraham was accompanied only by his wife who was designated 'barren' (Gn. 11:30; Lot was also with him, but was soon to leave him). Yet God in a wonderful way was to give them a child, and God in a wonderful way was to give Ruth a child. Leaving her own, Ruth has come to a people she did not previously know. The Hebrew expression means literally 'yesterday, the day before that', *i.e.*, it indicates that Ruth's knowledge of this people was very recent indeed. According to Gerleman the Targum on this verse (which, of course, is very late) has an ingenious solution of the difficulty of Ruth's acceptance into the Israelite community despite Deuteronomy 23:3f. Boaz discovers 'through the words of the sages' that the prohibition applies to men, but not to women!

**12.** Boaz concludes with a little prayer for Ruth. He has recognized that Ruth has shown kindness to Naomi, and now he prays that Yahweh will recompense Ruth for this. Despite the 'all' of the previous verse, *thy work* is singular. The noun incidentally is poetic, being rarely found in prose (though *cf.* 2 Sa. 23:20; 1 Ch. 11:22). This is in mind in the second part of his prayer, too. *Reward* with us has associations of free bounty, but the Hebrew *maśkōret* denotes rather 'wages'. Ruth has deserved well, Boaz thinks, and he trusts that Yahweh, God of Israel, will pay her wage in full. In due course, the prayer was answered through him who uttered it. He recognizes the religious aspect of Ruth's change of country by saying that she has *come to trust* (AV) under Yahweh's wings. The imagery is probably that of a tiny bird snuggling under the wings of a foster-mother. It gives a vivid picture of trust and security (*cf.* Ps. 17:8; 36:7; 63:7), though from the similar language of Psalm 91:4 in a bellicose context some have drawn the conclusion that it is something like a huge shield that is meant. However, that hardly fits the present passage, and in any case would itself have been derived from the bird imagery.

**13.** Ruth's reply acknowledges her appreciation of Boaz' kindness. *You are most gracious to me, my lord* (RSV) expresses the thought better than *Let me find favour in thy sight, my lord* (AV), though the latter may be defended as a literal rendering. But Ruth is not imploring Boaz to be kind. She is saying how glad she is that he is kind (Gerleman, Rudolph and others think her words are almost equivalent to 'Thank you'; the expression has something like this meaning in Gn. 33:15; 1 Sa. 1:18). Boaz' words must have meant a great deal to her. They represent the first cheerful thing recorded as happening to her since the death of her husband in Moab. She had had to face widowhood, exile from her own land and people, and in Israel grinding poverty. Her kind reception at the hands of Boaz represents a landmark. Ruth puts this in two ways. Boaz has comforted her. Doubtless she had been somewhat apprehensive as she started the day's gleaning in a strange land and among strange people where her knowledge of the customs was limited and her reception was unpredictable. Boaz' words and his whole attitude must have been indeed a comfort to her. Then she says *thou hast spoken friendly unto thine handmaid* (AV). This reflects a Hebrew idiom which literally means 'spoken to the heart of . . .'. It is a graphic way of saying that the words were kind. And Boaz has done all this though Ruth is not as one of his own maids. How she differed is not said, but the different nationality is sufficient explanation. The word for *handmaid, šiphâh*, differs from *'āmâh* (used in 3:9) as being the more menial. But Ruth in her humility does not even claim a place with Boaz' handmaidens.

**14.** The Hebrew here is ambiguous. It could mean that Boaz addressed Ruth at mealtime (so RV and RSV), or it could mean that he said 'At mealtime . . .' (so AV). There is nothing to decide the point finally. Boaz' invitation to Ruth was that she should share in the meal with his party (which perhaps makes it more likely that RSV and RV are correct). Joüon points out that the accents favour this meaning, since there is a stronger accent on *hā'ōkel*, 'meal', than on the name *Boaz*, indicating a slight pause after *mealtime*. Its simple nature is shown by the invitation to eat of the bread and dip her morsel in the vinegar, and by the reference to parched grain. This latter consisted of fresh ears taken from the new crop and roasted in a pan. W. M. Thomson describes it in this way: 'a quantity of the best ears, not too ripe, are plucked with the stalks attached. These are tied into small parcels, a blazing fire is kindled with dry grass and thorn bushes, and the corn-heads are held in it until the chaff is mostly burned off. The grain is thus sufficiently roasted to be eaten, and it is a favourite article all over the country.'[1] Her place beside the reapers showed that she was accepted as one of the party and Boaz' act in passing the parched grain was, it would seem, a mark of special favour. But it was more than a courteous gesture, for our narrator makes the point that Ruth had all she wanted to eat and still had food left over. Boaz gave her a substantial quantity.

The word rendered *reached* (AV, RV) is unusual and its meaning is not certain. Gerleman thinks it may have some special meaning connected with the preparation of food. LXX takes it to mean 'heaped up', a word it uses in 2:16 to translate a different expression. Joüon similarly thinks it means that Boaz 'made a heap'.

**15.** After the meal Ruth returned to her task. But her way was made easier by an instruction from Boaz to his young men to let her glean even among the sheaves and not humiliate her. He gave them the instruction personally and did not content himself with an order to the overseer. There was obvious danger in allowing the gleaners in general to come too close to the sheaves, but Boaz was prepared to allow Ruth this special privilege. The law gave the gleaners the right to go over the

[1] *The Land and the Book* (Nelson, 1880), p. 648.

field after the reapers. But that is the point. They must do so only *after* the reapers had finished their work and had taken all they wanted from the field. Boaz was now going beyond the legal rights of the gleaners and allowing Ruth to glean before the reapers were through. This point will stand even if with Joüon we vocalize the word translated *sheaves* so as to read 'Those who made the sheaves'.

**16.** He went further. He instructed his young men to pull out something for her from the *bundles* (RV, RSV; *ṣᵉḇāṭîm*, rendered *handfuls* (AV), probably differs from 'sheaves' as denoting bundles not yet tied up), and leave them for her. AV goes on *that she may glean them*, but we should probably not translate as a clause of purpose.[1] Rather Boaz is simply saying what will happen, 'and when she gleans do not reprimand her'.

**17.** Ruth completed her day's work, labouring until the evening. Then she beat out the grain she had gleaned and discovered that it amounted to about *an ephah of barley* (an ephah was about four gallons). *Barley* is plural in the Hebrew, the thought perhaps being that of a multitude of grains. The amount is large for a gleaner (*cf.* Naomi's reaction, 2:19), which probably means both that Boaz' servants had obeyed his instructions and that Ruth had worked hard.

## c. Naomi's reaction (2:18-23)

**18.** Ruth took up the result of her toil and went to the city. Depending on how we supply vowels to the consonantal text we may read *her mother in law saw . . .* (AV, Berkeley) or *she showed her mother-in-law . . .* (RSV, Moffatt). The absence of *'ēt*, the sign of the accusative, before *mother in law*, perhaps slightly favours the former. On the other hand, Ruth is the subject of the verbs before and after and would naturally be taken as the subject of this one also (yet Hebrew is not averse to abrupt changes of subject). Nothing much depends on our choice, for either way the writer is telling us how Naomi came to learn what Ruth had secured for her day's work. Ruth also produced the food she had kept after her hunger was satisfied

[1] See T. J. Meek, *Journal of Biblical Literature*, LXXXI, 1962, p. 153.

(verse 14). Boaz had not simply passed her some food as part of the general meal, in which case what remained would have been gathered up. He had evidently presented her with a quantity of food so that she was now able to bring what she had not eaten to Naomi.

**19.** Naomi asks Ruth where she has been gleaning. It is difficult to see what difference is meant between *Where hast thou gleaned today?* (AV, RV) and *where wroughtest thou?* (AV, RV) for there is no hint that she has been doing any work other than gleaning. We should probably take the words as poetic and see an example of parallelism. Naomi proceeds to pronounce a blessing on the man who noticed Ruth (the verb is that used in 2:10). From this it seems that the result of Ruth's gleaning was rather more than might have been expected. Naomi deduces that some special favour has been shown Ruth, and she looks for the source. Ruth replies that the name of the man is Boaz. Notice the repetition, where *with whom I wrought today* (AV, RV) takes up in direct speech the *with whom she had wrought* (AV, RV) of indirect report. It is perhaps worth noticing that the Hebrew behind the latter expression is ambiguous. It could mean 'what she had wrought with him'. But the following words make it clear that AV and RV are correct.

**20.** This news causes Naomi to break out in praise of God. She first bespeaks a blessing for Boaz, thus recognizing his kindness. But the bulk of her exclamation is concerned with rejoicing in God. Grammatically, it is possible to take *who hath not left off his kindness . . .* (AV, RV) with *he*, *i.e.*, Boaz. But the whole drift of the passage shows that Naomi is thinking of God (*cf.* Gn. 24:27). He has not ceased His loving-kindness (the word is that used in 1:8; it denotes both kindness and faithfulness) and she makes specific mention of the dead as well as the living (though *living* refers to Ruth and Naomi the form of the word is masculine; *cf.* 1:8, where see note). There is a strong sense of family, so that any kindness that God might show to Ruth and Naomi is a kindness to their dead relatives as well as to themselves. Then Naomi goes on to tell Ruth the reason for her expression of pleasure. Boaz is a relative. For the expression rendered *one of our next kinsmen* (AV) see Additional Note (pp. 282f.). The use of this term plus the reference to *the dead* may indicate that already Naomi had in mind the way events were to turn out.

**21.** It is curious that after all this time our author still refers to his heroine as *Ruth the Moabitess* (see on 2:2). He does not wish us to miss her nationality, *i.e.*, if this is the true text. It is omitted by LXX, Vulg. and Syriac. The word rendered *also* in AV and *Besides* in RSV does not follow naturally on Naomi's previous remark, nor on Ruth's last reported words. We should probably take it as denoting an addition to all the good things that had gone before. The list of blessings had not yet been completed, for in addition to what had been mentioned there was the further point that Boaz had told her to stay by his servants until the harvest was done. Or we might take it simply as a general word of assent (Moffatt, *Yes*). The word rendered *young men* in AV and RV is indeed masculine in form, but it may include the feminine also. In other words, it may well include the 'maidens' mentioned in verse 8 (this appears to be the case with this word in Jb. 1:19). *My young men, . . . my harvest* (AV, RV) in this verse employ, not the usual Hebrew forms, but a construction meaning literally, 'the young men which are to me' and 'the harvest which is to me'. It is curious to find this construction repeated within such a short space. No satisfactory explanation appears to have been put forward.

**22.** So Naomi told Ruth (here qualified as *her daughter in law*; note that Ruth is often qualified in some way, most commonly as 'the Moabitess', see on 2:2, and once as 'thine handmaid', 3:9, AV, RV) that the advice was good. She speaks of Ruth's going out with *his maidens* which strengthens the view that 'young men' (AV, RV) in the previous verse is really a word embracing both sexes. The expression rendered *that they meet thee not in any other field* (AV, RV) is variously understood. Knox renders, *in some other field they might say thee nay*, and Moffatt, *so that the reapers may not attack you in some other field*. The verb *pāga‘* means 'to meet, encounter' so that AV and RV are quite justified. It is true that in some contexts the verb means 'meet with hostile intent' (*e.g.*, Jos. 2:16). But in the present context what Naomi has in mind is the kindness of Boaz (*cf.* verses 8f.). It would not be well in the face of this for Ruth to be found in another field. It would indicate that she did not appreciate very highly what Boaz had done for her. AV and RV are to be preferred.

**23.** Ruth did as she was told. She stayed with Boaz' maidens to glean right up to the end of harvest. Our author particularizes barley and wheat harvest. She stayed right through the whole, and not simply to the end of one section of the harvest. But her working with the servants of Boaz did not mean any wavering in her determination to remain with Naomi. She still lived with her.

## Additional Note on the meaning of *g'l*

Words from the root *g'l* are used with a variety of meanings in the Old Testament, but the fundamental idea is that of fulfilling one's obligations as a kinsman. Indeed BDB give the meaning of the verb as 'redeem, act as kinsman', while O. Procksch says that it is a 'concept in family law'.[1] It may thus be used as a general term to denote one's relations, as when Zimri slew all the house of Baasha and left 'not one . . . of his kinsfolks' (1 Ki. 16:11). A good example of this basic meaning is to be discerned in Job 3:5, where the sufferer curses the day of his birth saying, 'Let darkness and the shadow of death claim it for their own' (RV), *i.e.*, acknowledge it as kin. Arising out of the family relationship is a variety of duties. The verb may be used of redeeming a relation from a state of slavery into which he has fallen (Lv. 25:48f.), or redeeming his field (Lv. 25:25). This last-mentioned duty may perhaps have been

---

[1] *TWNT*, iv, p. 331. C. Ryder Smith thinks that 'to do the part of a kinsman' is the best translation of the verb, and he comments, 'One could wish that there were some such English verb as "to kinsman" ' (*The Bible Doctrine of Salvation* (Epworth, 1946), p. 19). Interestingly he thinks that 'The Book of Ruth is largely based on the idea' (*ibid.*). Lattey thinks that 'The primary function of the Goel was to represent the clan in the assertion of its rights and duties; his first duty was towards the clan, in virtue of his solidarity with it' (Lattey, p. xv). Lattey's whole discussion is valuable. So also is that of A. R. Johnson in *Supplements to Vetus Testamentum*, I (Brill, 1953), pp. 67–77, though he probably goes too far in his idea that the word group has to do with protection.

connected with the idea that the Israelites were not the absolute owners of the land. All the land was God's. They did but hold it in trust. Thus they could not sell it. If times were hard and money short they could indeed part with the land, but there was always the right and the duty of redemption. When a man's financial state improved he must buy back the land on which God had set him. Or, if he could not do this, his *gō'ēl* must do it for him. That redemption of land was regarded as important we see from Ruth 4:3f., where the land is mentioned before the lady. When one of the family has been murdered it is important that the family honour be upheld, and the nearest relation is bound to avenge the deceased. There are few passages dealing with the order in which relations were reckoned, but closest were brothers, then uncles, then uncles' sons (Lv. 25:48f.). The participle of our verb may be rendered 'the revenger' of blood (Nu. 35:19, *etc.*). But the word does not mean 'revenger'. That is the outworking in a particular situation of the basic family in obligation.

In this book the participle is used to denote a kinsman in 2:20; 3:9,12 (twice); 4:1,3,6,8,14. ('Kinsman' in 2:1 translates a different Hebrew word.) The verb is also found in the sense of 'play the part of a kinsman' four times in 3:13, in each case the duty in question being the marriage of Ruth. The point of this is that Mahlon, Ruth's husband, had died childless. There was therefore an obligation resting on the next of kin to marry the widow and have a child who would be regarded as the child of the deceased and carry on his name (see Dt. 25:5-10 for an account of the custom). The same verb is found five times in 4:4, in each case being translated 'redeem'. Once again the family thought is basic. There is some land that Naomi is selling and which must be redeemed lest it pass out of the family. The next of kin owes a duty to the family here. The same is true of the three occurrences of the verb in 4:6, though in two of them the duty is being declined by the next of kin. A cognate noun refers to the same transaction in 4:6,7. Differing translations are necessary in the different passages, but we should not miss the connections nor overlook the strong family sense which is basic.

## IV. THE MARRIAGE (3:1 – 4:22)

The book now moves on to its climax. Naomi takes thought for Ruth's future and arranges things so that eventually Boaz marries her. As the story unfolds we are given a good deal of incidental information about the life and customs of a small community in ancient Israel.

### a. Naomi's plan (3:1–5)

We have very little knowledge of the customs prevalent in Israel in antiquity and the arrangements for marriage here outlined are not elsewhere attested. But then we have no other example of a situation quite like this. What was to be done where two widows were left to their own devices? This story gives us an answer as to what might happen, though we have no means of knowing just how common the practice described was. Apparently it was an Israelite but not a Moabite procedure, for Naomi had to explain to Ruth what she must do to show Boaz that she was interested in marriage with him. Though Ruth carried out the plan readily enough there is no indication that she knew anything about the custom until Naomi outlined it.

**1.** Naomi sets matters moving by asking whether she should *seek rest* (AV, RV) for Ruth. RSV renders *seek a home*, which may well be the sense of it, but the idea in the word *mānôaḥ* is not 'home'. It has to do with rest (*cf.* 1:9; *mᵉnûḥâh* there is cognate with *mānôaḥ* here, and there does not appear to be any real difference of meaning). Moffatt does better with *I must see you settled in life*. Naomi is thinking of the precarious livelihood shared by the two widows and she looks for something better for Ruth. This is reinforced with *that it may be well with thee* (AV, RV). The lot of an unprotected widow in the ancient world could not but be a hard one. Marriage would alter that and so it would be well with Ruth.

**2.** *Now* introduces the next logical step. Boaz is described as *our kinsman* (RV, RSV), though when the cognate term was used previously he was connected with Naomi only. He was called a kinsman of her husband's, and this was further explained by saying that he was 'of the family of Elimelech' (2:1). When precision is required this is the way to state it. But in the present passage the important point is the position of Ruth. Since her marriage to Mahlon she too has a family connection with Boaz and thus he is described as *our* kinsman. Next comes the reminder that he is not an unknown quantity. Ruth has been with his maidens (and has received marks of special favour). Naomi tells Ruth that that night Boaz will be winnowing barley at the threshing-floor. In this process grain was separated from the husks by being trodden out by animals. Then the mixture was thrown into the air against a stiff breeze, so that the wind blew the chaff away while the heavier grain fell more or less straight down. Threshing-floors were usually situated in exposed positions, so that they could catch the breeze (it was the measure of Gideon's fear and despera-tion that he chose to beat out his wheat in a winepress, a most unsuitable location, Jdg. 6:11). It seems curious that Boaz should engage in this work at night. Perhaps there were unusual weather conditions with a brisk night breeze. More probably we should understand *hallāylâh* as 'the evening' rather than 'the night'. (Hertzberg thinks the term here means the whole afternoon.) It is possible that the wind in the daytime was very strong or very gusty, which would make winnowing difficult. If these were the conditions, then work at night might well be preferable. L. P. Smith says that in summer the wind blows from about four or five o'clock until a little after sunset. But after work ceased the grain must be guarded. Perhaps Boaz did not do this in person every night, and this may be the force of Naomi's *tonight*. This would then be one of the nights when Boaz was on duty.

**3.** Naomi instructs Ruth to look her best. She is to *wash* (the word may signify 'bath oneself', and this is surely the meaning here) and anoint herself. The ancients made a good deal of use of unguents, especially on festive occasion, this being much the same as our use of scents. The word for *raiment* (AV, RV) does not denote any special type of garment. Many think that in the context *your best clothes* (RSV) gives the sense of it. Joüon, however, points out that Ruth is not told to change her clothing and he asks whether in her poverty she would be able to. He reads the word as a singular, with good MS and LXX support, and understands it to refer to a large mantle which would completely cover Ruth so that she would not be recognized. Lattey takes a similar point of view thinking it unlikely 'that Ruth in her poverty would possess "best clothes," which indeed the Hebrew does not here indicate'. Rust thinks that Ruth was 'to prepare herself as a bride', but the evidence scarcely supports this. The large mantle is probably right. Having prepared herself in this way Ruth is to go down to the threshing-floor but not to make herself known to Boaz. Let him finish his meal before she does anything. 'Go down' is rather curious: one would have expected a threshing-floor to be on a height (LXX actually reads 'go up'). The explanation is probably that Bethlehem itself is on a high ridge so that one would 'go down' to any place in the surrounding countryside.[1]

**4.** Now comes the critical (and most interesting) part of the instructions. When Boaz lies down to go to sleep Ruth is instructed to *mark* (lit. 'know') the place where he lies. Then (*i.e.*, 'some time later', not 'thereupon') she is to come and uncover his feet and lie down (the Syriac has 'lie down at his feet' which is almost certainly not the correct text, but which gives the meaning). The point of this perhaps was to awaken the man as his feet became cold. The position was also a lowly one, and perhaps represented Ruth as a petitioner. It is also possible that *feet* here is a euphemism for *pudenda* (as Ex. 4:25, *etc.*). Moffatt appears to adopt this meaning with his translation *uncover his waist*.

That represented the completion of Ruth's task (except for her invitation to Boaz to throw his skirt over her, 3:9). The

---

[1] G. R. Driver has produced evidence to show that the verbs 'go up' and 'go down' may occasionally be used in the senses 'go up country', *i.e.*, 'northwards' and 'go down country', *i.e.*, 'southwards' (*Zeitschrift für die Alttestamentliche Wissenschaft*, 69, 1957, pp. 74–77). It is thus possible that in the present passage the meaning is that the threshing-floor lay to the south of Bethlehem. But the passages Driver cites are few and the use exceptional. It is more likely that we should understand our verse to mean that the threshing-floor was below the level of Bethlehem itself.

rest was up to Boaz. The context makes it clear that this describes a way whereby Ruth signified to Boaz her desire to marry him. Ordinary methods of approach were no doubt difficult and this provided a suitable medium. But why it should be done in this way we do not know. Nor do we know whether this was a widely practised custom or not. It is not attested other than here. Lattey thinks that 'the action in itself is symbolic, suggesting that the mantle should cover Ruth as well, and thus preparing the way for her words in iii.9. To throw the mantle over a woman would be to claim her for wife.' In view of the widespread use of garments in a symbolic fashion now known to have been common at the time, this may well be the explanation. The narrator uses the utmost delicacy, but it is clear that Naomi's plan was not without its dangers. The fact that she was prepared to urge this course on Ruth is the measure of her trust in both the participants. All the more is this the case since in the Ancient Near East immoral practices at harvest-times were by no means uncommon, and, indeed, appear to have been encouraged by the fertility rites practised in some religions.

The opening words of this verse *And it shall be* (AV, RV) are rather unusual. The Hebrew is *wîhî* where we would have expected *wᵉhāyāh*. This in strictness means 'and let it be . . .'. It is probably a way of continuing the imperative when Naomi changes from Ruth's to Boaz' part in the affair.

**5.** Ruth's reply is simple, but comprehensive. She goes beyond a readiness to do what Naomi has just said and says she will do anything her mother-in-law requires, leaving it perfectly general.

## b. Ruth at the threshing-floor (3:6–13)

The next section of the book tells how Ruth carried out the plan, and how Boaz received her overtures. On this latter point D. B. Macdonald says, 'Boaz is shown quietly handling the situation like a gentleman, and not either as an old fool or a village lout. He may be countrified but he has dignity and restraint.'[1]

---

[1] *The Hebrew Literary Genius* (Princeton, 1933), p. 122.

**6.** This verse tells us that Ruth went down to the threshing-floor and did as she had been instructed. That is to say, she carried out the first part of the plan, taking up her position unobserved and waiting for Boaz to retire for the night. The fulfilment of the rest of her instructions had, of course, to come later.

**7.** It was harvest-time and therefore a time of feasting and enjoyment (*cf*. Is. 9:3). Boaz ate and drank well and *his heart was merry* (the verb translated *was merry* is that rendered 'that it may be well with thee' in 3:1, AV, RV). In due course he went to bed *at the end of the heap of corn* (AV, RV). At harvest-time people would camp out, and in those days (as is the case still with country folk in that region) they did not mind hard beds! Probably his servants were in other places near the threshing-floor and Boaz would have had a place to himself. Ruth now came quietly. The word rendered *softly* does not mean 'secretly' but 'quietly', 'so as not to be heard'. It is used of David when he cut the skirt from Saul's robe (1 Sa. 24:4, Hebrew verse 5). The narrative does not say that she waited for a time but clearly she did, for Boaz was asleep when she came. Otherwise the conversation of verses 9ff. would have taken place here. Then she did as Naomi had told her. She uncovered Boaz' feet and lay down.

**8.** The impression left is that Boaz slept for some time before discovering Ruth. At midnight something disturbed him. RSV renders, *At midnight the man was startled*, and AV, *was afraid*. Whatever it was that woke him scared him. The original meaning of the word is 'tremble' and it has been suggested that Boaz trembled on account of the cold, his feet being uncovered. This cannot be completely ruled out, but the verb more commonly means 'to be afraid' and it seems better to think that Boaz experienced a moment of terror on being woken suddenly. Then, as AV and RV put it, he *turned himself*. This may mean he *turned over* as RSV, or *bent forward* as KB, Moffatt. The word is concerned with turning, but not with a particular way of turning. Joüon thinks that the idea of turning leads to that of looking, with the meaning 'looked all round him'. The point is not important. What is important is that his turning motion disclosed to him a woman lying at his feet. The narrator adds a touch of vividness with *and, behold*. He sees it all happening.

**9.** Now comes the moment of disclosure. In reply to Boaz' question Ruth reveals her identity. She describes herself as *your maidservant* (RSV) thus taking a lowly place as before (*cf.* 2:13), but she uses a different word from that in the previous passage. There is probably not much difference of meaning, though the other word may have a slightly more menial flavour. What is clear is that Ruth is not taking anything for granted. Still at this moment she acts towards Boaz in humility. She proceeds to her plea. It seems that *therefore* of AV correctly interprets the Hebrew (*HS*, 56, 57R1). She looks for Boaz to take action simply because she is who she is. She employs an expressive metaphor and asks him to spread his skirt over her. It is used similarly for taking in marriage in Ezekiel 16:8. The spreading of the skirt over a widow as a way of claiming her as a wife is attested among Arabs of early days,[1] and Joüon says it still exists among some modern Arabs. *Cf.* also Deuteronomy 27:20, *etc.* Wright points out that the word is singular in passages like Deuteronomy 22:30 (Hebrew 23:1); 27:20; 1 Samuel 24:4,5; Ezekiel 16:8 and, indeed, wherever the skirt of a garment is meant. He accordingly takes it to refer here to wings: ' "*spread thy wings over thine handmaid*", a much more delicate way for Ruth to intimate her wish.' P. H. Steenstra in Cassel reminds us that the pointing of MT implies a dual with the suffix written defectively (it cannot be singular with lengthened shewa since it is not in pause). The word is more commonly used for 'wings' than for 'skirt', and it is used with this meaning, for example, when Boaz speaks of the religious aspect of Ruth's change of country, 'a full reward be given thee of

[1] See E. Neufeld, *Ancient Hebrew Marriage Laws* (Longmans, 1944), pp. 31f. There is also the well-known statement of Ṭabari quoted by W. Robertson Smith, 'In the Jāhiliya, when a man's father or brother or son died and left a widow, the dead man's heir, if he came at once and threw his garment over her, had the right to marry her under the dowry (*mahr*) of (*i.e.* already paid by) her (deceased) lord (*ṣāḥib*), or to give her in marriage and take her dowry. But if she anticipated him and went off to her own people, then the disposal of her hand belonged to herself' (*Kinship and Marriage in Early Arabia* (Black, 1903), p. 105).

the Lord God of Israel, under whose wings thou art come to trust' (2:12, AV). Ruth had put herself under Yahweh's 'wing' when she came to Judah. Now she seeks also to put herself under that of Boaz. KD understand the word to refer to 'the corner of the counterpane, referring to the fact that a man spreads this over his wife as well as himself'. But 'wings' seems more probable. Ruth concludes by reminding Boaz that he is a near-kinsman (*gōʾēl*; see Additional Note, pp. 282f.). Because of the family connection she has some right to look to him.

**10.** Ruth is not left long in doubt. Boaz' response is to call down a blessing upon her (*cf.* 2:4,12). He thinks that Ruth has shown *more kindness* (AV, RV) now than when she first came. The kindness *at the beginning* (AV, RV) will be that which Ruth showed to Naomi in not forsaking her and in gleaning to provide for her needs. Now to this she has added a further evidence of her regard for family relationships. She has not followed natural inclinations (in seeking a young man in marriage), but has shown a responsible attitude to the family in looking to her *gōʾēl* as her marriage partner. The word *kindness* is that used in 1:8 (see note on this). It includes the thought of faithfulness as well as that of benevolence. Ruth is steadfast as well as kindly in this action. Lattey renders 'piety' but this is hardly it, though Ruth has certainly shown dutifulness (with which in a note Lattey equates piety). Boaz sees her faithfulness in the fact that when she thought of marriage Ruth did not go after *young men* (the word means 'choice' men) whether poor or rich. She preferred to keep to family connections and thus showed her respect for the right. She did not simply let her own personal inclinations rule her. Knox translates, *now, more than ever, thou hast shewn the goodness of thy heart*; Berkeley, *This your later kindness is lovelier than any previous one*. There is an article with *young men*. It is not 'young men' in general that is meant but 'the young men', the definite group of young men in the village. We should not overlook the implied compliment to Ruth. Boaz clearly was certain that had she wished Ruth might have married a rich young man. There would be no point in praising her faithfulness to family obligations otherwise.

**11.** Boaz tells Ruth not to be afraid for he will do for her all she says. He gives as his reason that Ruth has such an excellent reputation. Much more than is recorded had clearly happened during the months the two widows had been at Bethlehem. The writer of the book has a definite purpose in view, and he leaves out what is not relevant. But quite plainly Ruth had become well known to all the villagers. The word translated *city* (AV) here is literally 'gate'. In Palestinian towns the usual place of assembly was the gate (see further the note on 4:1). 'All the gate' thus means 'all the people who assemble in the city', or, as E. A. Speiser[1] puts it in an important article, 'the whole body of my people'. 'It is a matter of common knowledge' will give the sense of it. The expression is an unusual one and is found only here. Boaz may have in mind the legal proceedings he was about to initiate. Ruth need not fear that her Moabite origin or anything else would be urged against her. All in the gate know her virtue and that will prove sufficient. It is also possible that 'the gate' stands for those who take part in judicial proceedings and thus means 'all the important or influential people', 'all the responsible elders'. But a reference to the whole population of the city seems more probable.

The expression which is rendered *virtuous* (AV, RV) or *of worth* (Moffatt, RSV) as a description of Ruth at the end of the verse is difficult to translate. It is that rendered 'of wealth' in 2:1 where Boaz is introduced to us. It denotes ability or efficiency or attainment in any one of a number of directions, which is what gives the translation of RSV its attraction. AV and RV are too restricted in meaning. The word certainly includes *virtuous* in this context but it includes more also. Knox translates, *all the city knows thee for a bride worth the winning.* This is too

---

[1] *Bulletin of the American Schools of Oriental Research*, No. 144, December 1956, p. 21. He draws attention to the Akkadian *bābtu*, familiar in the Code of Hammurabi in the sense, 'district, quarter', and which 'is known to be an extension of *bābu* "entrance, gate"' (*loc. cit.*). The Akkadian, I am told, more commonly refers to a 'ward' or 'quarter' of a city, but *bābu* may have a meaning rather like that in the present passage. The Chicago *Assyrian Dictionary* cites, for example, a passage referring to 'the people of Ugarit ... together with the aliens living within their gates' (*op. cit.*, B, p. 23).

free, but it does bring out the comprehensive excellence that
the word denotes. It is used of the ideal woman (Pr. 31:10),
and of her who is 'a crown to her husband' (Pr. 12:4).

**12.** *And now* is logical rather than temporal. Boaz is not
contrasting this time with another time but moving on to
another phase of the situation. He affirms with some emphasis
that he certainly is a kinsman. Actually the construction is
elliptical. He says 'Truly . . . unless I am a kinsman', and we
are to supply, 'may something unpleasant happen to me'.
It is an idiomatic form of speech to give emphasis, just as an
oath is sometimes employed. The Hebrew is undoubtedly
difficult, and Joüon resolves the situation by omitting three
words. This is a desperate course, and it is better to try to make
sense of the text as it stands. There is a case, however, for
omitting *'m* (with the *Q\*rē*). It could have resulted from dittography since *'mnm* follows the first *kî*. KD, however, reject this,
holding that *kî 'im* is used here in the same way as in the
formula employed in oaths, with the sense 'except that',
'only', *i.e.*, 'assuredly I am redeemer'. Cassel's translator cites
E. Bertheau, that *kî 'im* 'excludes from the assurance the
opposite of what forms its object yet more decidedly than the
simple *kî*, thus: truly, indeed, only a goel am I = truly, I am
certainly a goel – I am that and nothing else.' Fortunately our
uncertainties about the text do not extend to the meaning.
Boaz is affirming in strong terms that he *is* a *gō'ēl*, a kinsman
who could act for Ruth. But he goes on to point out that there
was a man nearer of kin than he. In a town as small as Bethlehem it seems unlikely that this would not be known to Naomi
(though conceivably Ruth may not have known all the com-
plexities of her late husband's family relationships). But
Naomi probably calculated that Boaz was more likely to take
action than the other, and therefore arranged for Ruth to
meet him rather than the unnamed closer relation. It is
implied, but not actually said, that in the case of a childless
widow the next of kin had the prior right to marry the woman
and raise up seed to the deceased. In Deuteronomy 25:5-10
it is envisaged that the brother of the deceased is to marry the
widow, and no mention is made of anybody else. If the brother

refuses to perform his duty that passage makes provision for the widow to humiliate him publicly. But it is not said that anyone else should take his place. However, this would appear to be a matter of common sense. And the present passage shows that it was not open for anyone in the family to perform the marriage. There was a due order. The next of kin had the privilege and responsibility, and only if he declined was it possible (and necessary) for another member of the family to take his place.

**13.** Boaz makes plain what is to be the order of things. First he tells Ruth to stay where she is. There is no point in her going elsewhere during the hours of darkness (*cf.* Ct. 5:7), and she will be quite safe where she is. In the morning Boaz promises action. The closer kinsman has the right to marry Ruth if he chooses to exercise that right. Interestingly Boaz does not use the word 'marry'. He speaks rather of the man's 'doing the part of a kinsman'. It is family responsibility that he emphasizes. If the other will exercise his right to Ruth, then Boaz will accept it. But if he has no delight in doing this, then Boaz will do it for himself. His 'I' is emphatic, and it is reinforced by the strong expression *as the Lord liveth* (AV, RV). Boaz wants there to be no doubt about his determination. This being settled he tells Ruth to lie down till morning.

### c. Ruth's return home (3:14–18)

**14.** Ruth resumed her place at Boaz' feet and slept till morning. But she was up before daylight. (Joüon amends the text to read 'and he rose up' since it must have been Boaz who took the initiative. The point may be conceded, but it is not necessary to emend the text to find it.) While what she had done must have conformed to custom in some way (Boaz needed no explanation, but realized from the action alone what Ruth meant and what he should do), yet there were obvious reasons why it should not be published abroad that Ruth had slept there that night. There is an interesting provision in the Mishnah that if a man was suspected of having intercourse with a Gentile woman he could not perform levirate marriage with her (Yeb. 2:8). In its written form this regulation is, of course, centuries later than the book of Ruth. But if the custom was an ancient one, as it may well have been, it would give an added reason for Boaz to exercise caution. So he arranged for Ruth to return to Naomi very early, in fact, before there was enough daylight for anyone she might meet to recognize her. Boaz also said that Ruth's presence should not be known. The word *said* may mean 'said to himself' (as in Gn. 20:11 where it is translated 'I thought'). The Midrash regards the utterance as prayer (vii. 1). Otherwise the words must be addressed to Boaz' retainers, though there is a difficulty in that there has been no hint that any of them were present. The first suggestion is best. *A woman* (AV) is better *the woman* (RV, RSV). Boaz' reference is definite. Knox translates, *He warned her not to let anyone know that she had been there,* but it is difficult to see this in the Hebrew. The words do not seem at all like an address to Ruth. They are much better taken as spoken by Boaz to himself.

**15.** Boaz had a sense of the fitness of things and apparently he did not regard it as proper that his prospective bride should return from her night's adventures empty-handed. So he told Ruth to fetch her cloak and hold it out. When she did so he measured out six measures of barley. Unfortunately, the text does not say what measure is meant, the Hebrew reading simply 'six of barley'.[1] In 2:17 the ephah is used, but six ephahs would amount to about 132 litres or 24 gallons. This seems an impossibly large amount so it is probable that we should take the measure here to be the seah, which amounted to a third of the ephah. Hertzberg points out that this would make a load of about 40 kilogrammes (*i.e.*, about 88 pounds), not impossible for a strong young woman. Gerleman suggests the omer, but this was a tenth of the ephah and it would make Boaz' gift less than the amount Ruth acquired in a day of gleaning. The impression we get is that he was being bountiful, which seems to rule this out. Gerleman does not notice this

[1] D. J. Wiseman points out that the omission of the standard of measure is common in Semitic languages generally (*cf.* Dt. 22:29). Thus in the Alalakh tablets the term 'shekels' is normally omitted when listing amounts of money. See his *The Alalakh Tablets* (The British Institute of Archeology at Ankara, London, 1953), p. 13.

point. There is also a point of syntax, namely that the gender of the adjective 'six' leads us to expect a measure grammatically feminine, whereas 'omer' is masculine. On the whole, it seems then that six seahs is what is meant. Since Boaz had to put it on Ruth it is obvious that it was a large load. The munificence of this gift we may estimate from the fact that on a full day of gleaning Ruth managed but one ephah (2:17), and that was considered quite an achievement. Such a large amount would not be easy to manage so Boaz put it on Ruth, *i.e.*, he assisted her get the load properly balanced as she carried it on her head. The Hebrew text says at the end of the verse 'and he went into the city' but this must be an early scribal error. The context makes it clear that it is Ruth's going into the city that is meant. Boaz went later (4:1), unless we are to think that he now went into the city to his house and later to the gate. It is objected that this seems ruled out by the fact that the very reason for Boaz' presence would have been to guard the threshing-floor. He would surely not leave before daylight. The objection may be countered by drawing attention to the fact that a man who has just become engaged to a pretty girl is unlikely to display such a preference for a heap of wheat! But the argument from context still stands and it seems that the verse means that Ruth went into the city. There is some doubt about the article of clothing into which the barley was measured. AV renders *vail*; AV mg., RSV, Moffatt, *mantle*; Berkeley, *shawl*; Knox, *the fold of that mantle*; FF, *wrapper*. From the fact that it was used to carry a substantial load of grain it is obvious that it was no flimsy article. Probably we should think of a heavy mantle.

**16.** So Ruth returned to her mother-in-law. Naomi's question *Who art thou?* is strange unless we are to think that it was still so dark that she could not recognize Ruth. RSV, *How did you fare?* (similarly Moffatt, Berkeley) makes better sense, but the Hebrew agrees with AV. Gerleman takes *mî* to be an interrogative particle giving the meaning, 'Is it you?' In Judges 18:8 there is a rather similar question addressed by the Danites to their spies, 'What are you?' (AV, 'What say ye?'). Knight is of opinion that 'where the question in English expects the answer of the person's name, the question in Hebrew expects an answer about the character or condition behind the name: "Art thou married to him or not?" ' The words are absent from the B text of the LXX, which may mean no more than that the translator found them difficult. We must conclude that something like RSV seems required by the sense, but that AV gives the meaning of the Hebrew text as we have it. RSV is supported by the further statement that Ruth told her what the man had done to her. This puts the emphasis on what Boaz had said and presumably therefore on his undertaking to carry out the duties of a *gō'ēl*. The gift of the barley is not mentioned until after this.

**17.** Ruth's answer is not reported in detail, but special mention is made of the six measures of barley. *These six* are pointed out with Boaz' injunction, mentioned here but not in verse 15, *Go not empty unto thy mother in law* (AV, RV). It may be no coincidence that the same word *empty* is used here as in 1:21 when Naomi spoke of being brought home 'empty'. Her 'empty' days are over.

**18.** Naomi's intimate knowledge of Boaz' character is revealed in her answer. There is no need for Ruth to do anything further and she is told to sit still till she knows how the affair will turn out. Boaz will see the thing through to its conclusion. Naomi affirms that he will never rest now, till he has finished the whole affair.[1]

### d. Boaz redeems Ruth the Moabitess (4:1-12)

In a passage of absorbing interest our narrator gives us the details of the process whereby Ruth became betrothed to Boaz. This vivid narrative is important as one of the few documents from the ancient world which tell how a legal process of this kind was carried out.

**1.** *Then* (AV) is not to be taken as indicating strict sequence. By avoiding the *waw* consecutive construction (the Hebrew is

---

[1] The Hebraist will notice that the first *dāḇār* (*the matter*) lacks the article, while the second (*the thing*) has it. The article on the second occasion is explicable as referring back to the first instance. But it is curious that the first is without the article.

*ûḇōʿaz ʿālâh*) the author simply indicates that Boaz went up, but he does not indicate whether this was before, after, or simultaneous with the preceding. It is a piece of paragraphing technique, turning our attention to Boaz. His first move was to go up to the gate and sit there. For *went up, cf.* 3:3, where the verb 'go down' is used of a journey in the opposite direction. The threshing-floor was apparently below the level of the town.

*The gate* played a large part in the cities of Judah of antiquity. Excavations reveal that Palestinian cities were generally very closely built and there were no large open spaces like the Roman *forum* or the Greek *agora*. Instead room was found at the gate, and the gate accordingly tended to become the centre of city life. It was the place for any important assembly, and, for example, we find the kings of Israel and of Judah sitting on thrones in an open place 'in the entrance of the gate of Samaria' (1 Ki. 22:10). Similarly King Zedekiah sat 'in the gate of Benjamin' (Je. 38:7). But pre-eminently it was the place for legal business. When Absalom wanted to make capital out of the way justice was administered he 'rose up early, and stood beside the way of the gate: and it was so, that when any man that had a controversy came to the king for judgment, then Absalom called unto him . . .' (2 Sa. 15:2, AV). The gate was the place to find such men. Similarly Amos can speak of 'him that rebuketh in the gate', and of the unjust judges who 'take a bribe, and they turn aside the poor in the gate from their right', and he exhorts the people, 'Hate the evil, and love the good, and establish judgment in the gate' (Am. 5:10, 12,15, AV; *cf.* Pr. 22:22). People were condemned before 'the elders of the city in the gate' (Dt. 22:15, AV), and the gate is mentioned in connection with executions (Dt. 22:24). Less formally it was a place for social intercourse (Ps. 127:5). It is the supreme tragedy of a city when 'The elders have ceased from the gate' (La. 5:14, AV). It is of special interest in the present connection that if a man died childless and his brother refused to marry the widow the woman was bidden 'go up to the gate unto the elders' (Dt. 15:7, AV) to begin the process of public humiliation of the offender. The gate was the normal place for public business, and specifically for the kind of business described in this chapter.[1]

Presently *the kinsman* (AV, RV) of whom Boaz had spoken to Ruth passed by (the participle signifies, 'was passing by'). There is no indication that he knew what was afoot. But Boaz knew that he was bound to pass the gate so he awaited him there. When he came Boaz called on him to break off his journey and sit down. The Hebrew uses two words of address with a meaning rather like our 'so-and-so'. It is a way of showing that a definite person is meant without mentioning his name. Hence *such a one* (AV) is nearer to it than *friend* (RSV). Moffatt renders, *Ho, you!* but this is hardly it. Boaz used the man's name (Knox, *called him by name*) though the chronicler does not care to give it (or perhaps does not know it). Some hold that the Hebrew implies that the 'naming' of the man was a specific part of the legal process. But in any case the kinsman is not an important figure. He appears only to renounce his claim on Ruth and then disappears. Thus his name is of no consequence. Cassel comments, 'it remains . . . an instructive fact that he who was so anxious for the preservation of his own inheritance, is now not even known by name.' The expression used here is found in two other places only in the Old Testament, and in both there may be a deliberate concealment involved (1 Sa. 21:2 (Hebrew 21:3); 2 Ki. 6:8). It is also possible, of course, that no more is meant than that a specific name was used in each case.

**2.** Boaz proceeded to empanel his jury, so to speak. He took ten of the city's elders (Moffatt renders *sheikhs*) and sat them down also. Elders exercised judicial functions. Thus if a man fled from 'the avenger of blood' to one of the cities of refuge it was the elders who determined whether he was to be admitted or not (Jos. 20:4). And when Jezebel wanted Naboth executed in a judicial manner it was the elders she coerced into taking the necessary action (1 Ki. 21:8,11). Such passages show that the elders possessed far-reaching powers. In the present case they appear to play little part other than as

---

[1] L. Köhler brings out the importance of the gate in an Appendix entitled 'Justice in the Gate' in *Hebrew Man* (SCM, 1956), pp. 149–175

witnesses. But their importance was such that any transaction attested by them was of unimpeachable validity. We do not know whether there is any significance in the number *ten.* Obviously this could give a solid body of witness, but whether there was any legal requirement met by this number or not our information from antiquity does not reveal. In more recent times, ten, of course, is a significant number. Thus ten men are required for a synagogue service. Slotki sees in the number 'The quorum required for the recital of the marriage benedictions. Boaz held them in readiness for the pending ceremony'. However, he cites no evidence that the custom is so old. The Midrash Rabbah regards this passage as giving justification for ten at 'the blessing of the bridegroom' (vii. 8).

**3.** The court action begins with Boaz addressing the kinsman. He tells him that Naomi *selleth a parcel of land* (AV) which had belonged to Elimelech. *Our brother* (AV, RV) means, of course, 'our friend'; the expression is not by any means confined to immediate family relationships. The verb *selleth* (AV, RV) is in the perfect in Hebrew, a tense which normally describes completed action. The construction here is described by A. B. Davidson in these terms, however: 'The perf. is used to express actions which a lively imagination conceives as completed, but for which the fut. is more usual in Eng. – (*a*) The perf. of certainty ... Naomi *is selling* the field-portion' (*HS*, 41). Actually the consonants could be read as a participle, and some advocate this. But the perfect, though at first sight more difficult, is to be preferred (*cf.* Gn 23:11 for the perfect in a similar situation, and *cf.* 4:9, where 'I have bought' refers to imminent action). The perfect could denote a past sale, and Wright, for example, accepts this view. It seems to be ruled out, however, by 4:5, which views the sale as future, and 4:9, where it is imminent. Moreover, had Naomi sold it, the *gōʾēl* would have been required to redeem it from the purchaser. The meaning is that Naomi is about to sell the land. Jeremiah 32:6–12 seems to show that land would normally be offered to a member of the family before being offered to anyone else. It is this that Naomi is doing.

For *parcel of land* see the note on 'part of the field' in 2:3

(the Hebrew is the same). The land in question was Elimelech's share of the common field. Being part of a field in common ownership it may well have been difficult for Naomi to realize on it. This may be the reason she still had it despite the poverty to which she and Ruth had been reduced. But in any case it is difficult to see how she could have disposed of it much earlier. It would have been Elimelech's before going to Moab, and she could scarcely take action until she returned to Bethlehem. There has been no mention of the land up till now, and no indication of how and when Naomi told Boaz about it. This is a further indication that there were contacts between Boaz and the widows which are not recorded. This means that Boaz' readiness to marry Ruth rested on a better knowledge of her than a casual reading of the book might indicate.

There are problems arising from the fact that the land was Naomi's. R. de Vaux says simply that a man's widow 'had no right to the inheritance'[1] and this does seem to be the position in the Old Testament generally. Such a comprehensive statement as that in Numbers 27:8–11 does not envisage a widow as succeeding to her late husband's property. The line of succession is first sons, then daughters, then the nearest male relative. The widow is not mentioned (though possibly she is presumed to be dead; if there were no sons she ought to marry the *gō'ēl* and the property would go to the son of the new marriage). Women could certainly succeed to land in later times. The woman of 2 Kings 8:1–6 was perhaps a widow, and Judith certainly was (Judith 8:7), while the Mishnah says that the schools of Hillel and Shammai both allowed a widow awaiting levirate marriage to sell (Yeb. 4:3). E. Neufeld thinks that, though the law did not provide for a widow to inherit, yet in practice this was not enforced.[2] This gives a state of affairs intermediate between Numbers 27 and Judith 8. H. H. Rowley suggests that custom may have given rights in property to such a widow as Naomi, and he also thinks it

---

[1] *Ancient Israel: its Life and Institutions* (Darton, Longman and Todd, 1961), p. 54. He contrasts the Babylonian and Nuzi usage.
[2] *Ancient Hebrew Marriage Laws* (Longmans, 1944), pp. 240f.

possible that Elimelech had willed a life interest in the property to her, a custom attested in Nuzi texts.[1] Selling the property, however, indicates the possession of more than a life interest. The Alalakh tablets give evidence that a widow could inherit[2] but it is not clear how far we can reason from Alalakh to Israel.

The position, then, is that Naomi had rights in the land, but we have no knowledge of any legal process by which she could have obtained them. Our best guess is that a common-sense custom gave them to her.

It is curious that Boaz speaks of the land before mentioning Ruth. It is possible that the land was in some way bound up with the marrying of Ruth. Thus Knight says, 'Our author is suggesting that Ruth the person cannot be redeemed unless her property is redeemed along with her'; 'Men are not separable from the environment in which God has placed them as living souls. Here our author insists that the fields are to be redeemed along with Ruth herself. Ruth's redemption implies the redemption of all that she has.'[3] This would be more plausible if it were not that Naomi is said to be selling the land.

Boaz may well have decided that it would be good tactics to approach the matter in this way. He may have feared that, if it were a matter only of marrying Ruth, or only of redeeming the field, the kinsman would carry out his responsibility. By linking the two he presented the man with a double financial burden, that of buying the field, and that of providing for Ruth's maintenance (see further on 4:6). But in doing this he must have had some law or custom behind him, for the kinsman raises no objection.

For the form *that is come again* (AV, RV) see on 1:22 (where the

---

[1] *Harvard Theological Review*, XL, 1947, p. 89, n. 45.
[2] See M. Tsevat, *Hebrew Union College Annual*, XXIX, 1958, p. 112. In Babylon it appears that a widow had a life interest in her dead husband's estate (G. R. Driver and J. C. Miles, *The Babylonian Laws*, I (Oxford, 1952), pp. 334f.). Among the Assyrians the widow could not inherit (G. R. Driver and J. C. Miles, *The Assyrian Laws* (Oxford, 1935), pp. 238f.). There was clearly a wide divergence of custom in the ancient world, with a tendency to restrict the rights of the widow. The diversity makes it difficult to reason from the custom elsewhere to that in Israel.
[3] Knight, p. 37.

identical Hebrew is rendered 'which returned', AV, RV), and for *the country of Moab*, on 1:1.

**4.** Boaz reveals his thoughts on the matter. His *I* is emphatic. He leaves no doubt that he is taking the initiative. *To advertise thee* (AV) is a picturesque expression, meaning literally, 'I will uncover your ear', *i.e.*, acquaint you with the facts. The expression may have been used originally of confidential information, and denoted the lifting of hair or headgear which would be necessary if one were whispering (so Lattey). But there is nothing of the confidential about its use here. Incidentally, the expression could be used of God (1 Sa. 9:15), as well as of man. But Boaz did more than pass on facts. He gave the advice that the kinsman should *buy* the land (or 'acquire' it; *qānāh* is usually translated 'buy' but it means 'get, acquire', see BDB, KB). The importance attached to preventing property from passing out of the family seems strange to us, but the law provided that a family's property should not be permanently alienated. If a man were hard up he might raise money by disposing of his land, but he could do this only as a temporary measure, and when things improved he had the right to 'redeem' his land, *i.e.*, buy it back again. If he were totally unable to do this one of his kinsmen could do it. If none of his family could do it for him then it was provided that the land should return to him in 'the year of jubilee' (Lv. 25:28). The basic principle is laid down in these words: 'The land shall not be sold for ever: for the land is mine; for ye are strangers and sojourners with me. And in all the land of your possession ye shall grant a redemption for the land' (Lv. 25:23,24, AV; see verses 25ff. for the detailed regulations). We see the firmness with which this might be upheld in the refusal of Naboth to dispose of 'the inheritance of my fathers' (1 Ki. 21:3) even to the king. A family's right to its own land was inalienable. All this lies behind the present chapter. Naomi was poor and could not retain her land. But it was a solemn family obligation to see that the land was not lost. It is interesting that AV takes the next expression as *before the inhabitants* and RSV, *in the presence of those sitting here*. Either could be defended, for the same verb can mean 'to sit' or 'to dwell'. It is perhaps more likely that Boaz refers to those sitting by who were witnesses. It is not probable that the inhabitants of Bethlehem as a whole were present. He specially singles out *the elders of my people*. It is not clear why he says *my* people, as presumably they were also the kinsman's people. It may be his way of retaining the initiative, or it may be an ancient legal formula. Now he invites the kinsman to make up his mind. *If thou wilt redeem it, redeem it* (AV, RV) shows clearly the legal position. The kinsman had a perfect right to go ahead, and if he did none could say him nay. Alternatively, if he would not redeem it (for *if thou wilt not redeem* (AV, RV) the Hebrew curiously has 'if he will not redeem', but the meaning does not appear to be in doubt) Boaz asks him to say so. *There is none to redeem it beside thee* (AV, RV) does not, of course, mean there is no other possible redeemer. In the same breath Boaz goes on to assure him that he himself is ready to take over the task. He means that there is no-one ahead of the kinsman. He has the first right. Berkeley, however, renders, *there is nobody to redeem it except you, with myself next*, thus making the kinsman and Boaz the only two possibilities. Knox (as also the Vulg. he is translating) is similar with his, *thy right comes first, and mine second; there is no other kinsman* (this reads something into the narrative as Knox also does earlier by rendering *gōʾēl* as *rival claimant* and *lēʾmōr qeneh* as *challenge thee*). It is not without its interest that Boaz' *I* is emphatic when he says, *I am after thee* (AV, RV), and that the kinsman responds with an equally emphatic *I, I will redeem it*.

**5.** Now Boaz brings out his real interest in the matter. Ruth, as well as Naomi, is concerned with this field. There is some difficulty about the right reading as illustrated by the translations of AV, *thou must buy it also of Ruth the Moabitess* (supported by FF), and of RSV, *you are also buying Ruth the Moabitess* (supported by Moffatt, Knox, Berkeley, Joüon; for *the Moabitess* see on 2:2). The former reflects the Hebrew text, but some of the versions, namely the Old Latin, Vulg., and the Syriac, give us the latter. This accords with 4:10, but for that reason may be a scribal harmonization. If it be accepted we should probably understand the verb to mean 'acquire' rather than 'buy' (see on verse 4). There would be no question of paying a dowry for Ruth, either to her parents in Moab or to Naomi. She would be 'acquired' but in no sense 'bought'. AV gives the more difficult reading and this may be right (scribes would be more likely to alter it to the other to fit in with 4:10, than to manufacture this reading out of that presupposed by RSV). If this is so then Boaz is saying that Ruth also has a stake in this field, and since she is the widow of a childless kinsman this involves marrying her to raise up a child for the deceased as well as treating it as a property matter. It was important *to raise up the name of the dead upon his inheritance* (AV, RV). Once again Knox paraphrases rather freely, *to perpetuate the name of the kinsman whose lands thou dost enjoy.* This may give expression to the rationale of levirate marriage, but it does not give the meaning of the text here. The text says nothing about enjoying the lands. It is concerned only, as AV and RV say, with perpetuating the name of the deceased, which would be done by raising up an heir to take over his lands. *The dead* here, of course, is Mahlon, the husband of Ruth, who has just been mentioned. But in raising up Mahlon's name that of Elimelech would also be continued. Joüon, however, takes it to refer to Elimelech, but to call Ruth his *wife* seems more than strange. Joüon also points out that in the case of a dead man the Hebrews spoke of his wife and not his widow, citing the case of Abigail (1 Sa. 27:3; 30:5; 2 Sa. 2:2; 3:3).

**6.** The knowledge that redemption of the field and marriage with Ruth went together altered the whole complexion of things for the kinsman. He does not say, 'I will not redeem', but *I cannot redeem*, and this is strong language. The reason he gives is *lest I mar mine own inheritance* (AV, RV). The meaning of this is not completely clear but probably the kinsman was not rich. He could redeem the field, but now he sees that it will not be an augmentation of his own property. It will mean rather a diminution of it, for he must pay to buy the field, and then it will belong not to his own family, but to the son of Ruth. Normally in a marriage of this type the field would presumably belong to the widow, not to the widow's mother-in-law. In marrying the widow the kinsman would secure the field which he could then set against the cost of supporting her. In this case he had to buy the field and in addition provide for Ruth. It might involve quite an expenditure. The kinsman was certainly ready to buy the field without marrying Ruth. He may well have been ready also to marry Ruth without buying the field (as Rowley thinks). What he could not face was doing the two things. Yet they went together. Perhaps we should mention the idea of Cassel (and others). He finds it incredible that a man should refuse marriage on the grounds that his son would inherit, and prefers the explanation that Ruth was a Moabitess, which is expressly mentioned here. One family had been extinguished subsequent to Moabite intermarriage and he did not care to repeat the experiment. There is, however, nothing in the text to indicate that this was the kinsman's meaning. It is much more likely that he could not assume the double financial burden of buying the field and supporting the widow. It would mar his inheritance (see further on verse 3). Under the circumstances he withdrew his claim to redeem and invited Boaz to take it up. *Thou* is emphatic and is strengthened by *to thyself*. *Right* incidentally is cognate with *redeem* and with *kinsman*. It is not the concept of abstract right, but the specific right of redemption that is meant. The kinsman repeated his statement that he was not able to redeem. He apparently wanted there to be no doubt on this point.

**7.** The narrator now explains a custom which had become obsolete. AV gives what is probably the sense of the opening of the verse, though there is nothing in the Hebrew to correspond to *was the manner* (AV). But LXX appears to be based on a different text. It seems to be a slavish rendering of *mišpāṭ* which will here mean 'custom', *i.e.*, 'this was the custom', and this may be original. That the writer finds it necessary to explain the custom indicates that he wrote some time after the events he narrates. The custom concerned *redeeming* and *changing* (AV) (*i.e.*, *exchanging*, RV, RSV). We have no means of knowing exactly what this latter term covered, though we should notice that Leviticus 27 deals with the possibility of 'redeeming' and of 'changing' beasts vowed for sacrifice;

indeed, verses 10,33 use our very word to denote an animal intended as an 'exchange' for another that was to be sacrificed. The only other Old Testament writer to use the word is the author of Job, who uses it of the emptiness which is to be the 'recompense' of the man with a badly based trust (Jb. 15:31), of the 'restitution' the wicked must make for his wronging of others (20:18), and of the impossibility of an 'exchange' for wisdom (28:17). The word thus appears to denote exchanges of very varied kinds. However, the *redeeming* and *changing* (AV) in mind here seem to be confined to situations where one kinsman takes over from another. The custom is misrepresented if it is said, as Cooke does, 'When *property was transferred*, as in the present case, to take off the sandal and hand it to the person in whose favour the transfer is made, gave a symbolic attestation to the act and invested it with legal validity.' The difficulty with this explanation is that no property was transferred at this point. It still remained with Naomi, and the man who drew off his shoe never did transfer the property. Boaz, on the other hand, who was concerned with the property transfer did not draw off his shoe. It is a transfer of rights, not property, that is in view. The custom is described simply. To confirm whatever was agreed upon, one man drew off (the tense is perfect; one might have expected a frequentative imperfect, but the perfect accords with the fact that the action was performed once only in each case) his sandal and gave it to the other. It is a curious custom, but at least its unusualness would mean that it attracted attention, and this probably was its object (*cf.* Knox, *thus did the Israelites put the grant on record*). People would know of the agreement reached. For AV, *this was a testimony in Israel*, we should read, 'this was the testimony . . .' There is an article and the meaning is 'this is the way in which attestation was carried out'.

Some have objected that this account of it shows an ignorance of the custom, and that Deuteronomy 25:5–10 tells us what actually happened. The present passage, they reason, shows that the author of Ruth lived at a time when the custom had passed into oblivion, and he misunderstood it. But there is no conflict. In Deuteronomy 25:7 we have the case of the man who refuses to help his brother's widow; he 'refuseth to raise up unto his brother a name in Israel, he will not perform the duty of my husband's brother' (AV). There is no mention of an alternative kinsman. The man is prepared to let his brother's name perish and that for selfish reasons. He is to be treated with opprobrium accordingly. The widow is to spit upon him and his sandal is forcibly to be loosed. In Ruth it is different. The unnamed kinsman appears not to be a close relative, certainly not a brother of the deceased.[1] And he may not have known Ruth. He can scarcely have known her well. There seems no reason why he should be humiliated. Moreover, Boaz is quite ready to marry Ruth. The question is not, 'Will Ruth be wed?' but, 'Who will be the one to wed her?' Under these circumstances the kinsman himself took off his sandal and handed it to Boaz. The loosing of the sandal is the action signifying that the transaction was completed: Ruth 4 shows how it was done when a man simply passed his rights on to another. Deuteronomy 25 shows how he was humiliated when he refused to carry out his responsibilities under family law.

That the shoe might be used in a symbolism which is not ours we see from Psalm 60:8, 'over Edom will I cast out my shoe' (AV), where the thought appears to be that of sovereignty and possession. There are several passages wherein the placing of the foot upon land and possessing it are connected (Dt. 1:36; 11:24; Jos. 1:3; 14:9). It may well be, as many commentators think, that this is the origin of the custom. The handing over of the shoe symbolized the handing over of what went with it. E. A. Speiser cites from the Nuzi documents examples of the ceremonial transfer of shoes as a means of validating transactions,[2] and he sees in the present passage a further example of the same practice.

**8.** The kinsman's speech is resumed. He concludes by pas-

---

[1] Rudolph is of opinion that a brother was obliged to marry the widow of the deceased, but that a more remote kinsman was under no obligation. He might do so if he chose (Rudolph, p. 62).
[2] *Bulletin of the American Schools of Oriental Research*, 77 (February, 1940), pp. 15–18. E. R. Lacheman also makes use of the Nuzi texts, citing passages which indicate change of ownership, *etc.*, like 'My foot from my fields and houses I have lifted up, and the foot of Urhi-Sharri I have placed' (this

sing the responsibility on to Boaz. *Buy it for thee* (AV) (for *buy* see on 4:4), he says, *i.e.*, 'Take it to yourself'. So *he drew off his shoe* (AV, RV). Some Greek versions (LXX and Aquila) add, 'and he gave it to him', thus making it quite clear that it was the kinsman who drew off the shoe and then gave it to Boaz to seal the transaction. MT and thus AV could possibly mean that Boaz drew the shoe off in the spirit of Deuteronomy 25:9. We have no reason, however, for taking this to be the meaning, for that spirit is lacking from this chapter. Yet Knox translates, *So now Boaz said to the rival claimant, Untie thy shoe.* LXX gives the sense of it, whether it preserves the true text or merely interprets it.

**9.** Boaz begins this last speech. In this he directs the attention of those present to the salient points to which they were the witnesses. He addresses *the elders* first, as we might have expected, but he joins with them *all the people*. There is a single preposition linking the two (unless with Joüon and others we accept the reading of the one MS which repeats the preposition). This points to a close linkage, for the preposition is usually repeated in expressions of this sort. But though the two are closely linked they are not identical. In other words, though the witness of the elders is very significant and may be singled out for special mention the witness of the people is also important. The people are not present simply as bystanders and spectators. Like the chosen elders (4:2) they are legal witnesses. Their witness is mentioned again in 4:11. It is clearly important. Boaz may feel that his transaction is safe, attested by them all. This was very important as it was apparently a day of few written records. Nothing is said to have been put in writing throughout the whole transaction. But with a crowd of reliable witnesses everything would be safely established. *I have bought* should probably be taken in the sense of a present tense, 'I acquire' (for this meaning of the verb see on 4:4): 'By these legal proceedings I acquire . . .' His next words reveal the transaction to have been more far-

text concerns a mortgage rather than a sale). The pulling off of the shoe he sees as a further development of the same idea (*Journal of Biblical Literature*, LVI, 1937, pp. 53–56).

reaching than we might have guessed from the preceding. Hitherto we have heard of 'a piece of the field which belonged to our brother Elimelech' (4:3), but now what Boaz has bought is *all that was Elimelech's, and all that was Chilion's and Mahlon's* (AV, RV). He is establishing his full right to the family possession, and this not only with respect to Elimelech, but to both of his sons too. It is not at all clear how Chilion comes into this. After all Boaz was not marrying Orpah. Probably in the absence of an heir to Chilion his 'name' would die out and his claim to a share in the property pass to Mahlon's heir.

**10.** Boaz comes to the heart of the matter. In buying the field he has also obtained Ruth to be his wife. *Ruth the Moabitess, the wife of Mahlon* stands first in the clause, thus receiving emphasis. This is important. For *purchased* (AV, RV) see on 4:4. This verb is not often used of the process of acquiring a bride, but it is perfectly understandable in the circumstances. Once again Ruth is described as *the Moabitess* (see on 2:2). We learn here (and here only) that she had been *the wife of Mahlon*. The two sons were mentioned in 1:2 and the two wives in 1:4 but which wife belonged to which husband was not there made clear. Boaz proceeds to give the justification for his levirate-type marriage first positively and then negatively. It is *to raise up the name of the dead upon his inheritance* (AV, RV), *i.e.*, to provide a son who would carry on the name of the deceased. Then, negatively, *that the name of the dead be not cut off from among his brethren, and from the gate of his place* (AV, RV). The *brethren* will be the whole family, all his relations. His name is not to cease from the family circle. *The gate of his place* (AV, RV) is probably the gate of the city (Berkeley, *from the gate of his home town;* FF, however, renders, *the gate of his Home*). As we have seen, the gate was the centre of social and communal life, so this is equivalent to saying that the name of the deceased would be perpetuated in the community. Having thus formally set forth the effect and the purpose of his action Boaz concludes by reminding his hearers that they are all witnesses.

Knight reminds us that this action of Boaz in redeeming the helpless Ruth has implications for the author's view of God. We must ask ourselves, he says, 'What reading did the author put on this act of redemption by Boaz? Did he realise that if a mere man, a creature of God, could behave in the manner described, and had indeed by his action exhibited the power to redeem an outcast and bring her into fellowship with the living God, then two things could be said of the Creator of Boaz? – (1) God must feel at least as compassionate towards all the Ruths of Moab and of Babylon and of every other land as his creature Boaz felt towards Ruth; (2) God must actually be a God of redemption, with the desire and the power to redeem all outcasts into fellowship with himself.'

**11.** The court session concludes with a statement from the witnesses. First *all the people that were in the gate, and the elders* (AV, RV) responded to Boaz' last statement by affirming that they were indeed witnesses. Actually their assent is given succinctly in the single word *witnesses*. It is of interest that *all the people* are here mentioned ahead of *the elders*. Clearly their part was considered to be more than a formality. The following prayer seems somewhat long to have been uttered by the whole people and LXX may well be right in inserting 'and the elders said' after 'witnesses'. This makes the people respond with one word and the elders carry on with the blessing. Notice that they do not content themselves with discharging their strict legal functions. They proceed to pronounce a blessing on Boaz and his bride.[1] They begin with Ruth. Their verb *is come* (AV, RV) (or 'has come') looks on the imminent act as already completed. They pray that God will make her *like Rachel and like Leah* (AV, RV). It is interesting that, though they are Bethlehemites and thus descended from Judah, son of Leah (Gn. 29:35), they place Rachel before Leah. She was, of course, specially beloved, and she had died in the neighbourhood of their city (Gn. 35:19). Their prayer is a prayer for fruitfulness. These were the only two wives of Jacob and thus from them (together with their maidservants who

---

[1] E. Neufeld thinks that this was part of the actual marriage ceremony and he cites Gn. 24:60 and Tobit 10:11f. as further examples of the same thing (*Ancient Hebrew Marriage Laws* (Longmans, 1944), p. 150). But it is difficult to see the marriage ceremony in any of the three examples cited. In fact we have very little information as to how a marriage ceremony was performed in ancient Israel.

became Jacob's concubines, but had no standing so that their children were reckoned as in some way belonging to their mistresses) were descended the entire nation. This prayer then looks for a numerous and distinguished progeny. Then they think of Boaz. *Do thou worthily* (AV, RV) is general, and expresses a hope for Boaz' prosperity in a broad sense. The word translated *worthily* is that rendered 'of wealth' in 2:1 (where see note). It points to excellence in almost any field with perhaps some emphasis on military prowess. In this context the stress is on wealth and prosperity rather than military eminence. It certainly looks for Boaz to be a happy and successful man. For *Ephratah* see on 1:2. *Be famous in Bethlehem* (AV, RV: lit. 'call name (or a name) in Bethlehem') goes on to the consequences of this. As a result of his goodly actions these well-wishers trust that Boaz will be renowned. Knox takes these last two clauses to refer to Ruth, but the Hebrew does not bear this out. KD understand them both of the begetting of children. This seems unlikely in the case of *do thou worthily* (AV, RV), which is quite general, but it is not at all impossible in the case of *be famous*. It may signify, as KD put it, 'Make to thyself a well-established name through thy marriage with Ruth, by a host of worthy sons who shall make thy name renowned.' But the Hebrew is unusual, and many propose alterations to the text. The exact meaning must remain uncertain, but clearly the expression is one of good will, and AV, RV are probably right.

**12.** They had looked for Ruth to be prolific, and now they repeat the thought with respect to Boaz. It is at first sight curious that they ask for his *house* (*i.e.*, his 'household', more specifically, his descendants) to be like that of Pharez, for this man is not usually regarded as an outstanding example of fruitfulness or of anything else. But there are several reasons. As the speakers here point out Pharez was one *whom Tamar bare unto Judah* (AV, RV). The story is told in Genesis 38, and, since Tamar's situation had been not unlike Ruth's, the story may be very relevant. Then we must bear in mind that Pharez was apparently the most important of Judah's sons. At any rate, he seems to be mentioned more prominently than

Shelah who was older. And of the twins, though he was not marked with the red cord meant to signify the first-born, yet he 'came out first' (Gn. 38:28f.). The tribe of Judah apparently depended on Pharez' descendants more than on those of others. As the book of Ruth is set in the territory of this tribe the comparison becomes apt. Moreover, as we see from 4:18–21 Pharez was one of Boaz' ancestors and thus a most suitable person to be mentioned. Indeed, it seems that Pharez was the ancestor of the Bethlehemites in general (1 Ch. 2:5,18,50f.). Moreover, Pharez gave his name to the section of the tribe of Judah that was descended from him (Nu. 26:20). The verse concludes with a reference to *the seed which the Lord shall give thee* (AV, RV). There is a simple piety here. It is not natural fecundity but the gift of God for which they pray. FF takes 'seed' to refer to one child, *the heir*. The references to *thy house* (AV, RV) and to *the seed which the Lord shall give thee* (AV, RV) are probably best explained if Boaz was childless. It is unlikely that he was a bachelor but he may well have been a widower. In that case the first son of the marriage would be heir to Boaz as well as to Mahlon.[1]

### e. Marriage and the birth of a son (4:13–17)

**13.** The court case over, Boaz proceeded to wed Ruth. *Was* of AV might be better rendered *became* (as RV and RSV), for the verse is speaking of the process rather than the continuing state. *Went in unto her* (AV, RV) is the usual Old Testament expression for sexual relations. Notice that the son that was born is regarded as God's gift. Throughout this book there is the consistent thought that God is over all and works out His will We have just seen that the elders and others regarded children as God's gift (4:12) and we see the same thought now from the author.

**14.** It is interesting to notice that it is Naomi who is featured

---

[1] This is accepted by H. H. Rowley (*Harvard Theological Review*, XL, 1947, pp. 98f.). This verse is strangely overlooked by many commentators who affirm the genealogy to be a late addition partly on the grounds that the book elsewhere does not regard Obed as the son of Boaz. Plainly the villagers did look for a son who would belong to Boaz and establish his 'house'.

in the closing scene, not Ruth. The women of the city are delighted at the birth of the child. We have previously seen their interest when they met Naomi on her return to Bethlehem (1:19). They come to her now rather than to Ruth possibly because they know her so much better, possibly because she is the one with the greater need of companionship. After all Ruth has a husband and a child to occupy her attention. The women congratulate Naomi, but consistently with what we have seen through the book, they ascribe what has happened to the hand of the Lord. *Blessed be the Lord* was a usual way of expressing thankfulness. The oldest Jewish form of prayer known to us (admittedly much more recent than this) is called 'the Eighteen Benedictions' because each prayer begins with 'Blessed art Thou, O Lord'. Yet, though this may be a conventional form of expression we should not miss the significance it has in this narrative. Our author does not go out of his way to stress the divine activity. Apparently he is concerned with a story of human activities and he tells it much as other stories were told. But it is basic to him that God is over all men and all things, and that He brings His plans to pass. So in this book now and then an expression of this sort allows us to see that it is God who is the principal participant. He it is who has given Naomi the blessing. The reason given for the thanksgiving is that God has not left Naomi *without a kinsman* (AV). Up till now we should have thought that *kinsman* (AV, RV) would refer to Boaz, but this statement carries on till it culminates at the end of the next verse with a reference to Ruth's having borne him. This makes it plain that the women are speaking about the new baby. God has sent the child to be Naomi's *kinsman* (Knox, *an heir*). *That his name . . .* (AV) should probably be as RSV, *may his name . . .* It is a prayer that the child would become famous, just as the men have previously prayed for the same thing for Boaz (4:11).

**15.** The women prophesy that the child will mean much to Naomi. *Restorer of life* (there is no 'thy' in the Hebrew as in AV) probably has little specific meaning. It is a general term of good (*cf.* Ps. 19:7; La. 1:16). There may be a hint at her poverty since returning from Moab, but it is difficult to make much of this since Boaz must have been looking after her for quite some time now. There may be more to be said for *a nourisher of thine old age* (AV, RV). Boaz was not young (3:10) and it is probable that by the time Naomi was old he would have died and she would be dependent on the son of Ruth. But again we are probably not meant to look too closely into the term. It expresses a hope for the future, and one not to be too narrowly defined. The women now go on to the reason for their hope. They put a certain emphasis on the word *daughter in law* (after *kî* one expects the verb before the subject, but here the subject comes first). The daughter-in-law they characterize as one who *loveth thee* (AV, RV). The love of Ruth for her mother-in-law shines through this book and it is appropriate that it be given this recognition at the end. The tribute, *which is better to thee than seven sons* (AV, RV; *cf.* 1 Sa. 1:8), is all the more striking in view of the place usually given boys in comparison with girls. A numerous male progeny was the ambition of all married people and thus to speak of Ruth as being worth more to Naomi than *seven sons* is the supreme tribute. For *seven sons* as proverbial for a perfect family, *cf.* 1 Samuel 2:5.

**16.** As was only to be expected Naomi took a special interest in the baby. Sne took it up in her arms, *laid it in her bosom, and became nurse unto it* (AV, RV). One imagines that there would have been no difficulty in obtaining a nurse for the son of Boaz. But for Naomi this child was special. She had expected a lonely old age when her husband and sons died. With none of those near to her left her future had indeed looked bleak. But thanks to Ruth's devotion everything was now different. She belonged to a family once more. She was loved and she had a recognized place. The babe in a sense symbolized it all, and Naomi gave herself over to caring for him. For the symbolism, *cf.* Numbers 11:12. It indicates that Naomi recognized the child as in some sense hers (*cf.* verse 17 where the neighbours say this in so many words).

**17.** *The women* of the village did not cease their interest when they pronounced their blessing on Naomi (4:14f.). They took an interest in how the baby should be named, and, indeed, actually *gave it a name* (AV, RV). They first pronounced, *There* *is a son born to Naomi* (AV, RV), and in the way families were reckoned this was indeed the case. The child was in effect the son of Mahlon, and thus, though Ruth was not her daughter, Ruth's boy counted as Naomi's descendant. Knox's translation understands the situation otherwise: *Noemi took the child to her bosom, and still it must be she that nursed him, she that carried him, till the neighbours, congratulating her, said It is Noemi that has a son.* But this is reading something into the Hebrew. AV and RV give the sense of it better. It is possible also that the expression should be understood along the lines that Boaz was primarily *gō'ēl* to Elimelech (4:3,9). He should accordingly have married Naomi to raise up a child to Elimelech. However, since she was too old Ruth was a substitute and the child in a sense was Naomi's. Gerleman understands Naomi to have adopted the child and he compares the way the children of Bilhah and Zilpah were 'adopted' by Rachel and Leah. This, however, does seem to be reading something into the narrative, which is more naturally explained along the lines we have suggested. Moreover, Naomi is specifically said to be the child's nurse (4:16) which would be a very strange way of describing her relationship to a child she had adopted. Rudolph aptly comments that Naomi's is an act of love, not of law. L. P. Smith in *IB* thinks that 4:16 'is usually interpreted as formal adoption' but adds, 'there is no clear biblical evidence on such a ceremony'.

The women gave him the name *Obed.* It is curious that these women from outside the family should be able to intervene in this fashion. It may be that their kindly interest so impressed Boaz and Ruth that they accepted their suggestion. Or local custom may have given the women a more prominent place than we would have expected. But it is a most unusual procedure. Joüon amends the text to read, 'The neighbours said, "There is a son born to Naomi!" and she gave him the name of Obed.' An interesting support is the statement by Josephus that Naomi named the child (*Ant.* v. 9.4). But as his account contains inaccuracies, too much reliance cannot be placed upon it. Rudolph is another who thinks the text requires emendation, though he is not sure how. But it is better to stick to the

Hebrew text. *Obed* means 'Servant'. The name is not found very frequently in the Old Testament, and we do not know anything about anyone who bore it, since it occurs only in lists of names and genealogies. From the frequency with which the cognate word '*ebed* is found one might have expected Obed more often. Perhaps it was avoided on account of its servile implications. If so, this makes it all the stranger that the women should use it here. Perhaps they imply that the babe will serve Naomi in whom they clearly have a special interest. The verse concludes with a little note connecting Obed with David. The child who was born as the result of the marriage which took place after such curious happenings as those narrated in this book was the grandfather of Israel's greatest king.

### f. A genealogy of David (4:18–22)

The book concludes with a short genealogy linking Pharez (the son of Judah; see on verse 12) with David. Some scholars think this to be no part of the original book, but a later addition. This is precarious reasoning, however, for as S. B. Gurewicz reminds us, 'it is hard to imagine that a Jewish scribe would ascribe to David, the king so greatly venerated and revered in Israelite tradition, Moabite antecedents without some valid basis'.[1] Moreover, David certainly had some links with Moab, for during a time of danger he entrusted his parents to the care of the King of Moab (1 Sa. 22:3f.). Herbert thinks not only that the genealogy is original, but that it emphasizes the main purpose of the book.

It is introduced with *these are the generations of* (AV, RV), thus making use of a formula found often in Genesis (as 2:4; 5:1; 6:9, *etc.*). The word rendered *generations* is found also in Exodus, Numbers and 1 Chronicles but nowhere else in the Old Testament apart from this passage. BDB give its meaning as 'generations, esp. in genealogies = account of a man and his descendants'. It often introduces quite long sections so that it evidently covered not only the genealogy but the story of those in the genealogy. There is an air of history about the term.

[1] *The Australian Biblical Review*, V, 1956, p. 46.

It has historical associations. Here, however, it applies strictly to the genealogy. The genealogy in this verse agrees with the fuller information given in 1 Chronicles 2:4–15.

It seems likely that the genealogy is somewhat compressed, with certain names being omitted. *NBD*[1] dates Joseph (and therefore Judah) *c.* 1750–1650 BC, with David's accession *c.* 1010 BC. To cover this span of *c.* 640 years the genealogy lists but ten names (including that of David). Another line of reasoning starts from the statement in Matthew 1:5 that Salmon was Rahab's husband. This dates him near the time of the Exodus but there is no name between Salmon and Boaz. It is not known at what time the events of the book took place (Josephus says that Elimelech migrated during the time of Eli, *Ant.* v. 9.1, but there is no confirmation of this from other sources). But it does seem likely that names have been omitted.

Some comments may be made on individuals. Amminadab (4:19) was the father-in-law of Aaron (Ex. 6:23). Nahshon his son (4:20) is mentioned several times at the Exodus period (Ex. 6:23; Nu. 1:7; 2:3; 7:12,17; 10:14). MT reads 'Salmah' in 4:20 and 'Salmon' in 4:21. One must surely be a textual error, but which? A third form is Salma' as in 1 Chronicles 2:11,51,54, which inclines us to Salmah (the -on ending may have been influenced by other names with this form). Notice that Mahlon is not mentioned and Obed is treated simply as the son of Boaz. In a sense he carried on Mahlon's name and succeeded to his property. But in an official genealogy he was reckoned as the son of his true father.

Why does the book end with a genealogy? It is hard to say. In the Introduction we have noted and rejected the view that the whole was written to lead up to the genealogy, and thus to provide an ancestry for the great King David. It is too obviously an appendix, a mere addition to the main story, for this to be at all plausible. But a genealogy is, to say the least of it, a curious way to end a book. The author does not tell us why he has done this, and we are left to guess. But at any rate we can make this comment. Throughout the book in all its artless simplicity there runs the note that God is supreme. He watches

[1] *NBD*, p. 218.

over people like Naomi and Ruth and Boaz and directs their paths. God never forgets His saving purposes. The issue of the marriage of Boaz and Ruth was to lead in due course to the great King David, the man after God's own heart, the man in whom God's purpose was so signally worked out. These events in Moab and Bethlehem played their part in leading up to the birth of David. The Christian will think also of the genealogy at the beginning of the Gospel according to St. Matthew. He will reflect that God's hand is over all history. God works out His purpose, generation after generation. Limited as we are to one lifetime, each of us sees so little of what happens. A genealogy is a striking way of bringing before us the continuity of God's purpose through the ages. The process of history is not haphazard. There is a purpose in it all. And the purpose is the purpose of God.